Grace
UNFAILING

To Phyllis

The Radical Mind
and the Beloved Community
of Richard Roberts

GWEN R.P. NORMAN

Gwen R. P. Norman

Grace Unfailing
The Radical Mind and the Beloved Community of Richard Roberts

Canadian Cataloguing in Publication Data

Norman, Gwen R.P., 1909–
  Grace Unfailing

Includes bibliographical references and index
ISBN 1-55134-090-9

1. Roberts, Richard, 1874–1945. 2. United Church of Canada – Clergy – Biography. I. Title

BX9883.R63N67 1998   287.9'2'092   C98-932686-1

United Church Publishing House
3250 Bloor Street West, Suite 300
Etobicoke ON
Canada M8X 2Y4
416-231-5931
bookpub@uccan.org

Cover sketch: Esther Lovett
Design, Editorial, and Production: Department of Publishing and Graphics

Printed in Canada
5 4 3 2 1   03 02 01 00 99 98

 980258

To my family
and to all who come after

O God, undone am I,
 My sin prevailing;
Send Thou me, or I die,
 Thy grace unfailing;

from a hymn written by Richard Roberts

The Radical Mind

That there is something typical about the mentality of the great rebels may be gathered from the comparative reading of a few biographies. All alike display an abnormal mental sensitiveness combined with great physical restlessness, a keen craving for fellowship combined with a fondness for solitude and lonely meditation, a vivid perception of present evils together with a passion for a future that should restore some primitive simplicity, a tendency once the first step in rebellion has been taken to extend the rebellious front to other issues, a frequent admixture of integrity of character with a certain irregularity of conduct. But the paradox of the rebel has always been that, while he has always been assailed as a subverter of the social order, his own driving force has been a social sense quicker and broader than that of his orthodox contemporaries....He endeavors to push out the frontiers of privilege in order that the poor and the outcast may enter upon a larger life. Indeed, it may be said that the whole historical struggle for freedom has been a struggle to broaden the basis of fellowship....The prime agent of this pursuit has been the dissenter. Dissent has again and again proved itself to be the social growing point. Yet the dissenter has usually been shot at dawn or hanged. We shall not have achieved a genuine freedom or the condition of a pacific and steady social evolution until we have reached a state of society in which there will be not only a generous toleration, but a serious encouragement of dissenting thought.

Richard Roberts
from The New Man and the Divine Society

The Beloved Community

We are longing for a life of peace and freedom and harmony which this world of sense cannot afford us, and we know not where to find it.…In this longing for wholeness and harmony of life is also the spring of that preoccupation with the ideal commonwealth which has brought forth the idea of Utopia. In Christendom the imaginative quest of the perfect home chiefly addressed itself to the finding of an idealized Jerusalem, whether Saint Bernard's "*urbs Syon aurea*" or William Blake's "Jerusalem," which should be built in "England's green and pleasant land." It has had other names: the Republic, the City of God, the New Atlantis, the City of the Sun, and Erewhon; but under all the names is the same dream of that to which Josiah Royce gave the most beautiful of its names "The Beloved Community."

Richard Roberts
from The Preacher as a Man of Letters

Canada, early 1920s

Contents

Foreword by Roger Hutchinson and Phyllis Airhart ix
Preface xi

Part I: "Look unto the rock whence ye are hewn"
1 David Roberts Rhiw 3
2 Margaret Roberts 8
3 The Community 12
4 Early School Days 18
5 College: Aberystwyth 24
6 Bala 28
7 The Forward Movement 35

Part II: "The Coming Man"
8 London: Willesden Green 43
9 Westbourne Grove 47
10 Crouch Hill 58
11 Crouch Hill: Extracurricular 74
12 The Fellowship of Reconciliation 83
13 Brooklyn, NY: The Church of the Pilgrims 97
14 Seeking New Fields 107

Part III: "He setteth the solitary in families"
15 Nan 115
16 RR and His Daughters 122

Part IV: "I press on to the mark of the high calling of God in Jesus Christ"
17 Montreal: The American Presbyterian Church 129
18 The Pace of Life 136

19 RR's Preaching 143
20 The City 149
21 Toronto: Sherbourne Street United 153
22 Theologs, and "that difficult person, the
     undergraduate" 166
23 To Serve His Church 171
24 Further Afield: Psychiatric Clinic and Later Japan 176
25 RR, the Oxford Group, and Retreats 180

Part V: "All my trust in Thee is found"
26 Moderator 189
27 Back to Normal Life 219

Part VI: "Be Thou still my strength and shield"
28 Sherbourne and the Future 231
29 Halifax 241
30 The Last Years 251
31 L'Envoi 259

Part VII: Contextualizing Richard Roberts'
     Thought: Liberal Protestantism and the
     Dilemmas of the Modern Age
     by Catherine Gidney 263

Richard Roberts: A Bibliography Compiled by
     William Whitla 287
About the Author 295
Index 296

Foreword

This biography of Richard Roberts provides an engaging insider's account of the public and private lives of the United Church's sixth moderator [1934–36]. Roberts won the respect of Canadians and, in particular, members of the United Church, as a well loved minister, writer, and speaker. He was in constant demand as a speaker for large evangelical revivals, but he was more at home in small fellowship groups designed for the cultivation of an intelligent faith and a quickened spirit. He was initially impressed by the work of the Oxford Group Movement. However, he preferred a more democratic style of leadership and insisted that fellowship must expand from intimate face-to-face settings to the larger structures of local, national, and international society. Evidence of that conviction was his support for social gospel reforms and the League of Nations, and the fact that he was invited to write the foreword for the Fellowship for a Christian Social Order's 1936 book of essays, *Towards the Christian Revolution,* edited by R.B.Y. Scott and Gregory Vlastos.

Gwen Norman's "daughter's-eye view" of Roberts' life is complemented by a fine chapter in which Catherine Gidney examines his thought. By refusing to choose between the traditional evangelical emphasis on God's transcendence and modern immanence, he served as a bridge between nineteenth- and twentieth-century theologies. On the one hand, his aim was to hold together Barth's emphasis on revelation and Macmurray's view of community. On the other hand, as he explained in his 1927 book, *The New Man and the Divine Society,* he meant "to hold fast to the great doctrines of Inspiration, Revelation, Incarnation, Redemption and Grace; and also to accept the elements of immanence-theology—the Inner Light, the Indwelling Christ, and the Kingdom of God, as a phase of the unfolding life and Jesus as the crown of biological evolution" (p. 16).

In his defence of his desire "to be a traditionalist *and* a modernist" Roberts struck a distinctly post-modern note: "I shall naturally involve myself in many verbal inconsistencies; but in a world of relative knowledge that is hardly to be avoided. If I am charged with uttering contradictory things, I will simply answer that I cannot help myself, things being as they are." This acceptance of relative knowledge and the need to respect different voices suggests that Roberts is also a bridge to the late twentieth century and that the publication of this book is very timely.

Roger Hutchinson and Phyllis Airhart
Emmanuel College, Victoria University

Preface

Should a biography have a history? In the case of this one, some explanation is needed as to why it has lain fallow for over thirty years. The original preface I wrote is dated, Matsumoto, Japan, 1966. Why, then, is it only now being published?

It was generally assumed in the family that my eldest sister, Peggy [Margaret P. MacVicar], would undertake the writing of our father's life. This plan seemed sensible. Peggy was on the spot. She had, since my mother's death in 1958, all of RR's remaining papers in her charge. Her own writing skills were known. Her letters, though few and far between, were informative and embellished with pithy and witty comments. "Few and far between"—that was the catch. Peggy hated putting pen to paper.

When my family and I were visiting the MacVicars during our furlough as missionaries* from Japan in 1959–61, Peggy and I set ourselves to put some order in the papers. Since that time, having worked in the United Church Archives, I occasionally wonder what precious gems we discarded in our amateurism. [One lost treasure that still lodges in my memory is a brief note from Healey Willan *apropos* a Sherbourne Street United Church announcement in the Saturday *Globe and Mail*: "Oh Roberts, how could you?!" I leave you with the mystery as I cannot remember the cause of this cheery dig, save that it had to do with an unfortunate wording.]

In the course of ordering the papers, Peggy suddenly said to me: "Why don't you do it?" "Do what?" I asked. "Write the biography?" We consulted my sister Doi [Dorothy Knowles] and the outcome was that a bulging, battered leather briefcase, fortunately steel-

---

Editor's note: "Missionary" is presently referred to as "Overseas Personnel" by the United Church.

banded, accompanied me back to Japan. Had we still been at Kwansei Gakuin University I would have been occupied with teaching and extracurricular university activities. But in Matsumoto, properly sorting and studying the papers kept me occupied, for at first I had no regular duties in the church or community.

Turning to these papers was never a chore. I kept meeting, in the papers, some whose names reverberated in my memory. Others were entirely new to me. It is hard to recall now a time when I knew nothing about my father's childhood, and only very little about his early manhood. The quality of Seth and Frank Joshua of the Forward Movement, and the impression of the Rev. Thomas Charles Edwards, theologian and mentor, were exciting. So were others of later years, some of whom I did know personally.

Among the papers, fortunately, were brief chapters of my father's autobiography. I have a feeling that someone had "pressed" him to write his own story. Perhaps the pressure was dropped; more likely he simply felt that writing about himself was not why he was here. It was, however, a bonanza for me. Part I of this book would have been spare, indeed, without this material. For Part II there was a good supply of information in correspondence, reports, minutes of meetings, and other diverse sources.

There is a change of pace in Part III. Here the pressures of his ministry, his part in the life of the larger church and community, have fallen away. He stands solely in relationship with his wife Nan [Anne Catherine Thomas] and his three daughters, Peggy, Doi, and Gwen. We called our father, Dad. Nan to us was Mam [she did not like Mum, which was what maidservants called their mistresses]. I would have liked to write this section of the book in the first person, and spoken of Dad and Mam, but my editors prevailed. Throughout the book, then, I refer to Richard Roberts not by his full name, nor any other formal appellation, but simply as "RR," which is the way he signed a good deal of his correspondence.

I am often intrigued by the long list of credits which follow a movie and the interesting titles the people involved in its creation bear. In the original version of this book, credits belong first and foremost to my two sisters, Margaret P. MacVicar [Peggy] and Dorothy Knowles [Doi], both now deceased. My nephew, Richard Inglis MacVicar, at my request, did some digging in New York for some of the facts about the persecution of radicals when war fever swept the

USA. Linda Newmarch of Toronto assisted my sister Dorothy in searching the records of the American Church in Montreal and Sherbourne Street Church [now St. Luke's] in Toronto. All of these generously checked facts of which I was uncertain, and distance prevented me from checking myself. Dr. Gerald R. Cragg, then at Andover Newton College, read the first half of the manuscript and provided valuable criticism and guidance.

When I typed the first manuscript I made two carbon copies, one for each of my sisters. Not long after that I asked Mrs. Ernest Bott [Edith], who was an accomplished typist, to make three more copies, one for each of my children. [The manuscript was 197 single-spaced pages; she would not accept any payment! For she, too, honoured my father.] I was pleased when the Rev. Glen Lucas, then Chief Archivist of the United Church, asked permission to photocopy the manuscript so that it could be available to others without my having to part with my copy.

So why was it not published sooner? I attempted to place it with more than one publisher, including the Ryerson Press, but got no takers. But I rested in the thought of all that I had learned and how much plain fun I had had in writing this biography, and left it to lie fallow. Gradually it dawned on me that the timing was wrong. It was either too soon after his death or not late enough. The climate was not right.

Now a new generation of students and professors has arisen, and there has been keen interest in Richard Roberts and his influence. I have had numerous letters asking for permission to quote from his writings. Students in our United Church theological colleges have been writing theses on his thought and influence. I would like to thank Professors John Young and Margaret Van Die of Queen's Theological College, and Professor Phyllis Airhart and Principal Roger Hutchinson of Emmanuel College, for their encouragement in pursuing publication.

I also thank the Emmanuel College Centre for Reasearch in Religion for support of the publication of this book as one of its projects.

Particular thanks are due to Catherine Gidney for writing the concluding chapter on RR's thought in the context of his age. I am grateful to Thomas Harding for undertaking the overall editing of the manuscript and for suggesting that it be submitted to the United

Church Publishing House. Thanks also to the United Church Publishing House for the publication of this book. A number of dates and identifications have been added to RR's autobiography and elsewhere in square parentheses.

My father chose titles for his own autobiography and I have adopted and adapted them for his biography. "Look unto the rock whence ye are hewn" is Isaiah 51:1. "The Coming Man" was a phrase used to describe him in two articles by R. E. Welsh in 1906 and 1910 as referred to in that part. "He setteth the solitary in families" is Psalm 68:6 "I press on to the mark of the high calling of God in Jesus Christ" is from Philemon 3:14. Two other parts use lines from famous Welsh hymns: All my trust on Thee is stayed" is by Charles Wesley from "Jesus, lover of my soul" (1739; tune: Aberystwyth), and "Be Thou still my strength and shield" by William Williams from his hymn "Guide me O Thou Great Jehovah," originally written in Welsh and translated by him (1745; tune: Cwm Rhondda). "Grace Unfailing," is taken from Richard Roberts' hymn printed on page 259 of the book; the subtitle is also drawn from his writings.

My children, Margaret, Nancy, and Dan, Bill Whitla, Nancy's husband, and Marilyn, Dan's wife, have all, in one way or another, been rooting for the success of the publication, as has my nephew David Knowles. Nancy and Bill Whitla deserve special mention. Nancy has typed, pursued, and arranged throughout; Bill has prepared an extensive bibliography of Richard Roberts' published work and prepared the complete manuscript for publication. Without the help and support of all these people, particularly Nancy, this publication would not have been possible. My thanks to all those named above.

Gwen R. P. Norman

Part I

"Look unto the rock whence ye are hewn"

———

1

David Roberts Rhiw

Richard Roberts came on his father's side of farming stock. His father, David Roberts, was born in a little farmhouse named Traian in the parish of Llanwnda, Caernarvonshire [now the county of Gwynedd], North Wales. As the farm was not large enough to support the five sons of the family, all but one went off to work in the slate quarries of Llanberis, 12 miles away as the crow flies. It was only after some years as a quarryman that David Roberts entered the ministry of the Calvinistic Methodist Church. His last pastorate, in which he remained some thirty or forty years, was Rhiwbryfdir, in Blaenau Ffestiniog, and long after his death he was revered throughout North Wales as David Roberts Rhiw. RR left this impression of his father.

I do not know just when my father's thoughts began to turn toward the Christian ministry. Indeed, he was so self-effacing that I imagine it was suggested to him, probably by the elders of his church. That must have been in the middle of the 1860s. His first step was to enter a famous Welsh academy named *Ysgol Clynnog* [Clynnog School] which was conducted by Ebenezer Thomas, better known to this day by his bardic name *Eben Fardd*, and held in high repute as a poet in Wales. From Clynnog my father proceeded to Bala in Merionethshire where two men, Dr. Lewis Edwards [1809–1887, the founder and principal of Bala College] and Dr. John Parry [1775–1846, a Hebrew scholar and author of a best selling Welsh catechism], were training men for the Calvinistic Methodist ministry and laying the foundations of a Welsh theology.

The journey from my father's house to Bala in those days was something of an adventure. Railway facilities were few and far between, and the greater part of the journey had to be made on foot. It took some three days, and many of the students carried with them a supply of food for the early weeks of the term. The Bala students lived hard and they eked out their scanty resources with modest fees earned by preaching on Sundays in little country churches that were within walking distance. But the men who came from Bala...were of a breed after their own kind. They bore the stamp of their great masters. For his teachers my father cherished a deep reverence to the end of his days. Of his Bala days he spoke little that I can recall. But whatever else may have befallen him there, he came away with the makings of a profound theologian. After serving two minor charges faithfully and with growing acceptance, he was called to the pastorate of a large and well established congregation at Rhiwbryfdir, in the Ffestiniog area of Merionethshire. There he remained until the end of his life.

In early Welsh Methodism, which was an outcome of the Methodist revival of the eighteenth century, the preaching of the Gospel was an itinerant calling, and the pastoral oversight of the local "societies" was in the hands of lay deacons elected by the societies themselves. In my father's early ministry the settled pastorate was still a novelty, and in many quarters it was regarded with misgiving. But in spite of a settled pastorate, the preaching office remained itinerant. My father preached to his own congregation only on the first Sunday of the month. On the other Sundays he preached to other congregations while other men preached to his people. These visiting ministers usually stayed at the manse over the weekend, and for us children there was always a mild excitement on Saturday afternoon in awaiting the preacher. With the years we grew to know most of the preachers as the majority were drawn from our presbytery. Naturally we had our favourites....There was, for instance, John Davies of Bontddu, who could be counted upon to have a supply of peppermints in his pocket. With others we could have good fun, but some were crusty and we took care to keep our distance from them.

My father received a modest stipend for his services at home; the rest of his income was derived from the fees which he received for his Sunday services away from home. The manse was rent free as a matter of course. But I doubt whether my father's income at any time was much more than 150 pounds a year. Sometimes he went farther afield to a preaching festival here or there, or to Welsh churches in England. I remember that once he went to London for six weeks to minister to the Welsh churches there. His preaching was not of the popular kind. His diction was quiet and deliberate, his subject matter scriptural and meditative. But the influence of his preaching was profound and lasting, especially in the places which he visited with some frequency.

I said that my father had left college with the promise of becoming a considerable theologian, and the promise was fulfilled. He remained a student to the end of his days, kept his Greek Testament constantly by his side and gathered together a library of books which was astonishing when his small income is remembered. He was deeply versed in the Puritan theologians. He began his ministerial life with a moderately strict Calvinistic bias, but his outlook broadened with the years. "I have learned," he said to me in later life, "that the Atonement is too great to be compassed by a single doctrine. There may be many doctrines of it, and all of them may be, each in its own place, true." His authority on matters of doctrine in his own community and presbytery was unquestioned.

As he was slow of speech, so he was slow with his pen. After his death we failed to find a single complete sermon in manuscript. All we found was a sheaf of loose sheets of memoranda. On the first Monday of the month he began to ponder and brood over next Sunday's sermon. My most familiar picture of him is as he sat in an easy chair in his study, with his Bible on his knee, so deep in meditation that my entry into the room went unnoticed; and I saw him so, times without number. In these broodings his sermon would slowly take shape and would be ready for delivery at the appointed time. On fine days my father would go out of doors and pace to and fro in front of the church; in those deliberate perambulations, he was minting the purest gold. He would preach this same sermon on the remainder of the month's Sundays to the congregations which he visited. (These engagements away from home were, as a rule, made several years beforehand, and there was a special pocket diary published which provided for engagements even ten years ahead.)

He was never appointed to any of the high offices of the church—the presidency of Synod or of General Assembly—and he was glad not to be, however much my mother might rage that lesser men than he were appointed to these offices. Two distinctions, however, gave him pleasure. In the annual service of ordination of candidates to the ministry...there are two deliverances which are regarded as of high importance. The one is an "Oration upon the nature of the Church," the other a "charge" to the ordinands. My father was chosen at different times to discharge these offices, and on both occasions his utterance was by general consent agreed to be classical.

However, it is likely that the chief quality which my father brought to such occasions was not so much what he said or how he said it, but his own generally known personal character. He was a man of unshadowed purity of heart, wholly without guile. There was a story, much savoured in our community, of a small boy who, while his mother was teaching him his catechism, refused to repeat the answer to one of the questions. The question was, "Who have sinned?" The answer was, "All have sinned." But nothing would induce the child to give the answer in the book. On being asked why he would not repeat the answer, he shot his last bolt: "It's not true...Mr. Roberts has never sinned!" In the community, public opinion was on the child's side—save for a few amateur theologians.

When the story was told to my father, he said nothing but smiled sadly, the smile of one who knows better, for he had a very sensitive and active conscience. Moreover, he was very gentle, though that does not mean that he could not be on necessary occasions as firm as a rock and as stern as a judge. But he offended no man willingly, nor in my experience of him did he allow a bitter word to escape his lips. I saw him once or twice deeply wounded, but even then he was not without charity. It was this combination of qualities in him that led him to being the arbiter usually chosen by his presbytery to resolve a dispute in a church within its bounds. It is no exaggeration to say that no minister in his own presbytery, or far beyond its bounds, was more deeply trusted, nor was there another whose leading was more readily followed by the laity. Once when a furious controversy was raging over the question of infant baptism, the principal of Bala Theological College where I was studying, asked me whether I knew where my father stood in the controversy. I had to answer that I did not certainly know. "Well," said he, "will you please tell him that I hope that he will take part in the discussion at the next presbytery, whatever side he is upon."

One task laid on my father gave him great happiness and much trouble. All through his ministerial life he had brooded long and deeply over St. Paul's Epistle to the Romans. One might almost say that he had lived in it! When he was asked to write a handbook in two volumes about the epistle, he was, in his shy way, delighted. He was slow to write at any time, as I have said, and when it came to writing a book the going was heavy. In the event, the two slender volumes proved to be a considerable success and afforded an excellent introduction to the epistle.

My relationship with my father was one of peculiar intimacy, especially in his later years. His ripe counsel was always available to me and, when we met, our fellowship grew ever deeper. After I left home our meetings were rarer, especially after I went to London. But when we did meet, it was as though we had never parted.

In 1906, his health broke down seriously, so seriously that at the end of February of the next year I was called home, as it was evident that he was not far from the end of his journey. I spent the last week of his life at his bedside. For most of the time he was in a diabetic coma, and the intervals of consciousness were short and few. On the Friday afternoon, however, his eyes opened wide, and seeing me at his bedside he smiled. He was evidently too weak to speak. I offered to read to him and he nodded a weak assent. I said to him, "I do not need to ask you what you would like me to read to you—first, the twenty-third Psalm; and after, the eighth chapter of Romans." Once more a nodded assent. When I had finished reading the Romans chapter, with its glorious crescendo and finale: "I am persuaded that neither death nor life...nor things present nor things to come, nor any other creature shall be able to separate us from the love of God which is in Christ Jesus our Lord," I asked him: "Does this hold now?" This time he answered audibly, "Yes, it holds." And again more faintly, "It holds." With that he relapsed into unconsciousness, not to wake again save into the ultimate realities in which he had, through his life, put his trust.

The funeral was a memorable occasion. It was on St. David's Day and, as someone said, this time it was a double St. David's Day. I was told that the procession which followed the body to its resting place was more than a mile long, despite heavy rain.

2

Margaret Roberts

RR's mother was born Margaret Jones. Her father, Richard Jones, was originally a glover. When his business was destroyed by the introduction of French kid into Great Britain, he had entered his father-in-law's shipping firm in Conway. Later the business was transferred to Liverpool, and it was there Margaret Jones grew up. Tradition had it that the family had gone to sea for some generations. Certainly Margaret Jones' uncle was captain of the Five Sisters, which went down in a gale with all hands lost off Flamborough Head. Margaret's mother Martha was one of the five sisters for whom the ship was named. Of his mother RR left the following sketch.

Where my father met my mother I do not certainly know; neither do I know the date of their marriage. I, their first born, saw the light of day in 1874. I was followed by a sister, Annie, and a brother, Robert David, known among us as Bob, who died in early manhood. My mother endowed me with her own temperament. We were both hasty and our relations were not always even. Not that we did not love each other, but it took very little to set us at odds. Consequently, I took my troubles to my father rather than to her. With the years he became more and more the repository of my confidences. None the less, my mother was a great woman. She was quite fearless, and in our small domestic world her forthrightness and fearlessness made up for my father's natural diffidence and shyness.

If the office-bearers of the church failed in their concern for their minister, and sometimes they did, they heard about it from my mother, and on such occasions she did not mince her words. Even my father did not escape her discipline. One day we were sitting at dinner, my father had been suffering from a cold, and that day he had been out of doors for the first time. At one point in the meal my mother looked at him while he was quietly preoccupied with his meat and potatoes. "David," she said abruptly, "what do you mean? You have been and got your hair cut, and you with a cold. It is just like you to do a thing like that. You never think of the children and me."

My father made no immediate rejoinder, and went on eating. Presently he looked up and said, "Margaret, I have not had my hair cut." My mother was up in arms at once. "Why then," she said, "didn't you say so before, and keep me from making an exhibition of myself before the children?" For the rest of the meal there was profound silence. Occasions of that kind, however, were very rare. Indeed, I cannot recall another with clarity. I would say that my mother's normal attitude toward my father was one of deep reverence, and she was sedulous in guarding his hours of study from interruption.

Another memory of my mother is in another setting. It was election time. The sitting member was a Scotsman named Robertson, but a faction of Liberals was favouring a native of the county, Morgan Lloyd, as their candidate. The most solid Liberals had no confidence in Lloyd, and among them was my father. Lloyd's following was very strong, however, chiefly because of his Welsh origin. One Saturday afternoon Robertson's supporters had called a meeting in our public hall to promote his candidacy. This provoked reprisals, and the leaders of the Lloyd faction called a meeting in the open air under the very eaves of the hall. The temper of this faction was ugly and some stones had already been thrown through the hall windows.

The leader of the forces was a trouble maker named Jenkins, a member of my father's congregation; he was in charge of the outdoor meeting. Somehow the news reached my mother of the doings outside the hall, and my father was in the hall. That was enough. She went to see for herself what was going on. After watching the rowdy scene for a time, she saw Jenkins mounting an improvised rostrum. Immediately she began to elbow her way through the crowd to the platform. When Jenkins was about to address the crowd, my mother addressed him: "Jenkins, if anyone is hurt or killed today, you will have to answer for it." This unexpected sally discomposed Jenkins, and it was a rather subdued orator who addressed the crowd. It is interesting to recall that by the next election, Welsh nationalism had grown so strong that there was a general movement to secure Welshmen to represent Welsh constituencies. Our constituency chose one of its own sons, Thomas E. Ellis [1859–1899, MP for Bala and Junior Lord of the Treasury, 1895] who became the chief whip of the Liberal Party in the House of Commons; and an adjacent constituency returned a young lawyer named David Lloyd George [1863–1945, Welsh politician, returned for Caernarvon 1889; Prime Minister, 1916–1922].

An episode in which my mother played a characteristic part had to do with the public health of the community. The death rate was a great deal higher than it should have been. This condition was partly due to malnutrition, especially among the children. It was proposed, therefore, that cooking classes be provided for the quarrymen's wives. When this proposal was made public, the women rose in a body to repudiate this slur on their domestic economy. Some of the women in our immediate neighbourhood brought their grievance to my mother, expecting sympathy and support. But my mother, who was known to be a good cook, answered that she was going to join the classes as there was a great deal she had yet to learn. When my mother's attitude became generally known, a great deal of the opposition died out; and the classes were quite successful.

It is due that I should put it on record that I owe my soul to her. In the summer of 1892, my father had received an invitation to visit and to preach in Welsh settlements in the US, and he had accepted the invitation. My mother was also included in the invitation. As I had no examination pending that term in college, I enjoyed myself hugely, did very little work, and spent much more money than I should have done. The day of reckoning came with my mother's return. She gave me a verbal trouncing so protracted and thorough that I lost all conceit for myself. But it was too thorough to induce penitence. I felt sore and bitter and no more. There was no doubt I deserved it, and even more. But I did not see it in that light. I flung out of the house, went up into the hills, and there spent the rest of the day. But I came back still bitter, and so I remained.

One day my father said to me in his quiet way, "If you have nothing else to do, you might tidy up the papers in my desk." For him I was always ready and glad to do anything at any time, and I set about the job. In the course of it I came upon a black notebook which I casually opened. It was a diary my mother had kept of her American experiences. It had been kept carefully until half way on the return voyage. My parents were travelling on the S.S. *Gallia*, which was then a veteran of the high seas. In mid-ocean it met with a fierce storm and in the course of it, the ship's propeller was damaged. For two days, during which the ship was mercilessly tossed about, the engineers laboured to mend the damage. Many of the passengers had given themselves up as lost and certainly they were in great danger. Of this experience my mother had attempted no account in her diary. The only sentence written during those days was a brief prayer which ran: "Lord, save my elder boy."

When I came upon this prayer I was stunned. For the first time I understood how deeply my mother loved me, even when a few days before she was lashing me with her tongue. And I realized, also, that I had need of her prayer. I closed the little book and went again to the silence of the hills. In the wild and solitary place to which I had gone, I had it out with myself, and there I made a decision which proved a new beginning to my life. What little service I have been able to give to man or to the kingdom of God began on that day.

In his book *The Spirit of God and the Faith of Today*, RR tells this story in the third person, and goes on to add this sequel:

...But so far as he could tell there was no specifically religious element in his thought or his experience that day. He was naturally of a sceptical turn and, in the relative freedom of college life, had taken leave of all his religious habits. It happened, however, on his return to college that fall that he met a woman, a fellow-student, with whom on one occasion he fell into a discourse concerning religion. He found that the woman believed very devoutly in the efficacy of prayer; and, in a rather flippant way, he said: "Then I wish you would pray for me." She took him at his word and said, "I will." To his own great astonishment, as he was going to bed that night, he knelt in prayer. And, according to his own testimony, his conversion was completed in that act of prayer. From that hour, life became a new thing.

RR concludes the sketch of his mother:

My mother died in 1911, at my sister's home in Llanberis. It was a strange turn of the wheel of time that from the house in which she died it was possible to see the slate quarry in which my father had worked in his youth and early manhood.

3

The Community

Rhiw, where RR grew up, was a centre for slate quarrying. The life of the community was typical of any such community in Wales.

When I was a boy the slate-quarrying industry was still prosperous; though it had, I imagine, passed its peak. Certainly my early recollections include frequent references to previous "good times." None the less, Blaenau Ffestiniog was still growing; it sprawled without any design from Rhiwbryfdir to Conglywal in one direction and to Tanygrisiau in the other. Its most obvious feature was its rocks. From the back window of my home we looked upon a steep craggy rock, one end of which had already been covered by the piled up rubble of the quarries. From our front windows we looked upon a smaller but no less rugged rock called *Y Garregddu* [the Black Rock], upon which we could sometimes see half-wild goats that had been driven from higher altitudes by bad weather. Beyond, at some distance, we could see Manod, which overlooked the other end of Blaenau. As a small boy I conceived the idea that heaven was on the other side of Manod.

Most of the land between *Nyth-y-Gigran* [the Raven's Nest], the height at the back of my home, and the *Garegddu*, had once been wet bog. But with the years it had been gradually drained and much of it converted into pasture and hay land. Still, some stretches of marshland remained; one of these lay across the road from our front door, and it was a happy hunting ground for small boys. I well remember the evil day when some men came into our paradise with picks and spades and began to dig ditches across it. Paradise was lost; henceforth we had to play in the street.

Another characteristic of the neighbourhood was its wetness. *Glaw 'stiniog*, the common vernacular for "Ffestiniog rain," was proverbial throughout North Wales. So it might well be, for the average rainfall was over ninety-nine inches. The prevailing wind was from the southwest and carried with it a great deal of moisture. For this moisture the semicircle of mountains, from the greater and lesser Moelwyns at one end to Manod at the other, was a perfect trap. The consequence was that the moisture was precipitated in a fine endless rain upon our heads, until it was exhausted. And then it began again. It was no uncommon experience to leave Blaenau Ffestiniog by the Northwestern Railway in heavy rain and to emerge from the tunnel to find the scene bathed in sunshine. We did have occasional spells of fine weather, but rain was our natural element.

The community appears to have been, from its beginnings, intellectually serious. But it is necessary to add that this seriousness had its roots in the common religious life. When I first went to school, I might be caned—and often was—for speaking Welsh in school hours...if I were caught doing so. [RR used to further comment: "The caning never taught me not to speak Welsh, but only made me determined not to be caught at it again."] That, I imagine, must have been a belated survival of the Tudor policy of extinguishing the language, and apparently it still lingered on in the conservative tradition of the Board of Education in London.

We owe the survival of Welsh speech and letters to religion. It was in the Sunday school that the boys and girls of my generation learned to read Welsh, and not for any cultural purpose but that we should be able to read the Bible for ourselves. Moreover, we were expected to learn by heart large sections of the Bible, year after year, and we even had annual examinations in the prescribed portions of the Bible. I venture to question whether any people have been so generally and deeply versed in the Christian scripture as were the Welsh folk of my boyhood.

Our passage through the Sunday school was a very important part of our education, for in Wales the Sunday school was not, as in England, a means of teaching only children, it embraced all ages. You might at one end of the room see a class of young children learning the Welsh alphabet and at the other a group of grey-beards discussing the mysteries of a Pauline epistle. Our men were very theologically minded. One day, as we were sitting at our midday meal, a lad brought a message to my father from a group of men in a slate-dressing shed not far from our house. The message was in Welsh, scratched on a piece of dressed slate with some sharp tool. It ran as follows:

> "To the Reverend David Roberts: Would you please set down the order in which the believer receives the following gifts and graces: penitence, repentance, forgiveness, justification, redemption, sanctification?"

It was signed, "Engine Penybont"—the engine, in that connection, being used as a corporate designation for the workers in that particular shed. The lad was to wait for an answer.

My father, after reading the message, went to his study and wrote the desired answer to the question. At that time I had been in the ministry for a few years and I realized that the slate was a social document of some interest. So I appropriated it, and it stood upon my study mantelpiece for some years. Unfortunately, it was broken in a house moving. Whether Ffestiniog quarrymen still debate theological subjects in the dinner hour I do not know, but that they still debate I am certain. I imagine, however, that the area of debate covers a wider and more varied ground.

> RR described the Calvinistic Methodists in a lecture entitled "My Wales," delivered sometime in the 1920s.

It is not until the Puritan movement in the seventeenth century that we find anything like a religious renaissance in Wales, but that was not general and was chiefly confined to the towns. What shocked Wales into a flaming religious life, more than a century later, is what is sometimes described as the Evangelical Movement. A group of men, tutors at Oxford, being greatly concerned with the state of religion in the Church of England, began to meet regularly for prayer in a room at Lincoln College, and out of that praying group emerged the Methodist Movement in England and Wales. But the movement was not identical in the two countries. It was led in England by the brothers John and Charles Wesley, and in Wales it followed George Whitefield.

Whitefield greatly moved some of the Church of England clergy in Wales and they caught his fire, and before long Wales was ablaze with a new religious life. As the English church in Wales as a whole was cool to the movement, it lost its greatest opportunity; a new church calling itself "Calvinistic Methodist" came into being and it remains to this day the strongest religious communion in Wales....

The Calvinistic Methodists—now the Welsh Presbyterian Church—in my time had six spacious places of worship, not to speak of two or three chapels of ease [small offshoots of central churches designed to make church attendance easier for people living in remoter districts]. The Congregationalists or Independents had four sizable chapels, the regular Baptists three, while the Campbellites or Scotch Baptists—known colloquially as y *Batus bach*, "the small Baptists"—had a couple of modest places of worship.

Of course the Church of England was represented, having a parish church at Llan Ffestiniog, some 4 miles from Blaenau, and two others in Blaenau. But in those days it was a state established church and therefore something of an outcast in that stronghold of dissent. In our more generous moods we might allude to it as *yr hen Fam*, "the old mother," but more generally, and particularly when the question of its disestablishment cropped up, we spoke of it as *yr Estrones*, "the stranger woman." My old grandmother's possessions were taken and sold because she would not pay tithes to the Anglican Church at the time when she was seeing my father through college to become a Presbyterian [Calvinistic Methodist] minister. But that story now belongs to the ghostly company of "old, unhappy, far-off things, and battles long ago," for not so long ago the Church of England in Wales was disestablished and is now the Church of Wales, a title which exaggerates its standing but is less offensive to Welsh sensibility than its former name.

In addition to the preaching services, the nonconformist churches had others in the course of the week. There was a prayer meeting on Monday evening, a children's meeting on Tuesday, and on Wednesday evening the *Seiat* was held. *Seiat* is Welsh for "society" [or "fellowship meeting"]; and the meeting on Wednesday was a meeting of the society, that is, the communicant members and their children. It was a sore trial for the children and none of us pretended to like it. Business affecting the society was transacted; that done, the minister would converse publicly with some of the members, whether men or women, upon their spiritual experience.

In my boyhood the Sunday sermons were the great event of the week, and we boys and girls were expected to learn the texts of these sermons and repeat them together at the *Seiat*. Moreover, we were encouraged to take notes of the sermons and to give a digest of one of them, which was good discipline and habituated us in the writing of Welsh. Finally, some of the senior elders would exhort the members to faithfulness, or warn them against the heinous sin of *gwag rodiana y Sabboth*, "vain walking on the Sabbath." In spite of my love and reverence for my father, who had to conduct these meetings, I have not a single happy memory of them. The *Seiat* was a weekly torture.

We were a musical people, though our music was, in my younger days, almost altogether vocal. Once every year we held a *Cymanfu Ganu*, "a singing festival," an institution which has had much to do with the unique excellence of Welsh congregational singing. Every year a booklet was issued for the festival containing hymns and tunes, old and new, and the hour before the Sunday evening service would be given to the practice of these hymns. Then the great day came, and with it a distinguished conductor. The largest chapel in the place would be packed with prepared singers, who entered into the proceedings with the greatest zest and enjoyed themselves immensely.

Not only did we have a musical festival, we had a preaching festival, the *Cymanfu Bregethu*. It was held at Easter. Each of the churches involved was expected to secure two distinguished preachers. These engagements were usually made some years ahead. The co-operating churches "pooled" their preachers and arranged their engagements so that two different preachers would preach at each of the three services on the two days of the festival. Twelve sermons were preached in each church during the festival. I recall many of those preachers: David Saunders of Swansea, Evan Philips of Newcastle-Emlyn, John Williams of Brynsiencyn, S. T. Jones of Rhyl, and perhaps greatest of all, Thomas Charles Edwards, of whom I have more to say later. These were all men of power which I, although only a boy, could recognize even though the sermon soared over my head.

But a certain element of competition entered into the *Cymanfu*, though men like David Saunders were, of course, innocent of it. Sometimes there was friction over the order of precedence, the last being the place of honour. From time to time there was a tendency to exploit the *hwyl* [a cadenced, sing-song style of fervent, emotional preaching] into some discredit. My father sedulously avoided it. There was also occasionally a tendency to introduce an element of "sport" into the *Cymanfu*, with preachers substituting for race horses! In later years I heard again and again that in the Glamorganshire colliery valleys, the colliers laid odds on the preachers.

Our interests, however, were not confined to religion. Toward the middle of the last century there came another spiritual awakening—a new intellectual eagerness, a literary revival, a new passion for education. We had always been singers and had sung to the harp. The singing festivals testify to this. We had great poets from time to time. From the late 1860s, all this side of our life increased with extraordinary vigour. It happened that we had an old institution ready to serve this new life, the *Eisteddfod*, literally meaning "the session." What takes place at the annual Eisteddfod is, in these days, too well known to need description. But beside the national Eisteddfod there were, and are, local *eisteddfodau*, in communities which are sufficiently populous to maintain them. Not the least of these was the one periodically held in the community in which I was born and bred.

4
Early School Days

There was a solid base for these voluntary cultural expressions in the educational structure which grew up in Wales in the latter part of the nineteenth century. This is described in RR's manuscript concerning his schooling.

I was fortunate in the time at which my school years began. Up to 1870, the day schools were under the control of the clergy of the Church of England, though the population was overwhelmingly nonconformist. Moreover, they were few and far between. Here and there were the so-called British schools, established by the British and Foreign School Society, a benevolent society founded and supported by well-to-do English nonconformists. The education provided by these institutions appears to have been of a mediocre quality, at least in Wales.

In my native place there were two schools, one belonging to the Established Church, the other a British school. In the early 1870s, my community was one of the first to take advantage of a new Education Act, making education compulsory. The act enabled a community to elect a school board, which might establish and maintain elementary schools and were empowered to levy taxes for their upkeep. My community elected a board and took over the two existing school buildings. But these buildings were soon superseded by a very handsome and well equipped new school. Before 1884, or thereabouts there were at least five such schools, each having separate departments for boys, girls, and infants. I think my own earliest memory is of being led by the hand, for the first time, to the infant department of one of these schools.

What I am able to recall of my early days at home and at school is faint and confused. At school I was considered stupid, and it was a considerable time before anyone suspected that my stupidity might be caused by defective eyesight. The suggestion once made, my mother lost no time in taking me to Liverpool where a friend of her family was in high repute as an oculist. I remember nothing of the visit to him nor of the subsequent visit to the optician. What I do remember is the first time I wore my spectacles in the street. Alice in her Wonderland had nothing on me in mine. I was in a new and exciting world—the passing drays, carts, cabs, and "buses," the bustle of all kinds of people on the sidewalk, the shop windows, the high houses. Even more exciting was the journey home, seeing the world out of the carriage windows; and more wonderful yet, seeing the sea stretching out, as if it were to meet the sky. The pair of spectacles made a great difference to my standing at school. Presently I was at the head of my class and remained there.

But that was not all the difference that the spectacles made. Being by nature inquisitive, I spent a great deal of time exploring the world around me, of which I had seen so little. There was plenty to explore—streams and lakes (some of them with fish), the craggy heights near home and two sizeable mountains, Manod and Moelwyn. And, within a boy's reach, there was a glorious glen. It took me a long time to explore my boyhood world, and it proved to be the prelude to much more ambitious enterprises in later years.

In the year 1884, there was established a higher grade school for such boys as seemed capable of an advanced education. It was called the Advanced Elementary School and was housed in one of the discarded buildings of the earlier order, adapted and furnished for the new. In that same year I had completed the elementary school, and my parents decided to send me to the new school if I could pass the entrance examination. Though I was a year younger than the rest of the class, I came out second on the list. The headmaster of this advanced school was Griffith John Williams, who had been headmaster of the school which I had been attending previously. There could not have been a happier choice. Indeed, in later years, I came to believe that he was the begetter of the enterprise.

The new school was a great success. While we continued most of our former studies, we were introduced to others, Latin, botany, geology, and algebra. The special interest of the Head was geology. The study of geology naturally attracted us boys, for our daily bread came by way of what geologists call the Llandwilo Beds, which our men quarried and dressed into roofing slates. But our Head was not content with book education, and now and again he would take us afield. I well remember an excursion to a bleak and rugged stretch of country to observe the striations which the Ice Age had left behind, and where some fossil remains of a still older time could be found. On another occasion he took us to the Conway Valley for a botanical excursion.

In those days no serious attention was paid to the physical education of the pupils in our local schools. No supervision of our games was provided save a casual oversight while we were at play on school premises, and that more for the sake of the premises than the pupils. So far as I can remember we had only two organized games. The first was a primitive version of a game which I was later to know as "Rounders," but which we called "Ring." (This is the game which developed in America to become baseball.) We played where we could—sometimes in a quiet street, sometimes on an unoccupied piece of ground. We knew nothing of matches with other groups of boys. The other game was called "Relieve ho," which was presumably introduced by the sons of English engineers who had been brought in in earlier years to attend to the machinery in the quarries. The players were divided into two groups. Each group had its end to defend and at the same time each had to make forays into the enemies' country. The victory went to the side that made the most captures. I remember, faintly, the coming of football into our parts, and the consternation that it stirred among the *unco guid* (those who are professedly strict in matters of morals and religion—and consider that they can tell others how to live their lives). The football was an invention of Satan and good boys should shun it. But the football got the better of the deacons in the end.

I remained at the advanced school for the three years of its curriculum; and never had as good a teacher as Griffith Williams. He was bent on my continuing my education, and presently the opportunity came. The North Wales Scholarship Association was formed to enable boys whose parents were not well-to-do to go to schools where they might be prepared for university. Griffith Williams "coached" me for the first examination of the association, and when I came back from it, he went over the papers with me. It was plain sailing until we came to the last paper and the last question. I told him frankly that I had bungled it. He looked over the question and considered my answer, and after a short pause he said angrily: "You could have won that scholarship if you had had your wits about you." I had a lean time at school for the next few days. Then came the report of the competition, and the sun shone once more. I had won one of the three scholarships offered. This scholarship had the effect of making me henceforth virtually a visitor to my birthplace.

In the meantime the educational enthusiasm of my home people grew, and not only did they provide a new building for the higher grade school, they also built a higher grade school for girls. When a bill concerning secondary schools in Wales was enacted, a secondary school for girls and boys was built so that the youth of that area had no need to go away from home as I had before qualifying for entrance to a university.

But where should I go with my scholarship? That was the great concern of my parents for the next few weeks. The trustees of the association had also provided a bewildering list of schools to which their beneficiaries might be safely entrusted. Some of these were Anglican foundations, which were out of the question for the son of a nonconformist minister. Others were too expensive even with the scholarship, which was for twenty pounds a year. In the end I think it was my mother that settled the matter. On the list of schools was that to which her brothers and some of my cousins had gone and its reputation was still high. So, at the next autumn term, I was entered as a pupil in the high school (as distinguished from the commercial school) of the Liverpool Institute. When I presented myself I underwent an examination to determine the form to which I should be assigned. I was sent to the lower fifth form, two forms from the sixth and highest, a good deal higher than I expected to be.

As the school had no provision for pupils away from home, it was arranged that I should live during the term at my mother's old home, which was not far from the school. It turned out to be an unfortunate arrangement for me. My grandfather had left but a meagre fortune and my two maiden aunts had to work for a living. For some years before my grandfather's death, my elder aunt had held a high position in the millinery department of an important Liverpool store. So the aunts set themselves up in business in a modest way. The venture was called a "Millinery and Fancy Work Establishment." My Aunt Hannah carried on her millinery work in a small annex to the shop. My Aunt Pattie looked after any customers who came to the shop in the daytime and made the motions of being busy with her "fancy work" in the evening.

It had now become necessary to secure a larger income if the old home was to be preserved, however, and so they took in "paying guests." Besides the two aunts, the company consisted of my orphan cousin Millie Jones, who earned a good salary as a clerk in a railway office downtown. Then there was John Bebb, a second cousin, and later his brother Alfred, both of whom were unfortunate in business. There was also a lodger on the second floor who was even more unfortunate than the Bebbs and was always behind with his rent. But there was also an angel in the house. Jennie had come [when] a young girl from Beddgelert in North Wales, to be a general domestic servant. By the time I joined the family she was no longer a servant but a member of the family, as well she might be. She was loved by all who knew her, and to me she was a second mother.

When I joined this household the only available room for me was a cubbyhole on the top storey. It was all very well as a bedroom for one who could rough it, but as a place for doing one's school lessons it was impossible. In the winter it was intolerably cold. I came home from afternoon school about five o'clock. I had then a clear hour before the household began to foregather after the day's work. After that I had no chance of serious work downstairs. Nor was the adult conversation in the evening attractive to me. In consequence I begat a habit of roaming the streets until bedtime and then going to bed with only half of my homework done, trusting to luck to see me through the next morning's work. Fortunately, a little later, I discovered the Picton Reading Room, and there I might prepare my Virgil for the next day, or whatever the overnight assignment happened to be. As I look back on my Liverpool year, I think that the Picton did as much for me as the institute did.

I went to the institute with a bent for mathematics, and that was fostered by Owen, the mathematical master, who was a very competent teacher. With two of the senior masters I did not get on very well. My Welsh accent was an offence to Burton, the English master. To old Kennedy, the "major," who taught us classics, I was "You Welshman," spoken in a tone that suggested I was some kind of vermin. With the other masters I got on fairly well, particularly with Ewart who introduced us to modern science, and Anthony Book who taught French, and did so in such a way that I have preserved a liking for French literature to this day. The headmaster was a clergy-man surnamed Sephton. With him I had little contact. Once I was sent by one of the masters to report to him a misdemeanour of my own. As it was my first serious offence he let me off with a warning and a little sermon, the while dangling a cane to give edge to the warning.

At the end of my second year Sephton retired, and his place was filled by a younger man named Hughes. With him I had only one contact. On one occasion Kennedy had badgered me beyond endur-ance and, at the end of the hour, I went straight to the head's office and laid a complaint. Then he did something that surprised me. I was by that time in the sixth form and a senior. It was, he said, very difficult for him to deal with a man so much older than himself. He asked me to bear with Kennedy until the end of term. "All this is," he said, "in confidence between you and me." I felt very important to be entrusted with "state secrets."

Hughes carried out his plans and his plans changed mine. I had often asked myself where my mathematics was taking me, as lately I had found it hard going. I took counsel with my father in the next vacation. His counsel was to keep up the mathematics, but to pay more attention to the classics. When I came back to school I found a new man in the "old major's" chair. The newcomer had but lately taken his degree at Oxford, and in a couple of months he had com-pletely won me to the classics. I settled down to work for a classical scholarship at Oxford. For the next eighteen months I worked hard upon the classics, but still under the handicap that resulted from the earlier years under Kennedy. I made two attempts to win a scholar-ship, but in vain.

5
College: Aberystwyth

When I went home at the end of the summer term, still sore after my Oxford failures, I announced that I was going into "business," as all but one of my cousins had done. That, I said to my parents, was all I was fit for. Wisely, my parents said very little at the time. But when my mother judged that I had sufficiently shed my soreness, she took me in hand. She told me that she had long prayed that I should become a teacher or a preacher, and she believed that God would answer her prayer. In the meantime, it was her wish that I prepare to go to college in the fall. My mother usually had her own way in family affairs, and presently I settled down to prepare for the entrance examination of the University College of Wales.

Up to 1870, there had been no university in Wales. But in that year a university college was established in Aberystwyth in mid-Wales; and thither young Wales, so far as it could at the time, hastened to go. It was to this college I went in 1891. Its first principal was Thomas Charles Edwards [1837–1900], a graduate of London and Oxford, a great Greek scholar but primarily a theologian. Just before I entered he had resigned in order to make a dream of his come true, namely, to create in Wales a theological school of the highest standard. I came to know him very intimately later on; he had put the Aberystwyth College on its feet, and it has been a going concern ever since.

But Aberystwyth was only the first. In quick succession followed the University College of North Wales at Bangor and the University College of South Wales at Cardiff. In the early days these colleges had no authority to confer degrees, but they were able to take advantage of the facilities of the University of London, which was licensed to confer degrees upon any person who passed its examination in the prescribed subjects. And so we were prepared for the degrees of

London University until the creation of the University of Wales, incorporating all three colleges, in 1893. (A fourth college, Swansea in South Wales, was added in 1921.)

At the end of the summer I sat for the preliminary examinations. I did well enough that a scholarship of twenty pounds a year for two years was awarded to me. My first business now was to pass the matriculation examination of the University of London, and that I did easily in the next January 1892. Then, in the following term, I settled down to the business of preparing for the intermediate examination in the BSc course. I had five years to prepare for it.

This generous leeway was my undoing. I soon became more interested in what may be described as the "public" life of the college than in the academic business that should have been my primary concern. It began with the first meeting of the "Lit. and Deb.," that is, the Literary and Debating Society. The subject of the debate was that the time had come to incorporate the Welsh colleges into a university, and I was the freshman chosen—according to the rule at the first debate of the year—to second the motion. As I delivered the speech it seemed to me to be a flat and sorry performance, but it turned out to be a considerable success judging from the applause that followed it. From that time I fear that I was more interested in my speeches than in my studies.

Nor was the Lit. and Deb. the only temptation. The sea was close to us and I spent a great deal of time with friends roaming along the rocks and sailing and rowing in the small craft that were plentifully available. Certainly the lighter side of college life did not suffer from lack of my attention.

There were distractions of another sort also. I presently joined a group of men who went every Sunday evening to conduct a religious service in a lodging house in a slummy suburb of the town called, if my memory serves me, Trefechan. The addresses which we delivered were naturally elementary, and probably none the worse for that; and we could boast of good singing. But the members of this group were later called to play a part in the quickening of a religious interest within the college. In the previous summer some students from English universities, who had attended the annual Conference at Keswick, arranged for a clergyman of the Church of England to visit the colleges and universities of Great Britain with the purpose of quickening the spiritual life of the students. He came to "Aber" but the good man left us rather bewildered. Most of us were Welshmen and nonconformists, and we were accustomed to much more weighty statements of the Gospel from our Welsh preachers. However, our visitor did stir us to plan for the next year, and the outcome was a weekly devotional meeting which was fairly attended.

The next year I was sent as a delegate to the student gathering which met at Keswick during the same days as the usual convention. I was still too young to have learned toleration of any religious idiom other than that I had inherited, which was Calvinism modified by a generous doctrine of grace. The convention idiom was distasteful to me, and the special student meetings were charged with the convention atmosphere. I knew that a student movement so impregnated had no future in Wales. I made the best report I could and we continued on our own way. In the course of that year, however, John R. Mott and Robert Speer visited the universities and colleges of Great Britain, and shortly afterwards the Student Association was removed from the ambit of the Keswick Conference and entered on a life of its own under the leadership of Tissington Tatlow. [Mott, 1865–1955, and Speer, 1867–1947, were Americans, Mott being founder of the World Student Christian Federation, and Speer being the chief administrator for the Presbyterian Church. Tissington Tatlow, 1876–1957, was later to become General Secretary of the Student Christian Movement of Great Britain and the author of its history.]

After the summer holiday, spent in the Mediterranean as purser on a cargo ship of my cousin's firm, I settled down in "digs" at Aberystwyth and set to work. But before the term was far gone I found myself becoming restless. This was partly due to the circumstance that the head of the biology department and I were not "kindred spirits." He was a person of scant patience and sharp tongue. The laboratory work soon became a trial; the myopia I suffered from imposed a very heavy handicap upon me when I was trying to dissect animal specimens, whether earthworms or rabbits. I had the same disability in seeing minute objects through the microscope. However, I carried on as well as I could with lectures and laboratory, for I had to face an examination at the end of the academic year.

But this was not the only preoccupation of that year. My visit to Keswick had awakened in me a persistent question whether or not I should become a preacher. There was no difficulty in blending a science degree course with a later course in theology. Indeed, an old teacher of mine had done that very thing. When I went home at the next vacation I mooted the matter to my father, and after a long conversation he seemed to be satisfied with my motives and plans. He reported the matter to his board of deacons, the local authority which had the power to commend me to the presbytery. After some trial preaching in a number of congregations within the bounds of the presbytery, and favourable reports from the congregations to which I had preached, I was accepted as a licensed preacher.

6

Bala

RR still intended to take his science degree at Aberystwyth. The examinations were held in London as the practical laboratory tests were accompanied by orals. There were four subjects: mathematics, physics, chemistry, and biology, and they all had to be passed at the same time. RR went up to London in 1893, and again in 1894, but on both occasions failed to meet the requirements.

I returned from London after my second try crestfallen; my parents were deeply disappointed and even more perplexed as to what to do with me. A return to Aberystwyth was out of the question. The remainder of the family funds had, in all fairness, to be devoted to the education of my sister and my younger brother. The only opening seemed to be, in view of my status as an accepted candidate for the ministry, that I should go forthwith to Bala. But would Bala accept a callow youth with a poor record?

As it happened, Dr. Thomas Charles Edwards, the principal of Bala, came to visit a friend in our vicinity, and my father sought him out and told him his dilemma concerning me. Bala had no age limits, and my father was invited to send me to Bala at the beginning of the next college year. As my father was taking leave of him, the principal, presumably sensing some doubt in my father's mind, said in good humour: "David Roberts, send your boy to us and we shall make a preacher of him." In conversation with one of his fellow ministers a few days later, I overheard my father saying, in allusion to the principal's parting sally, "I doubt whether the *old* Doctor [Dr. Lewis Edwards, principal of Bala in my father's time] would have said anything like that." It was my father's conviction that professors had their place, but it was the Holy Spirit who made preachers!

Bala is a little town in my own county of Merioneth in North Wales. At the end of the eighteenth century it became the centre, in those parts, of the Evangelical Movement which Wesley and Whitefield had set afoot. The incumbent of the Church of England in the parish had resigned his office and became a leader of the new movement. This was the Rev. Thomas Charles [1755–1814], B.A., a graduate of Oxford. One of his concerns was the grievous paucity of Bibles in the homes of his people, and his efforts to meet that need gave him a name far beyond his own parish. It reached a humble cottage in a remote glen, the home of a young girl named Mary Jones, who had saved her pennies in hope that someday she might buy a Bible. The day came at last. Rumour reached the glen that Mr. Charles of Bala had returned from a visit to London and brought with him a parcel of Welsh Bibles. So Mary gathered her saved pennies and, with a packet of food for the journey, set out to Bala 30 miles away. The way ran through rough and difficult country. It is rugged, mountainous, boggy, and with great stretches of moorland. But Mary set out with a stout heart, walking barefoot most of the way, condescending to respectability by putting on her shoes and stockings only when she at last walked into the little town of the Bibles. But when she arrived, Mr. Charles had sold all the copies he had brought home with him—all but one, which he proposed to keep for his own use. Face to face with the disappointed child, however, the good man had no heart to keep it for himself. So Mary had her Bible and went home happy.

That Bible is today honourably preserved in the Bible House in London; for it was the story of Mary Jones, told by Thomas Charles to a company of his evangelical friends, that fired them to lay the foundation of the British and Foreign Bible Society in 1804. What that society, with its offspring and its agents throughout the habitable world, and the great company of translators it has called to its aid, has done to make known the "grace and truth that came by Jesus Christ" to the peoples of this world, is one of the greatest and most romantic stories in the annals of mankind. And we Merioneth folk are still proud of the share our forebears had in the inception of this achievement.

The influence of Thomas Charles did not die with him. Not the least of his legacies was the Welsh Sunday school, of which something has already been said. Then, when the Evangelical revival begat in Wales the Calvinistic Methodist denomination, it became urgent to provide instruction for its preachers. A school was established at Bala for this purpose. The curriculum was not exclusively biblical and doctrinal. Owing to the lack of any public school system and the paucity of any other provision for ordinary education, the new school at Bala had to include in its plan the groundwork of a general culture, in addition to the study of the scriptures and the rudiments of theology. With the establishment of Aberystwyth and the other colleges, however, it was possible to make the Bala curriculum purely theological, and it was to do this that Thomas Charles Edwards left "Aber" and went to Bala. As his name indicates, he was of "Thomas Charles" ancestry; his father, Dr. Lewis Edwards, had married into the Charles family and was the most distinguished of his predecessors.

Thomas Charles Edwards was a man of high distinction, both in the range of his scholarship and in his reputation as a preacher in Welsh and English. Moreover he was an accomplished Greek scholar, both in the classical and post-classical language. While yet amid the preoccupations of Aberystwyth, he had written a commentary upon the First Corinthian Epistle which had a long and wide circulation among scholars and students. At the time of his death he was working on a commentary on the Epistle to the Hebrews, upon which he had already written a handbook in Welsh for the senior classes in the Sunday schools.

By the time Dr. Edwards had settled in as principal of the theological school at Bala, his own preaching days were over. The long and taxing years spent in setting up the University College at Aberystwyth, in building up its resources for the future and the unceasing travels that this had involved, was labour enough for a strong man. But he did more than another man's work in his incessant preaching far and near. It was no wonder that, by the time he had set up the new theological college, his health had been so seriously compromised that he was warned he must choose between the pulpit and the college. Face to face with these alternatives, his course was clear. For the rest of his days he must give himself to the college at Bala.

When I entered the college at Bala in the autumn of 1894, it was providing a fairly complete theological education. There were no elective courses. The principal himself gave courses in dogmatic theology and New Testament exegesis, the latter in particular being a memorable experience. The principal also reserved to himself the course known as homiletics, but treated it unconventionally. On Saturday mornings we were gathered for a religious session, and on those occasions the principal would address us upon the problems of the ministry. One of those sessions rises to my mind. He was speaking to us of the preaching office of the minister and particularly of the problem of the subject matter of the sermon. "Gentlemen," he cried out, "preach upon solid blocks of truth!" Certainly that was what he had always done, and in his day he was recognized among the first six preachers in Great Britain.

His two Welsh colleagues were Hugh Williams [1843–1911, an ecclesiastical historian] and Ellis Edwards, both of them men of fine scholarship. If Hugh Williams had a fault it was a tendency to pedantry, but we treated him with great respect, and to us students he was unfailingly kind and helpful. As with the principal, his classes were largely conversational. But Ellis Edwards suffered from a grievous deafness, and there was no place for conversational intervals during the class hour. But for that he made up by inviting us to his home in small groups or taking us for walks in the countryside. On these occasions he would discuss the matters which he had been treating in his classroom. I think that of all the professors we liked him best. Among ourselves we called him "old Ellis," but always in tones of affection. Besides these teachers we had a Scot who had been imported to teach us Hebrew, as so far we had not bred Hebrew scholars in Wales. I do not think that he was happy among us. However competent his scholarship and however promising ours, his "heart was in the Highlands."

We students lived in lodgings in the town, and, in the course of years, an unauthorized censorship of student conduct had grown up among the *unco guid* of the town. The generations before ours had submitted to this surveillance. But those of us who had come from the university colleges were not ready to submit to any discipline save that of the college. The crisis came over the formation of a football club. The *unco guid* among the students and in the town were shocked by this invasion of "the world, the flesh, and the devil" on the sanctities of Bala town and the morality of the student body. They appealed to the principal and professors to taboo it, and they were informed that it was a matter for the student body to decide. And so we did, and the opposition was overwhelmed.

There were other diversions available: boating and fishing on the lake and, for those who were partial to walking there was as beautiful and interesting a countryside as was to be found in all Great Britain. But the football prevailed because it provided, in an hour, exercise enough to keep a man fit for twenty-four hours. We hired a field within ten minutes of the college, and we elected captains. We provided ourselves with all the necessary gear and, all in all, our football club was a great success.

Another instance of the disadvantage of placing a theological college in a small country town arose out of a doubt whether we students were having an adequate diet in our lodgings. The question had been raised by a member of the college board, but how he came to raise the question I do not know. The students were summoned to a meeting of the board, and we were asked whether we would be in favour of a common table once a day. None of the senior men said a word and, lest the truth go by default, I, a junior, spoke up and said that I would like to have one good meal every day. There was some merriment following my remark, but when the story leaked out into the town I was a marked man in the local circles which censored student behaviour. In two or three days my landlady had heard the story and gave me notice for disparaging her cooking. In an earlier time that might have meant banishment from the college, for Calvinistic Methodist housewives had claimed a monopoly in housing and feeding Calvinistic Methodist students; it would have been bad form to live and have one's being in an Episcopal or Congregational household. But I had no trouble finding new quarters in a Congregational home and was in every respect better off. But my stock continued low among my own people until I left Bala.

Most of the students were able to maintain themselves in college by taking preaching engagements on Sundays. Bala was very well situated in the matter of travelling facilities, and most of North Wales was within fairly easy reach. Most of the men preached only in Welsh, a few only in English, and fewer still in both languages. Consequently I, who was in the third class, had more opportunities of preaching than most of my fellows. It was an excellent discipline for which I have not ceased to be thankful.

The principal had, as I have said, ceased from preaching at the behest of his medical adviser. But he found a way of using Sunday mornings to the great advantage of the least seasoned members of the student body. Some of his friends had presented him with a chaise and pony in order that he might have the advantage of relaxation and fresh air. Presently he had devised a scheme to help certain small congregations in the vicinity of Bala. His procedure was first to ascertain what congregation might have no prospect of a preacher for the next Sunday, and second to enquire what members of the junior class might be free of engagements. The understanding was that the principal and the student were to address the congregation, the principal briefly and the student to preach the last sermon he had composed. It was a major event for a congregation to have the great man among them, and the poor student shared some of the reflected glory of the "Prin," as we called him. I remember very well my excitement when the privilege came to me—for privilege it was—of going with the principal on his Sunday journey. But even more I remember the journey back. The principal spent all the leisurely return ride to Bala in discussing my sermon: generously praising what was worth praising and in gentle criticism of what needed criticism; and of that there was a good deal.

During my second year I began to grow dissatisfied with the courses at the college, and particularly with the lectures, which seemed to me to have lost their savour; all but the principal's New Testament exegesis class, which was full of life and light. Moreover I had discovered for myself that lectures were not the only means of imparting and acquiring knowledge.

(Later I learned from another source that college lectures are deposits from an age in which books were hard to come by.) After I had gone to Bala I developed a new interest in my father's considerable collection of books, and I realized that he had become the man he was because he spent his mornings reading and pondering upon what he read. No doubt he had learned much from his two great teachers, but the man he became was a self-made man. I should add that he would not so describe himself. He, like many great spirits, would have said: "By the grace of God I am what I am."

Another source of unrest was a visit which I had paid to Cardiff in the previous summer. I had gone there to give such help as I could to a remarkable "Forward Movement." The movement had been initiated by an inspired minister named John Pugh, who had been appalled by the poverty of the religious provision for the mounting population of the city. What I had seen and heard, both of the need and the scale upon which John Pugh was proposing to meet it, had impressed me beyond words. Already he had contrived to build a large mission hall designed to hold over a thousand people in a newly built area of the city called East Moors. This hall was filled every Sunday night. John Pugh had insisted upon my preaching there one Sunday night as the regular evangelist was away. I shall not forget my terror when I stood before that multitude, and the reassurance that came to me when I realized that they were taking me seriously. The whole movement looked and felt like a real "holy war": we went preaching on street corners; we were sometimes sent alone to preach in a mean street—and now and again had to beat a retreat before a fusillade of what missiles might be at hand. And we had now and again real conversions among the toughs and the roughs of the neighbourhood. I do not think that I have ever since felt a thrill comparable to that which I had from my first "conversion."

The effect of that and other experiences was to commit me altogether to the Forward Movement. However, I did not bind myself to join at any specific date, until I had taken counsel with my father and particularly had ascertained whether it would be expedient for me to take a third year at Bala—only two years being obligatory. I joined the movement at the end of the next year, having first passed the synodical [pre-ordination] examination in September, standing third in the whole of Wales.

7

The Forward Movement

The Forward Movement was primarily evangelistic, and only in second intention "church extension," and the need of it was very great. During the previous decade there had been an immense incursion of people from other parts of Great Britain; the general moral condition of the ports and the "valleys" had become deplorable. Associated with John Pugh in this movement was Seth Joshua. Seth and his brother Frank had been workers in the steel mills at Neath. Seth had also been a pugilist of some reputation and had led a somewhat dissolute life. Both brothers, however, were so soundly converted— radically converted—that they had felt constrained to set up a mission centre in their home town in which they carried on a remarkable work for a number of years. Then Seth received John Pugh's summons and obeyed it, leaving Frank to carry on alone in Neath, which indeed he valiantly did.

I joined the movement in 1896. After a few weeks at headquarters in Cardiff, gaining information and insight into the spirit and methods of the movement, in daily intercourse with John Pugh and sometimes with Seth Joshua, I went to my first assignment. This was to the movement's "centre" in a populous colliery village name Treharris, a community with an almost detailed family likeness to that pictured in Richard Llewellyn's story, *How Green Was My Valley*, save only that our village was not in a valley but above one. The centre was a tin tabernacle capable of holding some three hundred people. A small regular congregation had already been formed there, but it was very evangelistic and missionary in its temper. We preached and sang the Gospel at some corner or other most days of the week.

The colliery upon which the village subsisted was one of the most important in South Wales, and its pit was said to be the deepest. The colliers included Welshmen who had gathered there from the neighbouring countryside, and Englishmen, Scotsmen, and Irishmen who had migrated from their own countries, for in those days there was plenty of work in that region. The Welsh people were on the whole devout chapel folk and worshipped God in Welsh; our work lay among the others, not many of whom were devout or prone to worship. The community as a whole was fairly respectable, and there was as yet no suggestion of a slum in the village for most of the dwelling houses were recently built. We had a slum, however. The pit was at the foot of the hill on which the village stood, and nearby were the wooden shacks which originally housed the navvies who had been brought there to sink the pit. But they were still used as family dwellings.

By this time the Independent Labour Party under the leadership of Keir Hardie had come into being, and Hardie was already in Parliament [Hardie, 1856–1915, was elected MP for South West Ham in 1892, and first leader of the Labour Party in parliament 1906–1907]. I found a branch of the party in the village and joined it. By a happy coincidence the secretary turned out to be the secretary of my centre, a young tradesman whose deep religious devotion was matched by his eager socialism. Naturally he and I became fast friends, and I was as faithful to the open air party meetings as he was to our open air evangelisms; for him as for me, they were the complimentary parts of the same enterprise. Now and again the party headquarters would send some of its agents to visit us and confirm us in the faith. One of these, Tom Taylor, I remember very vividly—a tall, rugged figure, gentle in conversation but fierce as a lion toward capitalism and all its works. He was also a Primitive Methodist local preacher; after addressing a party meeting on a Saturday night, he preached in my tabernacle on the following Sunday evening.

Then a little later came Keir Hardie himself, on his first visit to South Wales. Later he was to become more familiar with that region, for he became the member of Parliament for the next constituency to ours. We were, of course, very elated to hear of Hardie's coming. But there were difficulties. Where was Hardie to stay? None of the party members could put him up—the young men were themselves lodgers and the older men had ample families. In the end I took him home to my own digs, gave him my bed, and slept myself that night in a chair. When I came down to breakfast I found him reading his Bible. Then, who was to preside at the meeting? The details of the meeting have passed from my memory, save that I recall vividly the sense I had of listening to a prophet as Hardie spoke.

My action in housing Hardie and presiding at the meeting got me into all sorts of trouble. My landlady, who rented one of the better company houses, took fright and gave me notice to quit lest she should have to quit, and a little later I received a solemn rebuke from the general secretary of the movement which I served. To this I wrote a tart reply in which I had a good deal to say about the huts I have already spoken of, for which the Christian owners of the pit exacted rent though they were not fit for cattle. Whether I was considered too dangerous a person to remain among the colliers I cannot say. I do know that I was removed from that charge because I presided at Keir Hardie's meeting. One of the owners of the pit was also the general treasurer of our mission.

Not long after, in January 1897, I was drafted to the growing seaport of Newport in Monmouthshire, to take charge of another centre in one of its growing suburbs. As I could not commence operations at once, and indeed did not for some twelve weeks as my hall was, for some reason, very slow a-building—I was directed to assist Seth Joshua who had, in the meantime, been moved there from Cardiff. It turned out to be a very fruitful experience for me.

Often while Seth held forth inside I was on a chair outside, haranguing the crowds. But what stands out most conspicuously in my memory of those months is that not a single Sunday evening passed that men and women were not converted to God. They were authentic conversions, provoked by no sensationalism or worked up emotionalism, but by straight and competent preaching on Joshua's part. Seth was entirely self-educated; but if ever a man had a vocation for the ministry, that man had. His was a plain, straightforward ministry, without noise or fuss or self-advertisement. But he had this thing called *power*, and he held that it was begotten of prayer. He himself often quoted the passage: "Ye shall receive power after that the Holy Ghost is come upon you." His own explanation of it was that "the Saturday night prayer meeting did it," and he was probably right. Like the apostolic company before Pentecost, we foregathered with one accord in one place, and continued in prayer and supplication; and on the Sunday night, Seth Joshua preached the Gospel with converting power. I have seen rough men weep their hearts out for very penitence, and I have seen the loveliness of the light of Christ kindled in young and tender eyes under that blessed ministry.

The Saturday night before the opening of the new hall to which I was assigned, I was engaged with some local sympathizers until after midnight, cleaning and dusting the interior in readiness for the next morning. It was a case of beginning on the ground floor, but under very favourable auspices. The centre was situated in a new working class suburb, and the immediate environment was beautiful. I discovered, among other things, that I had for neighbours the secretary and one of the leaders of the Newport branch of the Independent Labour Party; and both of them became loyal supporters of mine. I, on my own side, joined the local party branch.

While I was in Newport the National Eisteddfod was held there. Just about that time the Clarion van, owned and operated by *The Clarion*, the brilliant socialist weekly edited by Robert Blatchford [1851–1943, British socialist and journalist], had been carrying on a vigorous propaganda on the borders of Wales. When I heard that the van had reached eastern Monmouthshire, I conceived the idea of inducing those in charge of it to come to Newport for the Eisteddfod week. So I set out one day on my bicycle to find them. It was a glorious day; my search led me to Chepsted, then following the Wye Valley down the Whyncliffe, past Tintern Abbey. In Monmouth I had some tidings of the van and finally located it in a field a few miles away. I had no difficulty in persuading the vanners to come to Newport for the Eisteddfod week. We managed to get a good stance in the town which was full of Welshmen from all parts of the country. I recall, among other things, that we sold during that week over a thousand copies of Robert Blatchford's *Merrie England*, perhaps the ablest piece of propaganda writing of modern times. Its price was three pence.

One other memory comes back to me. The Independent Labour Party (ILP) local secretary was, as I have said, one of my supporters. Nonetheless, I suspected that there was a certain anti-religious animus at the back of his mind, and that his regularity at the Sunday evening service was due more to the gentle pressure of his wife than to his own choice. After every service we announced and held an after-meeting to which were invited those who desired to begin a new life. One Sunday evening my ILP friend, to my great surprise, remained for the after-meeting. I made my usual call to any who were moved to begin a new life and desired our prayers to declare themselves. My friend gave no sign. But when the people dispersed at the close of the meeting he remained in his seat. I waited for all the others to go out of the building until he and I were left alone. Then I went to him and said, "H___, is there anything troubling you?" He burst into tears and I could get nothing out of him. So I suggested that we should pray together. We knelt, side by side, and I prayed simply to God that we might both dedicate ourselves to His service. We remained there kneeling a while longer and then rose. We looked each other in the face and then, suddenly, he almost shouted at me: "I AM GOING TO BE A BETTER SOCIALIST THAN EVER!" Which was as it should be.

[The foregoing, with the exception of five sentences at the most, has been taken almost verbatim from three of RR's articles: "Radical Religion Forty Years Ago" (*Christianity and Society*), "Companies of the Upper Room" (*The Christian Century*), and a third which the author has only in manuscript form. The manuscript is untitled. Such few additions as have been made have been made in the first person, in order to not intrude an alien note.]

Another story from Newport days is of RR's brush with a wealthy chapel-goer. This man had reduced the wages of one of his employees, a family man, from one pound [twenty shillings] to sixteen shillings. The man laid the matter before his minister who immediately rang up the employer to plead his case. "No, Mr. Roberts, business is business," the employer responded. "I believe, Mr. S___, that you hold services down at the docks every Saturday night," RR said. "Well, and what of it?" "I'll be down there next Saturday, to tell the crowd just what sort of Christian you are." The shilling was restored!

There are other similar incidents and RR's cousin, D. Trevor Jones, recalls that some of his forthright comments concerning one of the wealthy men of the denomination called forth the indignant remark: "Talking like that about J___,...he [RR] ought to be put a stop to." In later years RR agreed with this verdict, though not with the reasons behind it. His judgement on himself was that he had failed in love in his attitude to these wealthy men, and that other tactics would have been more appropriate.

Whether it was in order to "put a stop" to him that he was recalled to Bala as assistant to Principal Edwards is not known. It is certain that the old man was failing and needed an assistant badly. That he had a warm affection for the young firebrand also is certain. It is entirely possible that, in need of an assistant, he saw a good means of withdrawing RR from circulation for a while. When the request came, RR went gladly to Bala. The exact nature of his work there is not clear. He did some lecturing, and probably relieved the principal of a great deal of the minor secretarial and administrative work of the college. He also assisted him in the preparation of his work on the Epistle to the Hebrews. This was never completed, however, as Dr. Edwards' health grew progressively worse. But it was all good experience, and the close association with a man of Principal Edwards' stamp was something many of his contemporaries must have envied.

RR always looked back on this time as a most fruitful growing period, and attributed his interest in New Testament studies to the principal's influence. There were some who knew both men and the temper of them, who doubted whether the association could last long. They expected some passionate disagreement. But it is clear that the "Prin" had a great fund of wisdom and consideration. When the old man was stricken with paralysis RR, as his cousin recalls, "lavished on him a kindness and tenderness which, indeed, did not surprise those who knew him."

During the summer of 1899, RR made his first trip to Canada, again through the good offices of his cousin in the shipping business. Apart from the fact that he loved the sea, the trip does not seem to have made any great impression on him. Dr. Edwards was still at Bala when the term opened in the autumn, but it was obvious that the situation could not long continue as it was. A more vigorous hand was needed at the helm. By November, Dr. Edwards could no longer carry on. A new principal replaced him, and RR resigned as his services were no longer needed. The next few months were spent in the church extension program of the Welsh Presbytery; then came the call to Willesden Green, London.

Part II

"The Coming Man"

———

8
London: Willesden Green

When RR went up to London in 1900, there were a number of churches of the Welsh Calvinistic Methodist persuasion scattered throughout the city. These served the very considerable Welsh population which had migrated there. Willesden Green, to which RR had been called, was one of them. In London, as in Wales, the preaching ministry was itinerant, and RR preached at other Welsh churches in regular rotation with his brethren. He preached, of course, in Welsh. He remained at Willesden Green from March 1900 until April 1903.

In London the church could not be the dominant element in the life of the people as it was in the Welsh towns and villages. Nor was it possible to reproduce in London the atmosphere of the church in Wales. RR's preaching attracted young people to the Willesden Green services, but that was not enough. RR was concerned to make the church vital in their lives.

Not far from the Willesden Green Church was the Primitive Methodist Church of Kilburn Lane. This congregation had a flourishing Christian Endeavour Society. As a part of its program, it had a great variety of athletic activities. The Primitive Methodist young people rented some tennis courts adjacent to the Willesden Green Church and RR took a keen interest in them. He was eager to learn the whole range of their program that his own young people might benefit from their experience. His interest was reciprocated, and on more than one occasion he addressed them. This, and other such contacts, took him outside of the confines of London Welsh society. His gifts as a speaker and preacher were becoming known in the English churches of London.

Nevertheless it was among the Welsh people in London that RR spent most of his time. His closest friend of college days shortly arrived in London bringing his wife with him, Tom [Dr. T. D., 1870–

1955] and Eirene Jones. The friendship lasted through the years. Of Dr. T. D. Jones, RR would later write: "...he has filled not a few positions in his rich life: professor; secretary to the cabinet under two Prime Ministers...; secretary to the Pilgrim Trust which he administers with insight and generosity; the begetter and fosterer of Coleg Harlech, an experiment in adult education; the counsellor and succourer of 'all poor devils'; and the perfect friend." Tom, Eirene, and RR agreed to meet on certain days for study in the Reading Room of the British Museum. RR recounts:

> One day Tom brought with him a copy of the list of subjects for competition at the next annual meeting of the Welsh National Eisteddfod....In the list were two that Tom thought suitable to Eirene and me—the former being an essay on Peace, the latter a biographical and critical account of that curious genius Robert Owen of Newtown in Wales, of New Lanark in Scotland, and of New Harmony in the United States. We settled down to our respective tasks and, in the event, we both won first prize in our respective competitions. Eirene did not know Welsh and perforce wrote in English. I wrote in Welsh, and eventually my essay was published as a book— the only book that I have written in my native tongue.

It was also in the Welsh group that RR found his wife, Anne Catherine Thomas from Llanerchymedd, Anglesey. The question of her Episcopalian background seems not to have entered into consideration. They met early in 1901, and were married on 1 January 1902. Their first child was born in 1903. Had he been asked what was the most important event of the years in Willesden Green, RR would undoubtedly have said it was his marriage.

In the meantime, RR was caught up in the Passive Resistance Movement against the Education Act of 1902. "Caught up" is in the nature of an understatement, for others have testified that, young though he was compared to veterans such as Dr. John Clifford [1836–1923] of Westbourne Park Baptist Church and President of the World Baptist Alliance from 1905 to 1911, RR was recognized as one of the leaders.

Nonconformist opposition to the Act of 1902 was no new thing. In 1870, it had been estimated that voluntary foundations, the majority of them Anglican, took care of the education of about one-half of the children of England, regardless of their religious affiliation. The Education Act of 1870 continued the practice, begun early in the century, of grants in aid to these voluntary schools. Even then nonconformists grumbled that, by this subsidy, the Anglicans were receiving far too many non-sectarian shillings. In 1902, there were still too few non-sectarian schools, particularly at the secondary level. Many nonconformist children had no alternative but to attend Anglican schools, where religious instruction was regarded as evangelistic in purpose. The new bill proposed to grant more of the "rates" to the Anglican schools, in proportion to the number of children under instruction. Nonconformists, however, believed that the educational portion of the rates should be used to establish new non-sectarian schools, rather than to bolster up those of the established church where, as one diocesan inspector of schools put it, "we trained the children of the nonconformists to be children of the Church." But in spite of vigorous opposition, both in Parliament by the Liberals and outside by the public, the bill was passed.

This was not the end of the matter, however. The country had been aroused. The nonconformists, led by Dr. John Clifford, organized meetings to keep the protest in the public eye. At one of these, held in St. James' Hall, RR was one of a galaxy of speakers which included Dr. Clifford and Herbert Asquith [1852–1928], later to be Liberal Prime Minister. It was said that Asquith, who rose to speak after RR, said of RR's speech that it was the most statesman-like utterance on the subject that he had heard.

A more practical application of the protest was the refusal of many nonconformists, particularly among the clergy, to pay the rates, on the grounds that it was a violation of conscience. Some, including Dr. Clifford, went to jail. Others were subjected to the attention of the bailiffs who seized certain of their movable property. In RR's case they seized his books. He promptly objected that they had no power to take the "tools of a man's trade," and the law upheld him. The bailiffs brought back the books, with apologies, and then, instead, took some of his silverware. Asked in later years what he did about the silverware, RR laughed: "Oh, we just bought it back." This was his wife's introduction to the lengths to which he would go in defence of his principles.

With the coming into office of the Liberals in 1905, the movement petered out, although a few half-hearted efforts were made to amend the bill. In retrospect RR was not at all sure that the movement had been justified. In 1916, he wrote: "It would be difficult to discover a case in which obstruction has achieved anything worth-while, *except when every other door has been shut*: and there are plenty of instances of the failure of obstructive methods, *e.g.* the egregious failure of 'passive resistance' to the Education Acts."

Freedom of conscience in matters small as well as great was always one of RR's basic tenets. At a presbytery meeting of the Welsh Church in London a motion was on the floor urging total abstinence. When the vote was called, two of the brethren refrained. After considerable persuasion one consented to sign. This he did with the *caveat*, "Drink a little wine for the stomach's sake." The other staunchly refused to alter his position. Whereupon one of those in favour of the motion rose to his feet and prayed earnestly to God that the one dissenter might be moved to change his mind. This, to RR, smacked of coercion, and he promptly protested: "Gentlemen, if you press this matter, I shall go out and drink a pint of beer to assert my liberty in Jesus Christ." The dissenter was thereafter left in peace.

RR's nearest ministerial neighbour in northwest London was R. E. Welsh, known at the time for a book he had published in 1895, *In Relief of Doubt*. Dr. Welsh was a Scot and some years older than RR, but the two men were soon fast friends. Later their paths met again in Montreal where "Daddy" Welsh, as he was affectionately called by the students, was professor at the Presbyterian [afterwards the United] College. In a tribute to Dr. Welsh on his retirement, RR wrote:

> I wish to say that I owe him much more than I can readily tell. It was he who persuaded me to leave the Welsh ministry and enter that of the Presbyterian Church of England, and he made my way easy. When, in 1903, I was inducted to the pastorate of St. Paul's Presbyterian Church, Westbourne Grove…it was Dr. Welsh who delivered the charge.

Welsh early recognized in his young neighbour the qualities which made him the subject of two articles published a few years later. One was in *The Christian Age* in November 1906; the other in the *Sunday Strand*, four years later. The title of both these articles labelled RR as "the coming man."

9
Westbourne Grove

St. Paul's Presbyterian was an old church, originally built in the middle of a field. By the time RR came to St. Paul's, however, the city of London had gobbled up the fields that had formerly surrounded it. It was reckoned, at the turn of the century, to be one of the wealthiest of the nonconformist churches in London, and the preaching of RR's two predecessors, the Rev. Walter Morrison and the Rev. G. A. Johnston Ross [b. 1865], had given its pulpit a position of influence in London [Johnston Ross was later to be professor of Practical Theology at the Presbyterian College, Montreal]. But it was not considered to be an easy church, for its parish lay in a part of London that had changed and was still in the process of change.

The steps by which RR came to Westbourne Grove are related succinctly in the Report of the Session and Managers for the year 1903:

> The year 1903 opened with the congregational pastorate vacant, but before many weeks had elapsed the present minister, the Rev. Richard Roberts, appeared in the pulpit to supply for one day, and it was immediately felt that if he were settled as minister he would be acceptable to all the congregation. But being a minister of the Welsh Presbyterian Church (otherwise named the Welsh Calvinistic Methodists), a Church with which ours has friendly relations but no arrangement for the mutual eligibility of ministers, he was not eligible to receive a call until he was admitted as a minister by the Synod of our Church. Steps had been taken by Mr. Roberts in this direction before he preached for us, and his application was cordially approved by the Presbytery of London North and passed on to the Synod which met in

May. The Synod, being satisfied that Mr. Roberts had been efficiently trained, accepted his application. Our call was put in his hands at the next meeting of Presbytery, and his induction took place on June 5th....

Since Mr. Roberts' induction the attendances at Church have much improved, and his influence in all departments of the Church's work has made itself felt for good in encouraging the workers and bringing in help.

In the same booklet is a pastoral letter, written by RR, which runs in part:

In a few weeks I shall have been at St. Paul's a twelvemonth, and I desire to bear witness to the kindness and forbearance I have met on all sides. To all the Office-bearers particularly do I owe a debt of thanks for their devoted activity and their wise and unfailing counsel. In coming to St. Paul's I was breaking what was for me new ground, and if I have been able to discharge my duties with any acceptance, as much is due to the Office-bearers as to myself.

RR was of the same mind in 1910, when he left St. Paul's to go to Crouch Hill. He always looked back on those years as particularly happy ones.

The congregation of St. Paul's was a mixed one. There was a solid upper middle-class group which was the financial backbone. In the list of contributors to the Missionary and Sustentation Fund are names which were household words for faithfulness, affection, and generosity: Miss Love, the Misses Lees, the Dunbar Walkers, and the Robsons. And it was through Dr. Stoddard Kennedy, a member of the congregation, that RR met the Roman Catholic philosopher of religion and writer on mysticism, Baron Friedrich von Hügel [1852–1925], of whom he wrote, after reading a volume of von Hügel's letters in 1927:

I find myself in these letters in an atmosphere so congenial that I am bound to conclude that the general outlook and colour of my present mind were largely determined by the intercourse I was privileged to have with Baron von Hügel....

It came about in this way...the doctor had been recently called in to see the Baron and had, in the course of his visits, spoken of me. The Baron expressed a desire to meet me, no doubt being impressed by what must have been my friend's excessively generous account....In due time I received this note:

13, Vicarage Gate, Kensington
3rd July

Dear Sir,
    Now at last my days are becoming clear and relatively free. If you will kindly be here on Tuesday next, 8th at 3:30, we could sit and talk in Kensington Gardens till 5. Or I could manage the same, Thursday next. But please let me know promptly. For I am off abroad for seven weeks on July 15th, and these last days want filling up now with various friends. With much pleasure at the prospect of an early meeting.

F. von Hügel

Naturally I went; and it was the first of many times on which I met him. I have a hundred times regretted that, when I left him, I did not take pen and paper and write down what he said in those conversations. The chief impression that remains is that of the extraordinary exaltation and fullness which I felt after I had seen him. It was as if virtue had flowed out of him into me; but this volume of letters serves to show that much of what he said lodged itself in my mind and has gone to make my mind, such as it is, what it is today. And I am only one of a very great multitude who have reason to thank God for Friedrich von Hügel.

This was no slavish adulation, however. On some points they disagreed. RR felt that von Hügel was incapable of fully understanding the Puritan temper. On the issue of the war in 1914 they were at opposite poles. After RR went to America he saw nothing of von Hügel until they met again in 1923, to find their friendship and fundamental community of interest unbroken. RR concluded: "I shall never cease to thank God that he gave me to know that great scholar saint."

But back to Westbourne in 1906. R. E. Welsh's article in *The Christian Age* reports a staff of sixty workers at St. Paul's, almost all of whom were volunteers. It lists a formidable number of organizations: Missionary Society, Women's Missionary Association, Dorcas Society, Ladies' Council of Service, Mothers' Bible Class, Thrift Club, Band of Hope, Bible Reading Union, Boys' Brigade, Young Men's Association, and a larger institute, not to mention a Sunday school of four hundred children. In the *Papers of John Pererin*, written in 1923, RR sadly described what had happened to the church with this proliferation of organizations:

> It was started as a fellowship, and we have turned it into an institution. It originated as a communion; it has become a corporation. It began as a comradeship; today it is a number of organizations, more or less loosely attached to a pulpit. Heaven help it.

Even as he wrote those words, however, RR would have strenuously denied them any connection with the church at Westbourne Grove, in spite of its multifarious organizations.

At St. Paul's, as at Willesden Green, RR threw himself into young people's work. During his time the Sunday school became a focal point of the work of the church. Visitations of the neighbourhood were made with the Sunday school register as their basis. The entire Sunday school was reorganized, and the classes were carefully graded beginning with the kindergarten and moving through the various ages. The teacher training class, held on a weeknight at the Newton Road Institute just behind the church, was undoubtedly the most important aspect of the program. It was natural, then, that at the presbytery meeting in 1910, when Westbourne Grove relinquished him to Crouch Hill, a Mr. Russell would say that, "the Sunday School teachers would miss Mr. Roberts—his training was so effectual...." The Newton Road Institute housed other classes and activities. Some of these were of a general educational nature, but there was also a considerable gymnastic program for the youth of the church.

The reorganization of the Sunday school, the time, energy, and passion he put into the project, and his own leadership of the teacher training class, were the active front line expression of RR's growing concern for that part of the church's life. He was well aware that there was a core of people in the churches whose devotion was unquestionable, yet the churches were making little impact on the world. In *The Christian Age* article RR was quoted as saying:

> If we are going to save the next generation from indifference we must begin *now*, and the obvious place to begin is the Sunday School....Principal Ritchie of Nottingham has investigated the statistics of the Wesleyan Methodists, and concludes that while only 20% of Sunday scholars have been retained for the Church, yet that represents 78% of the church membership. Still, the reflection is forced on any thoughtful Christian worker, that if so great a proportion of the membership is supplied by so small a proportion of the scholars retained, how vast a loss the churches suffer year by year by the failure to retain a larger percentage of those who enter our schools in their earliest and most impressionable years.

In the same interview RR goes on to summarize what he had written in his book *The Church and the Next Generation*, published in 1909. He spoke of the fossilized state of the Sunday school, the lack of adequately trained teachers, the lack of recognition by the churches of the importance of the work of the Sunday school, the inadequate facilities provided, the necessity of grading both the lessons and the classes, and the need for weekday groups related to the Sunday school. He was to remain vitally concerned with this problem until he saw that the churches were accepting the Sunday school as important and integral to their life.

But preaching was always central to RR's work in any of his pastorates. In the *Sunday Strand* article he is quoted as saying:

> I believe that my best pulpit work has been expository. I have even ventured to take some of the books of the Bible—an Epistle for example—and steadily go through them. I am sure such a plan helps to keep a congregation together....I am growingly convinced that exposition is appreciated by any thoughtful congregation. One winter I dropped this plan, but was asked to resume the practice. Of course, any such plan must be taken seriously by the preacher. I do not scruple to say that I have put my best work into these expositions, and I have had my reward in seeing my morning congregation

which is, perhaps, above average in point of numbers, steadily grow and increasingly appreciative.

RR did not neglect other kinds of preaching, and his book *The Meaning of Christ*, published in 1906, was largely the content of his sermon series "What think ye of Christ?" in which he sought to show what had been the judgement of great leaders, in thought and life, about Jesus of Nazareth.

While the regular care of the church and its many-faceted life absorbed a good deal of RR's time and energy, he remained very much aware of other young people in the neighbourhood, who formed another element of his parish. He tells something of this in his own words:

> I am not sure of the year, but I think it was 1906. For the previous four years I had been minister of St. Paul's Church, Bayswater....The church stood at the end of Westbourne Grove Terrace, once a fashionable street; but by the time I came to know it, it had lost prestige and the houses had been turned into quarters for the "shop assistants" of two important stores in Westbourne Grove—Whitely's and Owens'.
>
> In those days "the living-in system," as it was called, was general among the larger stores of London. It was apparently more profitable to the stores to house and feed their employees than to give them a full living wage. I became pretty familiar with some of these houses; and most of them were very dreary. Besides, the inmates were subject to a strict regime. Nevertheless they contrived to have some relief from the monotony of hall bedrooms by organizing clubs and societies of various kinds. Some of them had excellent athletic clubs; and without exception, I think, there was a Bible class in the house. It was in connection with the latter that I became familiar with the system.
>
> But the system was very unsatisfactory in several ways, particularly in the inevitable limits it imposed on individual freedom. The disaffection in the houses became so strong that the Shop-assistants' Union began a campaign for the abolition of "living-in." I had personally become convinced that the system was very unsatisfactory, and had on occasion said so semi-publically. So when the Shop-assistants' Union

organized a meeting to be held in the Queen's Hall, Langham Place, to protest against the "living-in" system, I was invited to be one of the speakers. Presently I heard that, apart from the chairman, there was to be only one other speaker—and he was [the Fabian socialist and playwright] Bernard Shaw! I went to the meeting in mingled hope and terror, the latter partly because of Shaw's distinction and partly because he had the reputation of being something of a bear. But I could have saved myself any apprehension. For when I was introduced to him in the anteroom, he turned out to be simple, kindly, and genial.

On the platform I sat next to him. The hall was full of shop assistants and their friends. It had been arranged that, after the chairman's opening speech, a collection should be made to defray the expenses of the meeting; and that took considerable time. Presently Shaw said to me: "Do you know much about shop assistants?" "Yes," I answered, "I know a good deal about them." "Well," he said, "tell me about them."

So I told him all I knew, how they were mostly migrants from the country to London, the conditions of their day's work, their trouble with "shop-walkers" who were their immediate superiors, their life after business hours, their living quarters. Among other things I mentioned the weekly Bible classes. That seemed to interest Shaw more than anything I had said and it was the one topic upon which he wanted more detail. In my account of the classes I had happened to remark that, generally, the attitude to the Bible was very conservative, and that "verbal inspiration" seemed to be taken for granted. Today that attitude would be called "fundamentalist." "But you don't hold that view, do you?" asked Shaw. "No," said I, "but I try to avoid stepping on any corns, as much as I can. And I know that my orthodoxy is questioned in some quarters. But I am able to serve them in other ways; and I am tolerated on that account." I have some vivid memories of Shaw's speech....[He] was an easy and clear speaker, without any trick of rhetoric or any purple patches. The impression made was that of a very competent and well-furnished mind thinking aloud. Humour was there, but of its own kind, and never exploited. It was to one hearer, at least, interesting to observe how he wove into his speech some of the information which he had received earlier in the meeting from his neighbour on the platform.

RR's move to Westbourne Grove had come about during the excitements of the Passive Resistance Movement. With that stand of nonconformist conscience no Presbyterian could find fault. His activities in the social field, however, were not limited to meetings such as the one described above. In an unpublished lecture on preaching he wrote: "In 1907–1908 I was the unofficial leader of some hundreds of unemployed men in the west end of London, marching through the streets at their head; but I am glad to say that my people then took no umbrage at this, though it was a radical departure from good form." It speaks well for the relationship between minister and office-bearers that he could take part in activities such as these and still retain their loyalty and affection.

Not far from Westbourne Grove lay Clarendon Street. It was regarded by the police at that time as the centre of one of the toughest districts in London. With all his other responsibilities there was little chance for RR to do anything constructive in the district, but he did have occasion to walk through it sometimes. Once he came upon an old crone, far gone in liquor, lying in a ditch. Hauling her to her feet and staggering and weaving under her limp weight, he tried to steer her home. Dismay on meeting some of his more respectable parishioners was drowned in mortification. "I wished the earth would open and swallow me," he later recalled.

Another time he came upon two women fighting. One was belabouring the other with a kettle. The other was giving as good as she got with a teapot. RR recounts the story:

> I got between them and held them apart at arm's length. But they were too much for me. As they tried to get at each other around me, I found myself spinning like a teetotum. Some louts had been loafing around enjoying the fun; but when I got in it, their laughter redoubled. Finally I called to them, "I say, you fellows, lend a hand." After a bit they did. But that experience...taught me never to come between two women.

In the spring of 1908, a group of nonconformists made up a party to journey to the Holy Land, to be in Jerusalem on Easter Sunday. RR joined them and wrote home of all he saw on the way. His comments ranged from the beauty of the Seine Valley and the wildness of Parisian traffic to the bestiality of the Pompeii frescoes in the museum at Naples. "I understand now, as I never did before, the meaning of the story of Sodom and Gomorrah," he wrote. On the whole, however, his reactions were enthusiastic and optimistic. From Constantinople he wrote of visiting the San Sophia mosque:

> Everything that was Christian about the building had been hidden or gilded over; but strangely enough, through the gilt with which the apse had been covered, over the place where the altar would have been, the figure of our Lord can be seen dimly but quite certainly. It reminded me of the word in the Gospels: "He could not be hid."

In a private note to his wife he added:

> ...all this journey is moving me profoundly. I have a clearer grasp of apostolic history and especially of the heroism and greatness of Paul. I find it hard to realize that, at this very moment, I am moving through a sea and along a course by which he once travelled. What Palestine will be, I can only imagine. May it make me a little more useful.

There was much in the Palestine experience that he valued: the sight of shepherds leading, not driving, their sheep; the sincerity and simplicity of some of the pilgrims—Russian peasants who had made their pilgrimage all the way on foot; sharing the Passover meal in the home of a Jewish rabbi; fellowship with English missionaries. But the exhilaration of these experiences was offset by depression. Years later he described in a sermon the feeling that came over him in Damascus, after entering with difficulty a mosque that had once been a Christian church:

> There was that mosque, the evidence of the defeat of Christianity in the very city in which St. Paul had seen the light of the Gospel and had dreamed the great dream of winning the Gentiles to Christ....And then one thought of North Africa, which in those far-off days had given the church some of its greatest saints: Clement of Alexandria, Tertullian, and Augustine; and today a Christian in those parts is despised and hated as an infidel.

The Easter morning service at the Church of the Holy Sepulchre was a crowning disillusionment—the pomp and ceremony, the crowd and the confusion. RR wrote: "I was never in such a babel, and I was glad to get away. And it was a very sorry business to see a regiment of Turkish soldiers in and out of the buildings, to keep the peace among the various sects of Christians."

He brought back from that journey misgiving and disquietude. In the sermon referred to above, however, he continues:

> But not long after returning home I one day picked up a report of the Bible Society and, opening it at random, my eye fell on a line which read: "This year the Gospel has been translated into the Chinook jargon...." The disquiet that had been vexing me disappeared in the twinkling of an eye. "This wonderful Christ," said I to myself; "they drive him out of Damascus, and lo, now he turns up in Alaska, speaking Chinook...."

During these years at St. Paul's, RR was indeed a "coming man." He was in frequent demand as a missioner for the Presbyterian Church of England, travelling widely and conducting special evangelistic campaigns. These were often in Presbyterian churches, but as frequently they were part of a general campaign in the nonconformist world under the auspices of the Free Church Council. RR recognized that these missions had serious limitations. Such campaigns were intended to reach the unchurched, but were largely attended by the faithful. He felt, nevertheless, that they were worth something if only they stirred up the people inside the churches to their responsibility for the redemption of the people outside.

The pace at which he was working throughout his ministry at St. Paul's was characteristic of him. Within the congregation, during the winter months, there were as many as thirty or forty meetings a week. Of course RR could not personally attend more than a fraction of them. The intense activity within the confines of his own pastoral charge and the district within which it lay, together with numerous and insistent calls from the wider nonconformist community, had put him under heavy strain. When an opportunity came for a fresh start, freed from all the accrued activities of his years in Westbourne Grove, he reluctantly concluded that he should move on. His reluctance was shared by the congregation of St. Paul's, as evidenced by a letter from the chair of the board:

Dear Mr. Roberts,

Having heard that you are about to receive a call from another congregation, we most earnestly and anxiously beg you not to leave us. Your going would be a serious blow to this congregation, and we urge upon you carefully to consider whether the benefit received by another congregation would outweigh the injury inflicted on this one.

Under your ministry the congregation has grown steadily in numbers and has largely increased its work. Some of the departments of work owe their existence to your initiative, and all of them owe much of their success to your energy and interest, and to the inspiration of your preaching.

We recognize that this is a difficult post to fill, but we believe that will only make you the more unwilling to leave it. We also believe that, under your continued ministry, there is a future before the congregation of still larger work and greater blessing than in the years that are past.

It is not merely as a congregation but as individuals that we urge you to remain, for your leaving us would mean to each of us a personal loss. You have gained the esteem and affection of us all, and to those of us who have experienced trouble, whether in spiritual matters, temporal affairs, or through the visitation of sickness or death, you have proved yourself a true friend and helper.

Were you satisfied that there was a clear call from God for you to go we would not venture to oppose it. Nor can we ourselves venture to pronounce dogmatically as to what the call of God at this time is, but we do express our conviction that the claims of your present congregation constitute a very strong call upon you to remain where you are.

We earnestly pray that at this time of difficulty and perplexity, you and we may be manifestly guided by the hand of God.

In the name and by authority of a congregational meeting held this evening after service....

10
Crouch Hill

The March 1910 issue of the *Monthly Chronicle*, published by the Crouch Hill Presbyterian Church, reports that on 3 March, a special meeting of the congregation had been called to implement, by the signing of a call, the election of a minister which had taken place on 23 February. The form of the call was read, and it was moved, seconded, and carried unanimously that the name of the Rev. Richard Roberts of Westbourne Grove be inserted into the call form. The Rev. Ivor J. Roberton, interim moderator, then "invited the members and adherents to adjourn to the Hall where the call was largely signed." The following Sunday a special effort was to be made to get onto the call form "the names of every member of the church and a long list of adherents. Mr. Roberts and the Presbytery will certainly be influenced in their decision by this."

The conduct of the meeting of presbytery recalls a time when the move of a minister from one congregation to another was dealt with in a more leisurely and less perfunctory manner than is the case today. The Crouch Hill *Chronicle* reported the proceedings. After the presbytery had been constituted RR was asked for a statement:

> Mr. Roberts replied that if the Presbytery placed the call in his hands he proposed to accept it....He had been happy for the last seven years in Westbourne Grove and had no expectation of greater happiness anywhere....He had gone to Westbourne Grove an untried and unknown man, and it was a considerable speculation on the part of the congregation to call him. If continued kindness and patience were marks of confidence, not a week had passed without that confidence being renewed. The advance of Westbourne Grove was much

less due to the minister than to the wonderful readiness to work displayed on the part of the congregation. The glory of Westbourne Grove was its session. No minister had had a session more loyal, devoted, and kind....[But] the recurrence of certain physical troubles meant that he must slacken the pace of his life, and the call to Crouch Hill gave him an opportunity of reorganizing the course of his life and relieving the bodily strain that was upon him....There was one element in the situation for which he was very grateful—that removal from Westbourne Grove did not involve separation from that Presbytery. The Presbytery had all conspired to make him feel at home.

The steps leading to the call were then described in detail by Mr. Roberton. Several speakers from Crouch Hill were heard urging the presbytery to accede to their request. These were followed by representatives of St. Paul's who spoke to the matter of the relinquishment of their minister. Sir Henry Robson, chair of the St. Paul's Board, spoke in a manner similar to the letter quoted previously. Mr. Russell spoke of RR's work with the Sunday school and its teachers. Alderman Pope said that:

> ...his friendship with Mr. Roberts had been unbroken. If Mr. Roberts did not make them "sit up" at Crouch Hill he had no hope of them. He would not only lead them in the green pastures of God's love, and by the still waters of His grace, but he would lead them to work, and show them how to work, and he (the speaker) wanted them to be kind to him, to extend their Christian sympathy and their love towards him. When he went into the pulpit they would get some of the finest and choicest meat there was at God's table. They (Westbourne Grove) gave him to Crouch Hill. They did not grudge him to them and he rejoiced that he would see him sometimes at that Presbytery.

Even the motion from the Rev. Alexander Ramsay that the call be placed in RR's hands did not bring the proceedings to a close. Mr. Roberton must thank Westbourne Grove for their attitude, and final details of the dates of the move were discussed and approved.

RR's pastoral connection with Westbourne Grove was terminated on 4 April, but he was not to be inducted at Crouch Hill until 9 June. In the meantime he was off to attend the World Sunday School Convention in Washington, D.C. The two-month period between pastorates might have been financially awkward but for a gift from Sir Henry Robson. It seems likely that RR had talked over with him the possibility of his going to the convention. The gift was accompanied by a note: "Enclosed I send you a cheque for £150. I always meant to make you a present...but I did not care to do anything until the call was settled in case I might be suspected of resorting to bribery and corruption."

The mention made in RR's speech of recurrent physical trouble probably referred to the migraine headaches from which he suffered all his life. He learned over the years that one sure cause was to be found in facing into a bright light for too long a period, and he sedulously avoided such situations when he could. But that was only one of several causes. When he was suffering from one of these bouts he simply withdrew himself from circulation, and Mrs. Roberts saw to it that quiet reigned in the house.

RR's first sermon at Crouch Hill recounted some of the details of his American trip. Not only had he been impressed with the scope of the plans for the Christian nurture of children the world over, he had been stirred by the enthusiasm for missions he had found among American lay people:

> It is a statement of fact and not hyperbole to say that today, in an American city of any size, the announcement of a missionary meeting for men would bring together, without any special effort, a gathering of one thousand or twelve hundred; and these numbering among them the most influential and responsible members of the community.

RR coveted this enthusiasm for Great Britain.

By autumn RR was well into his stride in his new pastoral charge. He was announcing a series of expository sermons on Ephesians for the morning services. The core of the mid-week meeting was to be a study of the Jesus of history. Nor was he entirely content with the order of service. A slightly changed order was announced in the bulletin with some explanatory notes:

My idea of a Sunday's services is that in the morning the emphasis should be upon the act of worship and the exposition of the Scriptures, and that the business of the evening is more especially hortatory and evangelistic.

Now, in all acts of worship there should be some coherent and intelligible idea to govern them. What are usually called "the pre-liminaries" consist of certain exercises which are intended chiefly to lead up to the sermon. They should, however, be not merely "pre-liminaries"—they should constitute an important and integral and indispensable part of the whole act of worship, and each element of them should have some concrete and definite meaning.

> With the hearty agreement of the office-bearers, the Offertory will, after Oct. 2nd, be taken not after but before the sermon. Please take special notice of the reasons.
>
> 1. The Offertory is an integral and necessary element in the act of worship. The usual idea of the collection is that it is an unfortunate necessity—an inevitable but quite foreign intrusion upon the spiritual business of the service. That is entirely wrong. The offering is as essentially worship as the singing of hymns. For
> 2. The Offertory should be the symbol and pledge of our own self-dedication to God. We give of our substance as an earnest of the gift of ourselves.
> 3. The Offertory is primarily an offering to God. The requirements are not satisfied by the furtive dropping of a casual copper upon the plate. The gift should be worthy of God and of the giver...and the amount of it is a question for the conscience and the honour of the giver. "Consider the grace of our Lord Jesus Christ who though he was rich, for our sakes became poor." That is the proper self-preparation for the offering.

The young people of Crouch Hill already had a variety of orga-nizations. There was the Athletic Club, the Swimming Club, the Gymnasium Club, the Literary Society, and the Young Men's Debat-ing Society. Apparently some of the older members of the church looked askance at the athletic programs, for in November RR wrote in the *Chronicle*:

I was greatly impressed last week by the tone and the atmosphere which prevail in the Athletic Club; and if there are any friends of the congregation who still harbour doubts as to the appropriateness and the legitimacy of this organization in connection with the church they may take it from me that the character of this particular club is not only wholesome but thoroughly Christian. It has clearly been the aim of its promoters to keep steadily in view the fact that it exists only in order to enable our young men to give their bodies as holy *living* sacrifices as their reasonable service to God.

With his American experience fresh in his mind, however, RR was anxious to see the young people drawn into a society for the "cultivation of spiritual life and of organizing definite Christian service." The original plan of holding the meetings of this new society on Thursday evenings had to be abandoned because such a large proportion of the young men and women of the church were already attending the Wednesday lectures on the Jesus of history. Instead it was determined to hold the special meeting of the young people for prayer and conference on Christian service right after the Wednesday meeting. At the end of 1910, then, RR's hopes were high.

The congregation at Crouch Hill was essentially a family church, though its membership also comprised a considerable number of transients boarding in the neighbourhood—young men and women employed in shops and businesses in London. At the time RR left St. Paul's, the membership had grown from approximately 230 to 336. Crouch Hill, when he came to it, had a congregation of from eight hundred to nine hundred. So, at a guess, it probably had a membership of about four hundred. Like St. Paul's, it had a mission. This was in Andover Road. And there was a full complement of activities for women, for young people, and for children. In order to get to know his people, RR and Mrs. Roberts held regular "at homes." He also set aside special times at the church for personal consultation. And, of course, he did the regulation pavement-pounding as he sought to visit his flock.

The move from Westbourne Grove to Crouch Hill hardly seemed to promise a more leisurely life. Nor did the move ease the pressure of outside activities. At the synod of the Presbyterian Church of England, held in Cardiff in May 1910, RR was appointed convenor of the Committee on the Instruction of Youth. Requests to act as missioner showed no decrease and he became increasingly involved in the life of the Free Churches. Some of his friends were anxious for him, as is attested by a letter from the Rev. E. P. Jones, a colleague of his Welsh Church days: "I dread lest the pace at which you go should shorten your course. You have time to go slowly *now* for the sake of 30 years hence."

In the midst of all these pressures RR had been working on a book, *The Renascence of Faith*, published in 1912. It received mixed reviews. In the *Letters of Principal James Denney*, edited by Robertson Nicoll, is this comment:

> I have never read so screamy a book as *The Renascence of Faith*. The man should be sentenced to read nothing but Horace for six months; it is a pity so right-hearted a person should be lost for want of knowledge and of self-control. His language in places is simply awful, yet he is a Presbyterian minister apparently.

Possibly it was this comment that led Nicoll to ask Dr. Denney to review the book in *The British Weekly*. Once, in later years, when some reference was made to Dr. Denney and what a lovely old man he was, RR said:

> Well, I don't know. I wrote a book—the first one of considerable length that I perpetrated. Dr. Denney reviewed it in *The British Weekly*—and oh—it was a scarifying thing. I wrote to him and said I was sorry he felt that way about it because there was a good deal of him and his book in it. Then he wrote me a very kind letter.

Not all agreed with Denney, however. Principal P. T. Forsyth of Hackney College, divinity school of the University of London, wrote that he had enjoyed the book's "alertness and push and tonic." But the letter which RR cherished most was from Edinburgh:

> My Dear Sir:
> Pardon a stranger taking up his pen to thank you for your fine book. I have spent a long evening in it; and with growing

admiration and gratitude as I went on. I thank God for you and for your book.

Alexander Whyte

"When I read that," concluded RR, patting the arm of his chair, "I was healed." Whyte was the much revered minister of St. George's Free Church and principal of New College in Edinburgh.

RR's work with the Presbyterian Youth Fellowship and with the Student Christian Movement, for which he was in frequent demand as a speaker, had shown that he had a peculiar ability to speak to the needs of young people. It was not surprising, then, to find that when the Presbyterian chaplaincy at Oxford fell vacant in 1913, his name was suggested. The chaplaincy combined the pastoral care of the Scottish Presbyterian students who were at Oxford with the ministry of St. Columba's Church of the North London Presbytery. The appointment was subject to the agreement of all parties involved. Bill Paton [1886–1943] of the SCM wrote:

> My Dear D.
>
> ...I'm all for the Oxford job. I talked to Tatlow [Tissington Tatlow of the SCM] about it (he's safe as a house. I hope you don't mind,) and we decided that he should write to old Whyte who, with his missis, has been having some hand in the Oxford business, and mention that there were rumours that you mightn't stay forever at Crouch Hill, and urge him to try to get you. Personally I think he'd rise, as he's talked about you to both T. and me. Have you considered salary? I don't think they can pay much and Oxford is devilish expensive.
>
> I don't feel with you about the doctorate. Inside Oxford it makes *absolutely* no difference. People like C.C.J. Webb haven't got doctorates, and Oxford wouldn't expect it, and if it weren't an Oxford doctorate mightn't be impressed! Furthermore, I doubt whether it would help much from the Presbyterian end....The Oxford people don't use degrees much....Would Mrs. R.R. like it—never a meal to herself?
>
> Meanwhile I'll pull discreetly such strings as I can.

This proposition which, in the event, came to nothing, was unsettling. Paton's reference to the rumours about RR's tenure at Crouch

Hill had a basis in fact. When he first began to consider the ministry, RR had felt strongly drawn to the foreign mission field. Never at any time did he lose the conviction that a church without a missionary calling was a moribund church. The missionary calling was, to him, almost as fundamental to the life of the church as prayer, and at the beginning of his ministry at Crouch Hill he said to his people: "A prayerless church is simply organized futility. A church breathing steadfastly the atmosphere of prayer is capable of great and enduring service."

In his preaching he did not so much plead the cause of missions as take it for granted that the foreign missions of the church commanded the full loyalty of every member. Not everyone at Crouch Hill shared this conviction, however, and there were murmurings. In fact, after a sermon on missions early in 1913, some members severed their connection with the church, and there was some growling over the loss of their pew rents.

Doubtless there were other sources of friction. For instance, some of the elderly in spirit grumbled over the pile of tennis rackets in the vestibule at the time of the mid-week service. They argued that it showed a lack of seriousness on the part of the young people. RR countered that the seriousness of the young people was attested to by their faithful attendance at the mid-week service. If they chose to bring their tennis rackets along so that they could adjourn at the end of the service to the tennis courts for the remainder of the long summer evening, it was not a matter for criticism.

The crisis came, however, over one of the women's organizations. The letters which deal with the trouble are tantalizing in their discretion. It would seem that a few of the members of the Women's Missionary Association had taken umbrage at some advice given them, and they began to circulate rumours of the affair which were less than accurate and which involved criticism of Mrs. Roberts. In some way the session also became involved in the skirmish.

On 5 December 1913, RR wrote to the North London Presbytery asking that he be relieved of the Crouch Hill charge. Almost immediately he left London for a "mission" in Birmingham. When he got back he found several letters awaiting him. David White, an elder of long standing, was in great distress over the whole business. He urged that RR meet with the session on his return, noting that the letter of resignation had been held in suspense. The session met and unanimously appealed to RR to withdraw his resignation. He did so, but troubles of this sort have a way of spilling over into the life of a congregation. Six weeks later RR felt it necessary to make a statement to the congregation:

> On Saturday, December 5 last, I sent in to the Clerk of Presbytery a letter in which I asked the Presbytery to release me from the pastoral charge of this congregation. It was my intention that it should come before Presbytery on the Tuesday following. But the Session Clerk, acting on his own responsibility, though against my judgement but with my knowledge, took steps to arrest the letter. In consequence of the subsequent action of the Session, I have since withdrawn the letter; and in consequence I am staying on in Crouch Hill.
>
> Some of you no doubt already know the circumstances that lie behind all this. It is not necessary that I should recount them in detail; but this much it is, I think, necessary you should know. Certain advice which I gave respecting one of the organizations connected with the congregation came, in the process of being passed from one person to another, to be very grievously misrepresented—so much misrepresented, indeed, that the Session thought it necessary to take some action in the matter—action which, ultimately, completely vindicated my position in the affair.
>
> But before the Session could take action, I took action on my own account. I resigned. The incident itself I could have afforded to ignore, but it came with a good deal of what seemed to me to be quite decisive background. To begin with, when a minister's action is canvassed in the particular way this was done, and subject to loose and irresponsible misrepresentation in this way, it simply means that he has somehow forfeited his people's respect and that his period of usefulness is at an end. But in addition to this, three months ago I very deliberately stated to the Session that I was of the opinion that I had failed to gain the confidence and the sympathy of the body of this congregation. Now, you do not need to suppose that I was in the least degree sorry for myself. I was not at all depressed. I simply had come to the bare and clear conclusion that here, in Crouch Hill, I was a round peg

in a square hole; and that it would be expedient for me to go where I could get the conditions that I needed in order to do my best work.

Now I need not detail all the factors which entered into this judgement. Since I have been here I have more than once refused to entertain proposals to go elsewhere; but one or two circumstances have led me to doubt whether I could continue to take this attitude. For instance, about a year ago I made certain very strong statements in order to make it quite clear than in any congregation with which I had to do, foreign missions could not be considered an open question. Some people left the church in consequence; and for some time afterwards I kept on hearing irritating echoes of criticism which seemed to me to indicate that the mind and the feeling of a considerable section of the congregation were hostile to the position I had deliberately taken up. Now I tell you quite frankly that I do not consider any congregation which is not deeply and sincerely concerned for the spread of Christ's Kingdom has any future at all; and I was filled with very real alarm and misgiving. Don't imagine that I claim to be immune from criticism; but I do claim that the strongest possible affirmation of a fundamental and axiomatic duty of a Christian Church should command the immediate sympathy and acclamation of all who profess to be its members.

But there was a second factor—namely the irregular and casual character of church attendance. Again do not misunderstand me. I have no personal grievance; I do not grumble because people prefer not to come to hear me preach. The size of a congregation does not now greatly affect me. But the loyalty or otherwise of people to the church and its worship do affect me profoundly; and the fact that a good many of the people who are supposed to attend this church do so only with a very considerable irregularity can only suggest that they do not do so on account of me. Now, I will be no hinderer or cumberer...anywhere; if I am an offence, I don't stay to fight. I simply go.

Now I may be right or I may be wrong in the inferences I drew. But right or wrong, they were the inferences which any minister would draw, and any minister worth having would feel exactly about them as I do. The Session assure me that my judgement is wrong; and it is because I respect their judgement that I am staying on. But I am bound to say that it is not without misgiving that I do so. I hold it generally true that it is a mistake to withdraw a resignation; and it is only a very pressing sense of responsibility that has overcome my general judgement in this particular case.

I know I have many deep and heavy limitations; but it is not of my own will and choosing that I am in the ministry. I recognize that the Gospel I preach is exacting and may even be disruptive; but that, I trust and pray, is only because it stands pretty squarely on the New Testament. I have also a defective social equipment; I find it impossible to sustain a satisfying pastoral relationship to so numerous a body of people; and I am not hopeful that I ever shall succeed in gaining an easy conscience on this point. But whatever my defects and limitations may be, I do not cease to give my freshest prayers and my best work to this congregation; God knows how poor and thin I recognize them to be; but I think I have every right to ask and to expect that, so long as I do not spare myself, the people who have called me will not fail to stand by me in the simple and primary loyalties of Christian discipleship, faithfulness in worship, and sympathy and generosity in Christian service and in the great causes of God's Kingdom.

During the week that followed this statement letters poured in. One of these, written on ordinary ruled foolscap and signed by sixty-two people, reads: "Just a few names of those who sincerely regret the recent trouble and who wish to assure Mr. Roberts of their sympathy with him." Doubtless whoever started this on its way took what paper was at hand in the church that morning and proceeded to collect the signatures. Many who signed were amongst the young folk, but their signatures were not far separate from those of their parents. Others wrote letters which expressed their own personal affection and regard, and in not a few there was a note of strong impatience toward the grumblers.

In spite of these spontaneous expressions of loyalty, RR's first judgement was correct. There was, in the congregation, a sufficient minority who found his preaching so uncomfortable as to make his position precarious. The next and final crisis came not many months later when RR, with many other ministers and lay people, became increasingly and publically involved in the protest against the war. To this end they came together in the formation of the Fellowship of Reconciliation. For as long as RR remained at Crouch Hill, however, even after the war broke out, there was never any doubt in his mind as to where his first duty lay. He continued to put his major effort into the church.

But the activities of the church changed. The interest of the congregation, which had been focused upon the Andover Road Mission, was absorbed instead in efforts for Belgian refugees and other charitable works connected with the war. To this kind of war effort RR gave his every support. And the personal lives and problems of the members took on a different cast. The withdrawal from the young people's organizations of the young men who enlisted, changed their complexion. RR saw these young men go with a heavy heart. He had no doubts as to their idealism and no word of criticism of their action. He knew where he himself must stand on the issue of war. But to him, another person's conscience was inviolate. There were probably some who joined up, as well as some stay-at-home belligerents, who despised him for his pacifism. But there were many who still looked to him as both pastor and friend. From wherever they were, they wrote to him fully and frankly:

On the Frontier, Sunday, 22.11.14.
...tho' I only received the beautiful little Testament yesterday, I can assure you it has been read at more than one peaceful interval since then—and, to my amazement, it has been requisitioned by the most unlikely of men; we are all— more or less—changed since we left England some 11 weeks back!

When I look back on events it seems as tho' they might all prove to be a terrible dream—but alas, the absence of so many of one's friends and the very obvious injuries borne by some of us still here, quickly prove the wished-for dream to be a grim and horrible reality....There has been a very heavy fall of snow, and it is bitterly cold. However, if the barn [in which they were quartered] is dank, it contains loads of straw into which we literally burrow. And so we sleep, eat—to

69

recuperate—no doubt for that fast-approaching time when we shall once more fill those dreaded Trenches!!...And so— you see—it is times like these which cause one "to think furiously," and your welcome little Testament has already been well-thumbed and read by flickering candle, all among the straw, while the cows stalled beneath "moo" their sympathy with us...and an occasional rat runs across to show that he too shares our habitation....However, in spite of everything, I am glad I am out here doing my little bit to prevent my own dear folk and country from being treated to the same sufferings as are being endured in this poor corner of the world....

N.A. MacPherson

Another congregational member, John Macmurray [1891–1976, later to become Grote Professor of Mind and Logic, University of London, and a noted philosopher of religion] wrote from a field ambulance corps:

What a queer anomaly of a Christmas this will be, with Christendom out to kill. I can do no thinking under these conditions: only week after week I just feel a steadier pressure of the hopelessness of expecting this war to end war, or do anything but weaken the whole moral resistance of Europe. The Press has been shameful, and the people have been only too ready to learn to slander and hate and boast blatantly. It makes me feel that [our] country is hardly worth fighting for....

I wonder what you are preaching about on Christmas day. I have never forgotten the Christmas sermon you preached a year ago—or is it two?—in Ferme Park, about the meaning of the Infancy of God. Crowds of extracts from sermons of yours are floating about in solution somewhere in my brain, but somehow that one stands out singularly clearly, along with another communion service when you talked about the sacrament as the claim to stand with Christ in the work for the salvation of the world.

What of the pamphlets and books that you are pouring forth about the war? I haven't seen any of the literature on the subject, which has been published everywhere I suppose....

Isn't it simply great to find how the Student Federation has stood the shock, and shamed all the churches? It seems to be the only institution which can see beyond nationality. That should give it a great future.

One of the most touching letters was from a young woman who had an "understanding" with one of a group of Germans, working in London, who had been attending Crouch Hill. The conflict of her loyalty to her country with her belief in the essential goodness of her German friend left her sorely troubled. It was to RR that she turned for comfort and guidance.

As the war progressed and the casualty lists mounted, RR must somehow give strength and comfort to those left behind. He would willingly offend no one, and he well knew and shared the anxiety and stress in the families that heard him preach. But it was inevitable that he should preach the Gospel as he found it, and some took offence. To certain people in the congregation his public utterances on the war and his vital connection with the Fellowship of Reconciliation were inexplicable and intolerable. He became convinced that to continue as minister of Crouch Hill could only do harm; that it might even bring shame and obloquy upon the church. Once again he submitted his resignation.

Even some who did not altogether agree with his stand about the war, however—and these included families whose young men were in France—did not let his resignation go by default. Considerable pressure was brought to bear on him, as on the previous occasion, to reconsider his decision. RR felt that it was no longer in his hands to make the final decision. He consulted Dr. Skinner [1851–1925], Old Testament scholar and principal of Westminster College, Cambridge, who responded in May 1915:

...Your surmises as to the attitude of the Office-bearers are entirely correct. Wylie's statement on that point was incomplete. He did not exaggerate the warmth of the testimony to the value of your ministry, and their appreciation of all that you have been and done to them; but at the same time there was a firm and general opinion that it would be unwise for the Presbytery committee to urge you to withdraw your resignation. How far this state of feeling was determined by the fact that you had already announced your decision...I cannot tell; but I have an impression that it goes rather deeper than that. Nor can I say how much of it is due to your attitude with regard to the war, and how far to a certain strain (such as you have been conscious of) of older standing. [But] the committee all felt that they could no longer press you to reconsider your decision....[As] regards your relations with your own congregation, things have gone too far for you to draw back.

And so the resignation went through. At the meeting called to appoint a selection committee to choose a new minister, however, there were still reverberations. One of the young men of the church, unable to be present probably because he was away in the Forces, sent a letter to the meeting which read: "By our apathy, by our lack of loyalty, by our unkind criticism, we have created the atmosphere which made Mr. Roberts' withdrawal possible at this tragic time, and have quite evidently given the session the idea that it was not advisable to press him to stay, if indeed some of the responsibility does not lie within that select body itself." Going on to say that many of the members felt the whole affair had been "sadly bungled" and were "thoroughly disheartened," he concluded: "Wouldn't it be better, before appointing the Selection Committee, to ask ourselves whether we want to call a minister to reflect faithfully our own opinions, or whether we desire to gain for ourselves a man who will put truth before pew-rents, a man who will be true to himself and therefore to the congregation? And having found him, shall we not be loyal through and through?" The *Hornsey Journal* reports that this communication was read "amid many expressions of assent."

The last sermon RR preached as minister of Crouch Hill reflects his mind at that time:

> Jesus Christ asks from us everything, or nothing; he demands the first place in our life, or no place at all. The moral law is one and the same in social life, in business, in politics, in international relations. We believe this in theory but in practice we generally tone it down. We regard the Sermon on the Mount as hopelessly idealistic, not practical politics. Well, practical statecraft has had its way, and the best it has been able to do for us is this awful welter in which we live today. Is it not time we gave the way of Jesus Christ a chance? It could

not be any worse, at least. It would probably involve a revolution for a great many of us in our ideas and way of life. The text says that the society of the redeemed, the Church of God triumphant, is to reign supreme over all principalities and powers.

This vision was recorded nearly 1900 years ago, and it has not come true yet; and seems farther from being true now than ever. We see the Church itself riven, broken, shattered by the war. We perceive how the national bond has everywhere proved stronger than the Christian bond, and in the midst of this welter the Church stands impotent and speechless—saying a good deal but virtually speechless so far as the wider and more ultimate interests of the Kingdom of God are concerned—just because there is a war, which is, after all, only an episode in the course of the world that the Church was sent to redeem.

It may need a revolution in the Church itself before the vision comes true. The Church has departed in many ways from the way of Christ. It has in many things accepted the ways of commerce even, and worldly wisdom, and the standards of worldliness. How does the Church, how does this congregation, how does any congregation judge its prosperity today? By figures and balance-sheets, just as they do in the City—utterly and wholly irrelevant to its main business. And yet this reigning Church will come on earth as sure as tomorrow's dawn. The crowning glory of the Gospel of Jesus Christ, as it came from His lips, was that the poor were having it preached to them. The poor are not in our churches today, and we have got to sweep out the things that keep them out—the impious exactions of pew-rents, the devices, the silly devices, we have for raising money—bazaars and sales of work and the like; the snobbishness and the middle-class exclusiveness of so much of our church life.

It is to the making of that reigning Church that you and I are called today—and we have got to begin sometime. And the beginning is just this: that we accept fully the redemption of Christ, and in the strength of that redeeming grace go forth accepting the sovereignty of Christ, fully, without reserve, over the whole area of our lives.

11
Crouch Hill: Extracurricular

In the preceding section references were made to certain of RR's activities outside the bounds of his immediate responsibilities at Crouch Hill. His appointment by the Presbyterian Church of England as convenor of the Committee on the Instruction of Youth, just seven years after his admission from the Welsh Church, shows that he was already being accepted as a leader in the English church. For RR his work at Crouch Hill and his work as convenor of the committee were but two sides of a single coin. He expected his people at Crouch Hill to see it in the same light. To that effect he wrote in the December 1910 issue of the *Chronicle*:

> It has occurred to me that the Congregation might like to know from time to time of the work which I am permitted to do for our Church. A congregation should esteem it an honour and a privilege to lend its minister for the wider purposes of the Kingdom...; and I trust that the work among children and young people in charge of which the Church has placed me will have a warm place in the interest and prayer of the Crouch Hill congregation. I believe that we are entering upon a new era in this department of work; and I am eager for Crouch Hill to feel that it shares with its minister the responsibility of wisely directing the new movements which are now emerging in connection with young people's work. I have no ideal short of this—that Crouch Hill congregation should assume real leadership in many (why not all?) departments of our Church's life.

Until he resigned from Crouch Hill in 1915, RR remained convenor of this committee and deeply involved in its concerns. The synod of 1911 gave its blessing to an early proposal for the inauguration of graded lessons throughout the Sunday schools of the church. The problem was that there was no material immediately available with a distinctively Presbyterian mark. The committee proposed to proceed by using a series already prepared by some other group. After considerable study it looked as though that of the Society of Friends was the most congenial, and arrangements were made. There was to be some extra material added with specifically Presbyterian missionary content. Other plans were set afoot to provide adequate training for Sunday school teachers, both in biblical knowledge and teaching methods.

These undertakings were, of course, only a beginning. In theory the young people, when they had made their way through the Sunday school, moved on to adult Bible classes. But many of them disappeared from the churches at this point. Others stayed in touch with the church, but chiefly through athletic, social, and recreational clubs. That the Bible class program lacked appeal was underlined by the steady drop in enrolment over a five-year period. In his statement to the people of Crouch Hill, RR goes on to write:

> The work among young men and women in our Church is in a very chaotic state; and a great effort is to be made to unify and coordinate existing societies. It is felt that in order to do this we shall need to inaugurate a new movement for our young men and women throughout the Church. Meantime, I am calling a conference of representatives from all the existing young people's societies in the London Presbyteries, to see what can be done....What the issue will be I cannot say....

What "issued" was the birth of the Presbyterian Youth Fellowship, later known simply as the Presbyterian Fellowship. RR was a moving figure in this venture.

Late in July 1914, the Presbyterian Fellowship held its third national conference at Swanwick. The conference concluded summarily upon the outbreak of war, but afterwards a leaflet was printed to capture some memories for the participants. A few of the more serious elements of the conference—concern for missions, for instance—peep through the heavy jocularity of the record. In its pictures and its prose, RR figures as one who could enjoy the high jinks of youth as well as appreciate their fundamental seriousness:

> One of the most pathetic incidents of the Conference occurred when Mr. Haldam Carruthers, a youth of great promise who had received a prize earlier in the week, endeavoured to cross to the island in the pond by means of a plank bridge. When he was half-way across the treacherous plank precipitated him into the water, in which he was immersed almost up to his knees, only, unfortunately, head first. With indomitable pluck the victim, after righting himself, instead of seeking the bank hoisted himself once more upon the plank. But to the horror of the few chance spectators he immediately fell off on the other side. A loud groan burst from all, and one running up was just in time to see the Rev. Richard Roberts strike himself violently upon the knee and to hear him ejaculate in a voice laden with emotion, "Well, I *am* glad I didn't miss that!"

And the young people carried away other memories of RR:

> One's mind runs on from one thing to another. I seem to see the Moderator again standing by the clock in the lounge talking to us in his own quiet way, just where Mr. Roberts stood on the last night, when we all saw things beyond mortal seeing, and our hearts answered to the simple words he said.

RR was never one to be limited by denominational lines. The work of the Free Churches in cooperation also laid claim to his loyalties. The Free Church Federation had been formed in 1892. RR's old mentor of the Passive Resistance Movement, Dr. John Clifford, and another who had been associated with them, Dr. Hugh Price, had been considerable figures in the early days of the federation. It bound together loosely the local Free Church Councils. These were voluntary bodies, and there was no delegated denominational membership. Their purpose was discussion and the framing of joint policy, and, at times, joint action on social and political matters which affected the life of the nonconformist churches. The resolutions introduced at the December 1911 annual meeting of the Metropolitan

Free Church Council give some idea of the scope of its interests: Sunday cinematograph shows, international peace, temperence, shops bill, and education.

The address of the outgoing president that December focused on the needs of the federation with special reference to young people. In view of his known interest, it is not surprising that RR was elected president for the ensuing year. Into this task he flung himself with his usual vigour. By the fall of 1912, a campaign to enlist noncon-formist youth in a united front was inaugurated with a number of rallies in the various districts of London. A letter sent out by the committee makes some pertinent suggestions for a cooperative ap-proach to the young people's organizations already in existence. RR was particularly anxious that the enthusiasm engendered by the cam-paign meetings should not be allowed to peter out in talk. At the conclusion of the letter he made this appeal:

> May we be permitted to suggest that the Councils should take upon themselves immediately the task of studying the social needs of their localities? The time is not far distant when young people will ask to be directed to definite work along these lines, and it would be a tragedy if the Councils were then unable to help them.

This sort of work, necessary as RR deemed it to be, was never-theless an extra burden to be borne. It was valuable work, but pedes-trian. There were many like-minded men involved in the council's activities; to them also it meant simply more work, more commit-tees. Of these a number felt an urgent need for their own refresh-ment of spirit. From time to time they would gather as small groups of friends to talk and to pray about their concern for the state of the Free Churches. In 1911, a few of them met at Mansfield College, Oxford, and together they conceived the idea out of which grew the Free Church Fellowship. "It began," wrote the Congregationalist theologian and social critic Nathaniel Micklem [1888–1953], in one of his "Ilico" columns in The British Weekly, "as a relatively small band of eager young ministers—Roberts, Maltby, Darlaston, Malcolm Spencer, Newton Marshall, Herbert Morgan, Warburton Lewis, and the like....They were from all the Free Church denominations, and there was a feeling of youth, of hope, of expectancy, of Pentecost about their meetings."

At the Mansfield College gathering an Inception Committee was established to further the project of a conference to be held in August in Swanwick. This first conference was limited to one hundred men who were invited on the personal nomination of the members of the original group. RR later recalled in "The Story of the Covenant":

It is difficult, indeed quite impossible, to convey any adequate impression of the joy and the strength which came to those hundred men. The immediate discovery of a new fellowship, considerable in its extent and deep and eager in its character, brought to every one of us a breath of new life. Whatever misgivings any of us may have harboured about the future of the Free Churches were dissipated forever during that week. Many of us had prayed, and had eaten our hearts up in a dreary isolation, but that week we walked into a new world, and things have never since been quite the same to any of us. If one attempts to analyze the experiences of that week, it is not with any hope of reproducing them adequately. The great discovery of a new fellowship was only one element....There was a new realization of the power of prayer; and there came to many of us with a shock of joy the conviction that we had discovered a new method of approach to the problem which had called us together. *That was the fusion of hard praying and hard thinking together*; and we felt that to this method nothing was impossible.

These men found that they had "a sure, inalienable faith in the Church as the divinely appointed organ of redemption and revelation in the modern world." They gave themselves up to the dream of a United Free Church of England and, beyond that, One Universal Church. And they faced the reality of the Church divided and dismembered—weak, mediocre, and poverty-stricken in Christian experience and service.

We set ourselves to an analysis of our problem; and we concluded that our present situation arose from a two-fold defect in our Christian experience—first, a defect of impulse; and secondly, a defect of knowledge. The former we traced partly to our ignorance of a real method of sustaining and developing the life of devotion, to a shallow and fragmentary understanding of the laws of prayer. In view of this we felt that we needed to rediscover the science and practice of prayer for our generation. Hence, this fell in as part of the second problem. The defect of knowledge is obviously the consequence of defective education; and we realized that, to save the situation, we needed to discover and formulate a new and sufficient policy of Christian education.

This, however, opened out two further problems. If we were going to educate, what was to be the subject matter of the education? Face to face with this question we were confounded, first by the obvious lack of agreement as to the content and range of Christian truth in view of the modern advance of scientific knowledge and the results of Biblical criticism; and second, by the absence of any authoritative guidance regarding the applications of the Christian ethic to modern social, economic, political, and international conditions. The second problem related to the people whom we wished to educate. We could not treat them as a single mass, and we were confronted with the necessity of a psychological analysis of the people with whom we have to do—from the child upwards. The solution of these two problems appeared a very considerable task; but the attempt seemed so inevitable, so imperative, that we agreed to make it. And in the new strength of our Fellowship, we did not feel unequal to it.

A résumé of the thinking of the conference was published under the title, "The Challenge of the Modern Situation." It was for private circulation only, and a committee was appointed to prepare a syllabus for a second conference. As they worked on the syllabus the committee soon realized that the basis of the entire movement must first be clearly stated if the movement was not to go astray. Malcolm Spencer jotted down a few heads. A draft of these was presented to the second conference in April 1913, as "The Grounds of our Fellowship" [later, "The Covenant of our Fellowship"]. But it still fell short of what the group wanted. A small group was set to work on it. As RR recounts:

For two days we discussed the matter and had reached a

common mind. But we found it exceedingly difficult to state it. At length it was suggested that a certain member of the Fellowship [Nathaniel Micklem] should withdraw and draft a statement, while the rest of us remained in silent prayer. In a very short time the draftsman returned, and read to us what he had written. It said what we meant—and how much more! We accepted it without discussion, and spontaneously sang the Doxology.

In its earliest days the group had no official name but was known, familiarly, as "the Boojum." "Swanwick Echoes," from the second of the occasional papers put out by the group, gives some account of this appellation, and also indicates something of the effervescent spirit of the group:

Some of the members of our Fellowship, attending in their customary way Autumnal Sessions of various kinds, have rejoiced to hear on every hand the authentic note of Swanwick; and with great gladness they have listened to their brothers "boojing."

(To "booj" is the verb derived from the noun "boojum," and means the speech of a man who has the burden of Swanwick. The Boojum was a term of affectionate familiarity applied in the day of the incipience of the conspiracy which brought us together. What it means, and how it came to be thus applied, are matters upon which to consult *The Hunting of the Snark*, by Lewis Carroll, and after that to take a long breath and guess. Failing that, ask the Secretary, but not by letter.)

At the Autumnal Meeting of the Congregational Union it was heard; still more loudly in the London Congregational Union Autumn Session; and in the Free Church Federation of London it was prolonged with great success....

It is good to know that the true work of the Fellowship is being done in this way by the means of existing societies— good too, that on every hand the message is heard and welcomed. We came into being, it would seem clear, in the fullness of time.

The 1913 conference affirmed that, without the inclusion of

women, "the Fellowship is not likely to realize the full measure of its possibilities," and went on to explain:

> There are certain parts of our work which we simply cannot do without the help of women; and there are things to be done which only women can do. The one thing which seems to be imperilled by the admission of women is the somewhat boisterous expressions of comradeship which we have in the past indulged in, and possibly something of the unreserved and unstudied outspokenness in discussion which has hitherto characterized our fellowship.

The only serious difficulty, the members thought, would be that if there was a sudden influx of women who had not had the experience of the previous conferences to guide them in the ways of the Boojum, problems of communication might arise. The solution was not hard to find. A special conference for women only, to bring them up to date, was to be held before their admission as a group to the main body. After that, any member, whether male or female, would be introduced on the nomination of an established member.

By the third year of the fellowship attendance at the annual Swanwick Conference had more than doubled. A number of people were present who did not altogether understand the underlying principles of the Boojum, however. The meeting on the first evening was, as a result, chaotic. The next morning RR spoke, and "Ilico" described the scene:

> I can see him now, leaning forward on the rostrum with both hands gripping the rail; he was not the less formidable in appearance for a curious cast in the eye; there he stands silent but with the movement of the lips as if he could scarcely forbear to speak, and at last an unprepared speech, with prophetic fire and moving eloquence, a real declaration "in the Spirit."

Of the fellowship itself, Ilico continued:

> If they had kept together as a small, homogeneous company of friends meeting annually and growing together, they might, as I have often thought, have achieved a wonderful leadership

for the Free Churches. But they were otherwise led. It was decided...that they must share their experience and enlarge their membership as widely as possible—no ignoble ambition, nor has it been fruitless, but it may well have been a great mistake. Yet, I imagine that they could not have kept together; the war put a great strain upon them, for they were deeply divided about the moral issues that it raised.

As the Rev. David Anderson recounted sadly in November 1914:

I think the church is really broken far more than most people imagine, and new groupings and fellowships will have to arise as a result....It seems in one sense tragic, because we all felt so near to a new unity of spirit which promised to regenerate the church; and now it seems as far off as ever.

12
The Fellowship of Reconciliation

When the conference of the Presbyterian fellowship was adjourned on the morning of 5 August 1914, RR made a hurried trip to Aldburgh where his family was on holiday, and then went straight to London, feeling that he must be in his own pulpit on that first Sunday of the war. The sermon he proposed to deliver was, in his own words, "a potpourri of conflicting emotions." Clarity came with a shock just before he rose to preach. Some young Germans engaged in business in London, who had been regular attendants at the Crouch Hill morning services, were no longer in their accustomed pews. RR later recounted in an article for the *Journal of the Fellowship of Reconciliation* entitled "How the Fellowship Began":

> I stood petrified for some minutes; then I found words to say to my people that my duty was to report what I had discovered, and to ask them to consider, as Christians, the appalling circumstance that lads of that congregation, who had worshipped God together in that church, might, under the orders of their superiors, be called to murder each other. What more I said...I cannot recall. But I knew when I left the church that morning that, as a minister of Christ, I could take no part in a war.

He found himself in the midst of a dilemma. It was a dilemma in which many church leaders and members found themselves. The church was torn. Dr. Alexander Ramsay gave notice of a resolution to be brought before the North London Presbytery and RR was troubled by the wording. He wrote the following letter:

My Dear Ramsay,

I have just received the Presbytery agenda, and want to say that your resolution puts me in a position of grave distress. As a citizen I can assent to all its terms—though I think *righteous* is rather a strong word. But my difficulty about it is two or three-fold:

First, there is in it no acknowledgement that we, as a nation, have any responsibility for the situation which preceded the war. I could agree with the resolution if there were no history prior to July 1 last. But our participation in the circumstances which made Europe an armed camp, charged with mutual suspicion and misunderstanding, involves us in a very serious responsibility for the war. Our subscription to the doctrine of the Balance of Power in Europe, our assent to the secrecy of diplomatic negotiations—these things alone are pretty serious counts against us.

Second: While I as a citizen may have my views and responsibilities as to the war, a court of Christ's Church which takes up the attitude indicated in your resolution does, in my view, come dangerously under the suspicion of denying Him. War means killing men, our brethren for whom Christ died. And I do not see how His Church can approve any war. Third: War itself generally, and this war in particular, is the result of the failure of the Church to impose the mind of Christ upon the nations, and to make His Law operative between them. It seems to me that the only possible attitude of the Church at this time is one of great heart-searching and penitence.

I associate myself with the expression of pride in the loyalty and devotion of our young men; but I cannot forget that out of the number gone from my congregation are eight young Germans called to *their* colours. And if my Christianity means anything, my bond with them is as close as with the others. I cannot think of my young men fighting each other without heartbreak. They are brethren in Christ; and we have failed to make it impossible that they should be called perhaps to kill each other.

That in the present state of the world war is sometimes inevitable, one has freely to admit. But we Christians ought not under any circumstances go to war save with bowed heads and broken and shamed hearts. And it is that aspect of the whole thing that I frankly feel most deeply today. I am proud of England, but I am very sore for the Church.

...I have no doubt you have thought of these things, but I think it right I should tell you how I feel. I cannot express these views in Presbytery as I am in the chair, or else I would.

A few sentences from Dr. Ramsay's reply indicates the conflicting loyalties Christians were facing:

I do not follow your criticism, which seems to me to be directed against something other than my motion. All that I affirm is the righteousness of Britain's cause in this war. Of this as a Christian man I am convinced. That does not mean that we have nothing in our past relations with Germany to seek forgiveness for, altho' I believe that our nation...and our government have sought for friendship and good understanding....The question of the righteousness of our cause is vital to our fervour of intercession, and it was because of this that I named it. The motion is intended to be not an approval of war, but a call to prayer....I think we also might take note of the large number of our young men who are going on service....Let them go in the name of the Lord and with our spoken benediction!....It never occurred to me that we ought to say all we feel as Christian men about the war, and yet I have so far sympathy with your point of view that I should willingly see my resolution amplified in some such sense!

This conflict of loyalties was widespread. In the hope of finding some sure course, RR telephoned a number of the men with whom he had come into close fellowship, both through the Boojum and through his work with the SCM. He continues the story in "How the Fellowship Began":

We held a meeting shortly after in our empty home on Crouch Hill. My own immediate ministerial neighbours came, and with them Dr. Orchard [William Edwin Orchard, 1877–1955,

Free Church theologian and later a convert to Roman Catholicism] and others representing the Free Churches. On the Anglican side was G. K. A. Bell, Edwyn Bevan, and several others. [Bell, 1883–1958, was later to become Bishop of Chichester, a noted ecumenist, and one of the few people in Great Britain who protested the saturation bombing of Dresden during World War II; Bevan, 1870–1943, was an historian and philosopher at King's College, London, a strong supporter of the SCM.]

We were a bewildered company. Since the Boer War at the turn of the century we had had no occasion to consider the Christian attitude to war. Henry Hodgkin [a Quaker] had promised to come, and I remember how anxiously we awaited him. Surely he would bring, out of the long testimony of the Society of Friends against war, some clear word that might resolve our bewilderment. But so far as our course of action was concerned, Henry was as puzzled as we were. The only two things about which we were fairly clear were, (1) that Great Britain was bound in honour to go to the succour of its ally France, and (2) that war was unchristian.

We did decide, however, that we might try to do something to safeguard the Christian faith and testimony from being swamped by what seemed likely to be the greatest war in history. We decided to meet again, and at the next meeting we came to the conclusion that we would issue a series of tracts under the title *Papers for Wartime.* We appointed, as editor, William Temple, [1881–1944], later Archbishop of Canterbury.

The first paper was written by Temple under the title "Christianity and the War"; the second was mine, entitled "Are We Worth Fighting For?"...

Unhappily, as more papers were published and time went on, a strong drift toward another emphasis became apparent. Some of the group took the line that the *Papers* should take on a more propagandist tone, and put more stress upon the winning of the war; and it became evident that the majority favoured that policy. Henry Hodgkin and I found ourselves in a hopeless minority. We agree that we could not serve usefully any longer upon the Committee, and that we must create another body that would be more forthright in maintaining the Christian front during the war.

It had not taken long, in fact, for war fever to grip England, and almost simultaneously to invade the churches. Before August was out some church leaders had gone overboard in support of the war effort. William Paton appealed to RR:

Have you seen Robertson Nicoll's letter—"stirring appeal"— in the *Daily News* today, [encouraging] young Nonconformists to enlist? [Nicoll, 1851–1923, was editor of *The British Weekly* and *The Bookman*.] Nat [Micklem] and I have just had a long talk over it. We are both very weary of the continued silence of the Church's leaders, broken only by platitudinous utterances or calls to arms. Nicoll's letter is the crowning blow, and seems a challenge to everything we believe in. It is impossible to let it go unanswered, and if the old 'uns won't say anything, Nat and I and also Chris Angus would like to say a word. We personally take the Sermon on the Mount line literally, though I don't for a moment wish to ignore the high motives and self-denying courage of men who are going up to the front. But where in all the Church's official talking...is there any note of penitence, or thought of a spiritual order of which we are members, which forbids us to fight? All that kind of thing is respectfully admired in the Quaker, but never seen elsewhere. Anyway—will you join us in a short letter...?

A few weeks later, Principal Skinner of Westminster College wrote to RR:

My Dear Roberts,
I feel as if I owed you an apology for an unconscious injustice I had done you in thinking you a rabid advocate of war. I believe the report which misled me rested on a confusion of your name with that of a certain Richard *Richards* who seems to be exceptionally eager to shed his Christian principles. But indeed in this Gadarene-swine race of the churches down a steep place into the sea it will be difficult to assign the first prize. Anyhow it is not going to you! It was only last night

that I saw your letter in the Christian World; and I want in a word to thank you for it, and to say how thoroughly I agree with it.

In a letter written in October 1914, Skinner commented on a conference for church leaders he and RR had attended:

I have been wondering what you thought of that Conference at Lambeth. It seemed to me the most futile waste of time that I have endured for long. To begin by making it clear that, at all hazards, you are in favour of this war and prosecuting it to the bitter end, and then to go on to consider what crumbs of Christian comfort you can extract from an admittedly deplorable situation (which is what most of the speakers did) did not seem a very hopeful line to take if men really want to know what Christianity has to say about war. I did not hear very well the speeches from your side of the hall; but Orchard seemed to be trying to speak the truth. Of those I did hear Hodgkin alone raised the real issues; and every subsequent speaker most triumphantly ignored them. They never got within a hundred miles of what seemed to me to be the realities of the question.

Henry Hodgkin [1877–1933] and RR did not formally resign from the group issuing *Papers in Wartime*; they simply ceased to attend its meetings. RR continues the story:

But we were not idle. There was a house in Pimlico, near the Thames, which was the home of a loosely organized body of forward-looking people called the Collegium, presided over by a Quaker lady, Lucy Gardner. To this house we invited all the people of our convictions that we knew of, and as time went on our numbers grew until we had the makings of a respectable and active association.

The problem before us was...to work out a Christian pacifist philosophy that could be accepted by the group, or at least by a substantial majority of it....We had not much to go on. The existing Peace Society of London had accepted the war as inevitable, and no light on our problem was forthcoming from that quarter. We went on with our search, and at length the moment came when we had reasonable certainty that we had solid and stable ground to stand on. We also gathered together a considerable number of people, some of whom were firmly anti-war in conviction, and others who were outraged by the war and were inhibited from supporting it, and were seeking for light.

A conference was called to meet at Cambridge, in Trinity College, during the Christmas vacation. And there the Fellowship of Reconciliation was born in the last four days of the fateful year of 1914. A good central committee was appointed to carry on for a year; Henry Hodgkin was elected chairman, Lucy Gardner continued as honourary secretary; and we continued to meet at the Collegium house.

It soon became apparent, however, that this arrangement was not satisfactory. The house was too inaccessible to be a good headquarters for a young and vigorous society. The Fellowship should be near the main arteries of London traffic. And since it would be impracticable for Lucy Gardner, in view of her other commitments, to go daily to an office far from her headquarters, it became necessary not only to find new headquarters but another secretary as well.

Henry Hodgkin was insistent that I should take the task, but at the moment I was disinclined to do so. It would necessitate leaving my church and my position as convenor of the Youth Committee of the Presbyterian Church. Presently, however, my relations with my church officers took a sharp turn for the worse, and I saw that I should have to resign my charge. So it turned out that I was free to accept the secretaryship of the Fellowship. I entered upon it on the first of July, 1915.

In the October 1947 issue of the magazine *Reconciliation*, George Davies recalls the group's difficulties in finding an office:

They had been refused accommodation after a score of applications. Accidentally, or perhaps providentially, I had wandered into Red Lion Square in my quest, and I noticed a card above the door which announced that offices were to let. The panelled walls and wide staircases, the pleasant ancientness of the rooms, seemed too good to be possible for this suspect pacifist society. When at last I interviewed the estate agent and learned the terms, a misgiving smote me that I [had not been] sufficiently frank with him. I ventured to explain that the F. O. R. was not too popular at the moment. He expressed surprise. I said, "You see, it believes in taking Christianity seriously, even in time of war." He replied, "Well, that seems pretty 'armless." And so the bargain was clinched, and kept for over 20 years.

RR's narrative continues:

The staff of the new office consisted, at first, of the secretary and a competent typist, plus some voluntary help for addressing and mailing circulars and the like. But help of another kind came, too. A young Scots student, Lewis MacLachlan, came to London and offered me his services, and served us well. If I remember rightly he remained with me until he went to Holland with a Friends' refugee unit.

George Davies was another. He was a banker in North Wales who had himself been an officer in the territorial army, but had been convinced of the evil of the military system and resigned from it. It is impossible to describe George Davies without recourse to superlatives. When he came into my office unannounced, I could think of nothing that described the effect he had on me save some superlative like "the sun in splendour!" What he meant to us while he was with us can never be told. Later the Military Service Act sent him to Wormwood Scrubbs Prison. While he was in that prison a friend who was visiting him was leaving through the prison gates when my brother-in-law, an officer in the Army, met the friend and, recognizing him, said, "What on earth has happened to you?" The man answered, "Well, I seem to have been in the presence of Jesus Christ...I have been with George Davies."

Of all the people in the FOR, George Davies was perhaps the most remarkable. The brother-in-law mentioned above, Dan Thomas, had served under Davies both in the bank and in the territorials.

It fell to Dan to arrest his former boss and commander. So he wrote to Davies, telling him the circumstances and asking him to come by a certain date. His brother officers could not understand why he did not go out to "get his man." But George Davies inspired that kind of trust. There were several occasions when, as a prisoner, he travelled unescorted from one prison to another. The authorities recognized him for what he was. In a letter from prison in Birmingham, Davies himself described one such occasion:

> As I was passing through Cardiff on my way from Dartmoor to a Home Office Work Camp in S. Wales, I saw Lewis (the ship-owner) talking on the platform to a middle-aged lady. I jumped out of the train, apologized for interrupting, and shook hands. He was astonished to see me; and then, indicating his companion, said, "You know Mrs. Lloyd George, don't you?" I was astonished, and she a little embarrassed I thought. I told them I was on my way from prison....

The tag "pro-German" was attached at that time to anything less than violent propagandist patriotism. Those were the days when women went about giving white feathers to any young man walking the streets in "civvies." The FOR, of course, came under suspicion. Amongst the pacifists and conscientious objectors were undoubtedly some to whom the pro-German tag was applicable. But the people of the FOR were, rather, pro-everyman. In the course of time a detective came to the office in Red Lion Square to investigate them. George Davies remembers how the detective was transformed into "a man in tears seeking Dick's [RR's] comfort in the loss of his brother by bombing."

On leaving Crouch Hill RR had taken his family to live in New Barnet. He commuted daily to Red Lion Square when he was not out of London engaged on some errand of the fellowship. He became conscious of the fact that, for several nights, he had been followed home. It was winter, cold and rainy, so he stopped at the gate and waited until his "shadow" came abreast. As he was passing RR spoke to him, inviting him in for a cup of tea. In they came together, had their cup of tea, and talked awhile. After that, RR and his shadow commuted together, and communed the while on pacifism, Christianity, and a variety of other subjects. There is no knowing what report the detective made on his work.

Shortly after the move to Red Lion Square the fellowship started a monthly periodical entitled the *Venturer*. The title was suggested by a passage in F. W. H. Myers' poem, "St. Paul":

Lo, as some venturer from his stars receiving,
Promise and presage of sublime emprise
Wears evermore the seal of his believing
Deep in the dark of solitary eyes....

RR continues the story:

We chose the word *Reconciliation* in the Fellowship's title, partly because there was a British Peace Society with an office in London and it was important that we should not be mixed up with it by using *peace* in our name. And for another reason we preferred the word reconciliation. Through all the years, peace had been chiefly conceived as the absence of war. For us peace was something to be waged, as war was waged. Peace is not a passivity, a state of rest, a lull between wars. It must be conceived as an activity; and the name of that activity is *Reconciliation*, which is the finest of all arts, the art and practice of turning enemies into friends. It is the essential core of Christian divinity and of Christian ethics. Its chief exemplar is God—and its classical statement is to be found in St. Paul's Second Epistle to the Corinthian Church..."If any man be in Christ, he is a new creature; old things are passed away; behold all things are become new. And all things are of God who has reconciled us to Himself by Jesus Christ, and has given us the ministry of reconciliation: to wit, that God was in Christ reconciling the world unto Himself, not imputing their trespasses unto them, and has committed unto us the word of reconciliation"....

This implies that Reconciliation is a universal principle, to be practised on every plane and in every department of life. It is to be practised toward the stranger and toward the difficult neighbour, and is to follow us into the store, the office, the workshop, the field. It is the fundamental principle by which we should regulate our public relations, our politics, whether domestic or international, and our commercial and professional concerns.

According to one or two of the original members, it was RR who found for the new fellowship the word "reconciliation."

RR was the first editor of the *Venturer*. As secretary other tasks also fell to him. With Henry Hodgkin, chair of the FOR, he arranged meetings and conferences in various parts of Great Britain. They themselves were frequently the main speakers, though they also called on other members of the fellowship whenever these were free.

A great deal of the work of the FOR was in the field of civil liberties. The Military Service Act set up tribunals to examine conscientious objectors. The operation of these tribunals varied greatly with the personalities which composed them. In some places they were eminently fair; in others they were harsh beyond all bounds. The Central Tribunal sent out a directive which differentiated between the validity of religious and moral grounds for conscientious objection. The directive also stated that the age of the applicant for exemption should be taken into consideration. Finally, exemption could be granted "upon conditions as to performing work of national importance, the terms of which will be found in cases decided by the Central Tribunal."

The FOR, in conjunction with the No Conscription Fellowship and the Men's Service Committee of the Society of Friends, protested this directive in a letter addressed to the presidents of the local government boards. They pointed out that to draw a line between religious and moral grounds was unsound. With regard to the age of the applicant, they pointed out that "if a man is old enough to fight, he is also old enough to have an opinion whether it be right or wrong to fight; and if he is not old enough to have such an opinion, it is a moral outrage to compel him to fight." With regard to "performing work of national importance," since the Central Tribunal, at least in one case, had qualified these conditions with the words "useful for the prosecution of the war," it rendered the exemption granted "wholly nugatory."

But it was not always easy for the three protesting groups to find a completely common mind. In a letter to Fenner Brockway of the No Conscription Fellowship, RR raised objections to one of their circulars. His objections reflect vividly his tenderness as to another person's conscience:

We are out, I take it, immediately for two things: first to bear witness against war and militarism; and second to secure the defeat and repeal of the Military Service Act....My fear is that the attitude of the National Committee in its emphatic (and practically exclusive) endorsement of the Absolutist position is looking to the defeat of the Military Service Act by a process of obstruction which seems to me to be a practical denial of the democratic principle. So long as there is enough freedom of speech left to allow us to use the normal democratic implements of persuasion and conversion, we are, I think, precluded from the extreme course of obstruction. Obstruction is only legitimate as a last resort, when reason has failed; and great as the limitations on liberty undoubtedly are, we are not yet in the last ditch....

That the Absolutist position is the only one that many men can accept, I know; it is the only one that I could take myself....But we should be exceedingly careful that we do not allow our own position to dominate us when we come to consider that of others, and to think that what is right for us must be right for everybody, and that those who do not go as far as we do are only (as I heard it put) "semi-conscientious objectors."...

The one point common to us all is that we can and will take no part in direct war processes. The Non-Combatant Corps man goes that far. He is usually a man who believes in the verbal inspiration of the Scriptures, and as the Scriptures say "Thou shalt not kill," he will not kill. But they do not say anything about not making military roads or repairing military railways, and therefore he thinks these things permissible. The attitude involves a number of presuppositions which I do not understand or share. But that gives me no right to say that the man has an inferior [attitude]. If I do so, I arrogate to myself an authority and an insight which I deny to the Tribunals. The man has gone as far as his conscience compels him; I have no right to expect more; I respect him that he has gone so far....

All this is infinitely the stronger in the case of the Alternative Service man. He may say not only that his conscience permits him, but that it compels him, to do alternative service. He sees the community in need of certain services; it is no concern of his what the need arises from....And if the community asks him (even in terms of a clause in the Military Service Act) to render such service, he finds himself governed by the conception of *need*, and goes and does it. He may quite reasonably say that he *must* (as the price of continuing in recognized citizenship in the community) accede to any demand which the community may make upon him which his conscience permits him to discharge, even though it be mediated by a Military Service Act....His conscientious objection is not to the Military Service Act...but to what the Military Service Act would compel him to do, namely, to go to war....The position is entirely a rational and intelligible one; it may not appear to be an effective method of countering the Military Service Act; it may on the face of it seem that such a man is helping to work the Act (though I think that is a superficial and indiscriminating judgement); but the main fact is that none of us has any right to suggest that this is an inferior conscience.

Indeed, it may turn out that this is the really full-blooded conscience after all. For it must be remembered that the Absolutist position involves a virtual declaration of war on the community. That may be necessary, but it is a terrific responsibility in a democratic order. And I can understand the man who says that his conscience forbids him to do that on the same grounds that it forbids him to go to war—namely, that it is a breach of fellowship. And we must remember, surely, that a basis of fellowship is the first condition of a process of conversion.

But RR was as ready to take himself to task as anyone else. George Davies recalls him speaking about a letter he had written to the *Nation*. The letter pointed out that pacifism meant not only physical disarmament, but the disarmament of our minds from that habit of disparagement or condemnation which so quickly besets us. On re-reading his own letter, RR had discovered three instances in it of that very fault he deprecated.

The FOR, as one of its tasks, prepared bulletins informing conscripts of their rights under the Military Service Act. These bulletins set forth clearly the steps to be taken by conscientious objectors in their applications for exemption from military service. The fellowship also circulated the questions which were in the purview of the tribunals, and described the nature of the proceedings at the hearing so that those called before them should not be taken unawares. Also they advised on how to apply for a rehearing of a case.

Nor did the concern of the fellowship end there. In cooperation with the No Conscription Fellowship they kept an eye on the conditions in which the "conchies" served their imprisonment, and brought these to the attention of the authorities. A typical case was that of the men who were sent to the Dyce Quarry Camp near Aberdeen. They arrived with just the clothes they stood up in. For the first fortnight the men not only slept in the clothes in which they had worked all day in the pouring rain, but in beds damp because of old and leaky tents—tents which had recently been condemned by the Scottish Local Government Board Sanitary Authority. Many had come directly from solitary confinement and a diet of bread and water. Under these conditions they fell ill. Medical attention for the sick during that fortnight was non-existent. One man, who later proved to have scarlet fever, was nursed by his companions in a dilapidated cottage with the roof falling in and no doors or windows. To a request that this man might be sent home, the reply was received that it would create a precedent; it was suggested that "he be taken to the prison hospital attached to the prison from which he came." Another man died of pneumonia. It was thanks to the efforts of the FOR and kindred bodies that the authorities, who had scant sympathy for conscientious objectors, were forced to formulate a more humane policy.

So it was a mixed bag of duties and responsibilities undertaken by the Fellowship of Reconciliation, and there was never any lack of useful work for its secretary.

13

Brooklyn, New York: The Church of the Pilgrims

RR had hardly taken up his work as General Secretary of the Fellowship of Reconciliation when he received an invitation from Brooklyn, New York. The Church of the Pilgrims asked him to preach at the Sunday services for a period of weeks, with no weekday or pastoral work. For the rest he was to be free to further the cause of the FOR in the United States where its work was already being watched with considerable interest. The invitation came through Dr. G. A. Johnston Ross who had been RR's predecessor at St. Paul's, Westbourne Grove, and who had recently taken up a professorship at Union Theological Seminary. RR, however, refused; he took exception to a proviso that he should promise to accept a call from the church if, after a trial period, it should decide it wanted him.

But the matter was not dropped. Henry Hodgkin had gone over to the United States in November 1915 and, at a meeting in Garden City, New York, the Fellowship of Reconciliation of America was born. The infant society was soon in rough waters, however, and Dr. Ross became urgent in his appeals to RR to come over to strengthen and guide it. He consulted with the office-bearers of the Church of the Pilgrims and wrote to RR in January 1916. The offensive proviso had been dropped and new terms offered:

> ...[T]hese terms, though generous, are not princely. They say nothing about entertainment and nothing about your travelling expenses. But then (a) it is kept in view that you are really coming over for the F. O. R., and (b) it is held that, inasmuch as the church leaves you free for week-day work, the expenses of travelling should come from the F. O. R. As

to the entertainment, as long as there is a bed in my house, that matter is not prohibitive.

So, it was primarily as an emissary of the FOR that RR went to America.

At the end of his contracted term with the congregation, the Church of the Pilgrims extended a call; RR was strongly drawn to the idea of returning to the pastorate. But such a pulling-up of roots as this would entail could not be decided on the toss of a coin. RR returned to England to consult first with his wife and then with some of his close friends. In May 1916, he wrote to Dr. Skinner, setting forth the pros and cons:

> I had hoped to have had a little time with you during the last week in order to tell you more about this American proposal. All my own personal inclinations are very much against going, but I am not sure whether I would be right in resisting the pressure of all the circumstances connected with the case.
>
> I went to America with my mind quite definitely closed against any suggestion of staying there, but in spite of myself the feeling grew upon me that I had no right to shut the door so uncompromisingly, especially before I had taken into account all the facts....It has become increasingly evident to me...that I must get back to preaching as early as possible; that is my own job, and I find that the necessity of regular production is essential to the preservation of what cutting edge my mind has. I have been aware of a certain dulling of my mind during the last few months, and I think I am as much afraid of that as of anything in the world. But over and against this has to be placed the fact that I am not likely to receive a call here in England for some considerable time.
>
> Let me tell you something about the thing from the point of view of the church. It is an old church, as American churches go, and in point of temper the nearest thing to Westbourne Grove that I have ever met. The people there are decent folk with a strong spiritual sentiment....The church has been two years vacant, after a very disastrous ministry of crude new theology and still cruder socialism. It is of some significance to me in the matter that I am the first man upon

whom the congregation has, during the two years of vacancy, been able to unite cordially.

Now, as to the Fellowship. In the first instance, I committed myself to the Fellowship and the Fellowship to me for a year. This was not in any sense a rigid affair, but I recognized from the beginning that, for me, it was of the nature of an experiment; and so far as I am concerned I am grateful to have had the experience. It has been a very illuminating time in many ways and I think I have been able to make some little contribution to its life. But it has become increasingly clear to me during the last few months that the position could only be a temporary one, and while I am committed to the Fellowship for good and all, so far as my thought and loyalty are concerned, I could not have continued in any case very much longer as its paid servant....If I were to be persuaded that my remaining here was essential to the development of the life of the Fellowship, I should not in the least hesitate; but I am quite clear in my own mind that I am not essential to the Fellowship here, and there are in it plenty of strong men available for its work....I have to consider this in relation to the future of the Fellowship in America. It is perfectly clear to my mind that, so far as the immediate future is concerned, I have a very definite contribution to make to it in America....As things are in America, the Fellowship has had no one yet to devote time to think out deliberately its implications over there. Most of the leading members are men who are already overworked, and if the Fellowship is to have any future there at all, it is necessary that someone should go over for a time to bring to them the thought and experience which we have gathered in this country. This opportunity has come to me not merely unsought and unbidden, but in spite of myself, and every instinct in me at the present moment bids me refuse to go; but I cannot shut my eyes to the possibility that it may be my duty to go, even in spite of the misunderstanding that may follow from it.

By October RR had made up his mind and was in the throes of making plans for moving his family across the Atlantic. On 9 January 1917, he began his formal pulpit ministry at the Church of the Pilgrims.

The Church of the Pilgrims was a Congregational church with a long history. From one of its walls jutted a small chunk taken from Plymouth Rock. Its fine stained glass windows were in keeping with the beauty of the building. But the building was large far beyond the needs of its congregation—a relic, like most of the other churches in the neighbourhood, of the days when Brooklyn Heights had been a prosperous residential district. It had a seating capacity of fourteen hundred and, in 1916, a membership of 250. There were still some spacious family dwellings, but already many were being turned into two and three family units. Others had been torn down and apartment blocks and residential hotels were taking their place.

Nevertheless there were still a number of old families in the congregation who formed a solid dependable core. In all his relationships with office-bearers and congregation, RR was happy. In later years he used to paraphrase Isaac Walton on strawberries: "No doubt the Lord *could* have made finer people than the best Americans, but he never did." He undoubtedly placed his friends of the Church of the Pilgrims in this category. And surely he would have numbered among them a little old lady of very strong premillenarian convictions who, he used to say, taught him the meaning of tolerance. He had spoken at some length and with some heat of the folly of this point of view in a sermon. After the service the old lady rebuked him gently and concluded with a sweet smile: "You'll go on thinking of Him in your way, and I in mine. But we'll both go on loving Him just the same."

As always, for RR, the responsibilities of his pastorate came first, but he did not lose sight of his underlying reason for being in America. Even before the United States entered the war there had been a growing sentiment in favour of taking part in it. With America's declaration of war on 6 April 1917, war fever broke out under the guise of a fervent patriotism. Edmund Wilson, in his book *Patriotic Gore*, gives a brief summary of this climate: "This cost us 50,000 lives,...and a persecution of everything German in a country with an immense German population, which had always been thought one of our more valuable elements, together with a hissing and hounding of opposition sentiment that far outdid the repressions of Lincoln."

RR and many like-minded Americans were to experience personally that "hissing and hounding." An example of this persecution in the name of patriotism was the dismissal of several professors from universities throughout the United States. Not all of them were out-and-out pacifists. The war psychology enabled some authorities to discharge certain radicals whose presence had proved embarrassing, but for whose dismissal it would have been difficult to find a satisfactory public explanation. The most publicized dismissals were those of Edward Salisbury Dana [1849–1935, professor of physics at Yale] and James McKeen Cattell [1860–1944, eminent psychologist, head of the department at Columbia, founder and editor of the *Psychological Review* and the *Scientific Monthly*]. They were both dismissed in 1917, for criticizing the US War Draft. There were colleagues who staunchly defended the right of these men to their opinions. Among those who resigned in protest were Charles A. Beard [1874–1948, historian and political scientist, founder of the New School for Social Research in New York and the Workers' Education Bureau, and a vigorous critic of American imperialism], Henry Raymond Mussey [b. 1875, professor of political science, Columbia], and Ellery Cory Stowell [1875–1958, professor of international law, Columbia]. Not one of these three was a pacifist, and the infringement of civil liberties exemplified in these dismissals troubled RR greatly. At an FOR conference in England in 1917, to add a lighter note to the proceedings, bogus telegrams were read as coming from absent members. One, purporting to be from RR, read: "From the frying pan into the fire!"

Dr. John Lathrop provides the following impressions of Brooklyn in the early years of the war:

> The First World War was on, but America had not yet entered. It was the hope of President Wilson that, by keeping out, it might be possible for America to act as mediator between the warring countries. A pacifist such as Richard Roberts was therefore warmly welcomed. At the other Congregational church on Brooklyn Heights, however, the Rev. Newell Dwight Hillis [1858–1929] was whipping up the war fever by preaching such anti-German sermons as the famous one, "Murder Most Foul." A considerable body of Brooklyn citizens who opposed America's participation in the war formed an organization called War on War. Richard Roberts assisted in some of its efforts. Some of Brooklyn's most prominent men and women became his admiring listeners at the regular Sunday morning service and at vesper services which he

instituted. Among the clergy of the Heights were outstanding liberals who warmly fraternized: Rev. John Howard Melish of the Church of the Holy Trinity, Rev. L. Mason Clark of the First Presbyterian Church, John Howland Lathrop of the First Unitarian Congregational Church, and others. Roberts was welcomed into the group and became a potent influence among them, especially in the interest of calming a war-torn world. In the short period of his Brooklyn ministry his influence spread amazingly over the borough, the greater city of New York, and the country at large, through his writing in periodicals and in his work in organizations, chiefly in the Fellowship of Reconciliation.

RR had close connections with the FOR and its magazine, *The World Tomorrow*. He was on the council of the American FOR for as long as he resided in America. He was a member of the editorial board of *The World Tomorrow* from its inception in January 1918 until he left Brooklyn at the end of 1921, frequently contributing signed articles and occasionally writing the unsigned editorials. Norman Thomas, the chief editor in those years, writes:

> He was an invaluable aid. This I can testify. I had enormous respect for his judgement and his experience which, in this field, was much greater than mine. He was busy with his parish and outside speaking in the hysterical years when he and John Haynes Holmes were about the only conspicuous clergymen who were able to stay in their parishes. He did not, as I recall it, spend a great deal of time in the World Tomorrow and F. O. R. offices, but was always available on the telephone for advice.

Norman Mattoon Thomas [1884–1968] was a Presbyterian minister, socialist, pacifist, and the founding editor of *The World Tomorrow*, editor of *The Nation*, and co-founder of the American Civil Liberties Union. He was a repeated Socialist Party candidate for the US presidency. John Haynes Holmes [1879–1968] was minister of the Unitarian Community Church in New York for more than forty years. Also a pacifist, he was, with Norman Thomas, a co-founder of the American Civil Liberties Union and one of the founders of the National Association for the Advancement of Colored People. The dimensions of pacifism reached into other areas of human concern and social justice.

But RR was far from settling down in the "New World." A letter to Miss Stevenson of the FOR in England summed what he was feeling:

> We have been in America now 18 months, and we do not know what the future has in store for us at all. The one thing that seems clear is that we have no continuing city in Brooklyn, and it is no use disguising the fact that my wife's heart and mine are "over there." On the other hand, the children are domesticating themselves here rather ominously: and that will have to be taken into account....[But] we shall be guided when the time comes as we always have been.
>
> For there is not in my mind the slightest doubt that we were guided to America at this time. The signs are plain. The F. O. R. and what it stood for here would have been seriously handicapped when the war came had it not been that I was on the spot with the British experience to fall back upon. And I hope that I have been able to some extent to steady things in view of such shocks as the subtle persecution of the F. O. R. through the YM [Young Men's Christian Association] International Committee. That is a pretty bad story which will need to be told some day. Meantime, we'll keep our heads above water—and "The World Tomorrow," our new periodical, is going ahead. And to me the experience has been in many ways tremendous. I have learnt a multitude of things and have gained an insight into certain aspects of the political and social problems relative to the Kingdom of God which otherwise would not have been possible. I don't think that I have ever been able to think so clearly and so soundly as during the last year. Just at the moment I am trying (using my long holiday for it) to rough out the draft of a book— "The unsolved problems of Democracy" or something of that kind for a title—in which I am endeavouring to gather up my thinking. By the way, Headley's are to bring out soon a little tractate of mine which I have called "The Red Cap on the Cross." It is frankly revolutionary—but I think it must be so. The Christian World cannot grow; it must happen. The Holy City comes down out of heaven.

I am (I regret to say) becoming increasingly sceptical about the Church's future. Religion is very down at the heels here, as in England, and I see no signs of a revival....Probably one gets a worse impression of the church here than at home. But there is a curious lack of touch with the things we have been accustomed to regard as fundamental. Something has happened for the worse to America since the days of Emerson, and it is rather significant that the only philosophy which has emanated from America in recent years is pragmatism, a sort of philosophy of payment by results. And that is the trouble. We are busily trying to get things done—and there is very little in the way of systematic thinking beyond this.

And my experience here has also set me in full flight of reaction (perhaps excessively so) against all sorts of authority and order. This is generally supposed to be the land of liberty. But it isn't. It is an egalitarian democracy which is quite another thing. "Jack's as good as his master!" ergo Jack, his master, and I and everyone else, have to toe the same line. The whole temper is one of uniformitarianism: and the intolerance of dissent is ferocious. While owing to a Liberal War Department the conscientious objector problem will be solved here much more satisfactorily than the English bungle, yet on the other hand, what Bertrand Russell [1872–1970, mathematician, philosopher, and pacifist] gets six months in the first division for, and Joe Rorke gets fined 50 pounds for, men get 15 and 20 years in the Federal Penitentiary....But to me, toleration is the first condition of social life—and so I am in full revolt against Authoritarianism, Order, and Uniformity—and I am become a fierce Libertarian. Not an individualist, tho'. I am more Catholic than ever, certainly less a Protestant. And for the old claptrap about Liberty and Order I am preaching such a Gospel as I can of "Freedom and Fellowship."

All this brings into focus something which lies deep in the memories of RR's children. On Saturday afternoons RR wanted exercise, and Brooklyn Bridge was not far away. It was the nearest thing to the wide open spaces that he knew, and thither the entire family would often go. The children looked forward to this moment in the week for it was a time when their father seemed to be peculiarly their own.

There was, however, some apprehension mingled with the anticipation. They loved him; they thought they loved him so much that they would have dived through flaming hoops for him. But, in the middle of Brooklyn Bridge, when he broke into the semblance of an Irish jig, they hoped desperately that the passersby would not think they belonged to him. Over the years the children thought that this was intended as a thrust at the stuffiness of their teenage conformism, and that it certainly was. After reading the correspondence of those years, however, the author wonders if it were not also a small catharsis for RR as well.

The war and pacifism were by no means his only concern. RR was deeply interested in what, to him, were closely related matters: the rights of labour and the right of free speech. His involvement in these areas is attested to by a letter which he kept, regarding it as a sort of accolade. The letter was from the US Attorney General's office in New York, requesting him "to call at this office...room 251, at your convenience within the next few days, and bring with you any communications which you may have received from Floyd Dell, Max Eastman or the Masses Publishing Company, within the last few years" [Dell, 1877–1969, was editor of *The Masses* and *The Liberator*. Eastman, 1883–1969, was a writer and radical political activist].

Early in 1918, RR had written to Ramsay MacDonald [1866–1937], labour leader and statesman and the first Labour Prime Minister of Great Britain [1924]. RR asked to be enrolled in the British Labour Party, apparently with some view in mind of returning to England and turning to political organization. Alexander Ramsay commented on this in a letter. After marvelling at the "skilful engineering" of the American Church in achieving Prohibition, and the enormous financial resources the church in America commanded, Dr. Ramsay continued:

> On the other hand, what you tell of the repression of freedom and of the tyrannical measures against labour agitation and personal liberty gives me pause. These elaborate musical services [in the churches] and the big stipends...and the close alliance with wealth makes me wonder how far a social conscience is alive in the church, and to what extent the labouring classes are found in its membership. I am much impressed with the idealism of labour in our country and of the vast possibilities in its future, and certainly in this respect

America lags a long way behind....I do not wonder that Labour attracts you, and that you have made up your mind to throw in your lot with it. We certainly need your help in the church, but I am not sure that unattached and as a liaison officer you may not do a bigger work for the kingdom of God...than by undertaking the duties of a pastorate and its inevitable limitations....There is a curious unreality about our church. Committees legislate in the air; the Synod hangs between heaven and earth. There is no contact with reality....All this you will put down to the maunderings of an old man or to the ripe wisdom of mature years, as your bent may be. Anyhow, I am the last man to say that out in that social field to which you are drawn you may not be able to do a bigger and better work than within the regular ministry, unless indeed you could lead us out on a new crusade. But whoso does this in one sphere or the other must be ready to pay the price. Paul was a wise man to remain unmarried in order to fulfil his career, and a wife and three children are hostages to prudence.

Always on the lookout for what he termed a "spiritual break-through," RR had gone to America full of hope. He had thought that, freed from the shibboleths of the old world, the new would provide fruitful ground for some fresh element to appear in religious life. His disillusionment had produced a longing for old friends and old places. It had also stirred in him the desire to shake off the inevitable im-pedimenta of church life and to carry the battle for the kingdom into the political and social field. The question remained: How was he to do this?

14
Seeking New Fields

As early as 1917, the FOR in Great Britain had begun to look forward to the days of social and economic reconstruction which would follow the war. Henry Hodgkin wrote voluminously to keep RR in touch with the situation. Each letter contained one or more suggestions as to how the challenge was to be met: the formation of groups representing the church and labour to think through problems of reconstruction from a Christian standpoint; a group of people who would spend considerable time travelling about the country as apostles of the new order; a weekly paper, explicitly religious in character, but with a pro-labour bias, to be produced by the previously mentioned apostles under one general editor. It emerged, tentatively, that RR would be the right person for the job. Then quickly another suggestion was put forward. RR was to spend six months on the continent establishing connections with like-minded men and women, particularly in former enemy countries. That RR knew no German and little French was passed over lightly. Only at the end of the six-month period would he settle down to edit the new weekly. It was all very high minded and hardly practical.

Philip Burtt of Headley Brothers, the London publishing house, was also interested in the new weekly, but could see that the schemes proposed by Henry Hodgkin were too vague and insubstantial. He set himself to make provision for some basic financial security for RR. In March 1919, he wrote:

> My present mind about yourself is to ask you to take full charge of all our religious books: what precisely "religious" means I don't know, but I am prepared to give it the widest possible meaning....I should like this to represent 30 books a year, and the 100 pounds I spoke of in my last letter...might

anyway go to 250 pounds; and that for a part-time job. Whilst I get keener and keener in favour of *the journal*, I am very much impressed with the magnitude of the scheme; and already there are two or three—or more—attempts to launch journals which may overlap part of our prospective field.

Hodgkin, Burtt, and RR continued to plan, but not all RR's friends were so rashly optimistic. W. E. Orchard had written very frankly in February:

Then about yourself. I am not surprised how you feel about the general pastorate, especially after your American experience; but I do hope that you will think considerably before you quit it forever. If you could only get some free centre like this [Orchard's church at King's Weigh House], I believe that you would find the opportunities are far and away greater than anything else could give you.

The Labour World is divided here between tame tabbies, vulgar jingoes and wild men. You would find that it would break your heart quicker than a Presbyterian Church. Whatever faults the Old Girl has, they are simply nothing compared to the alternatives. It is not just from my Catholic dogma, but from actual experience that I think that.

Then the F. O. R. We had a most unfortunate conference at K. W. H. [King's Weigh House] this year. The war being over, officially—God knows in no other way—they find themselves absolutely without agreement. The deep rift between the "Love identified with Jesus" people, like Halliday, and the "Love of which he is a not inalienable symbol" folk, of which there are not a few, is one crack; the rift between the Catholics and the Quakers is another. This runs down to practical things, for the Quaks are rather inclined to do nothing while the Cats are all of the firebrand variety. We have decided to hang together, but that is about all.

Now that helps to bring up the question of your return. I should love to see you back out of that ecclesiastically ruinous atmosphere. America is all very well, but give me Blighty with all its dullness and its entrenched evils and controversies about nothing at all. This is the only place for you, or for any gentleman; but do be careful of to what you come back.

Hodgkin has large plans about your being Continental Evangelist for the F. O. R., or Editor of a new Paper. I am keeping in touch with these proposals as much for your sake as for theirs. My advice is, if you are heart and soul Quaker you will be happy. If you are either definitely Labour and inclined Catholic you will find yourself miserable, tied up, if only with gossamer threads. You may have shifted more Quakery, as I have shifted more Catty, so you can discount both sides for yourself accordingly. But I don't want to see you wasting your obvious gifts in something that will take you nowhere and break your heart.

Orchard did, in fact, keep in touch with the proposals. He discovered that there were several people who felt, even more strongly than Philip Burtt, that the new weekly would find itself with a great deal of competition. It was further felt that a new journal might seriously harm some of the good existing journals which in part covered the same interests. This he faithfully reported to RR, with chapter and verse, and then added:

> I quite understand your not wanting to take up pastoral work and general church organization again, but I shall never be content until we have got you back into the ministry, impedimenta or not. And, by the way, would you like to preach at the Weigh House during the whole of August?...Perhaps I shall be chucked out by the time you come home and then you could succeed me!...Now do come home, even if you have to beg your bread.

RR accepted the invitation, and during the summer of 1919, was able to talk face-to-face with his friends and make a personal assessment of the various proposals which were in the air. He was also able to feel out the ecclesiastical and political climate of Britain.

One factor in the political situation at the time was the trouble in Ireland. The Anglo-Irish war was still only in its early stages, and the public reports were confusing and disquieting. RR's sympathies were, by and large, with the supporters of the Dail [the Irish Republican Parliament], but he felt that he must go over and see for himself what was happening. Nothing that he saw made him change his opinions. One incident of the Irish trip is worth recording, however. Dining out in a home in Dublin, RR discovered that his host had a problem. One of the Sinn Fein leaders was in hiding with him. The house was under police surveillance. How was the host to get the man out? Boldness was the answer. At a time when a dinner guest might be expected to leave, wearing RR's hat and overcoat the "mouse" walked briskly out of the house and away, hardly noticed by the "cats" waiting outside. Some time later RR left, rigged out in a coat too tight for him, with a ludicrously small hat perched on his head.

In the autumn of 1919, RR returned to Brooklyn. He had come to no decision about the future. The Headley proposition was still open; there was still talk about the new weekly and the FOR mission to the continent. But it was still all talk, and you cannot feed a family on other people's talk. Quite apart from his "hostages to prudence," however, the summer in England had given him a clearer view of what he might be getting into. Would not the "gossamer threads" of a responsibility divided three ways—Headley's, the FOR's continental and industrial schemes, and the new journal—be a greater handicap to constructive work for the kingdom of God than the "inevitable impedimenta" of the church? But he had still every intention of getting back to England.

Late in 1919, or possibly early in 1920 [the letter is undated], Dr. Orchard wrote again:

> ...I was undisguisedly glad at the prospect of your continuing in the ministry, for although I think you could run Headley's alright, I do think you would be thrown away on that sort of thing. Secondly I should like you to be in the ministry over here, where goodness knows you are needed badly. But there is no opening that I see at all. I sounded about the City Temple, but I found that there was little hope there....It is rather melancholy not to be able to see anywhere that is ready for you. It might be easier if you were over here preaching about; and that is the only thing that would reconcile me to you going to Headley's temporarily....One is forgotten when one is not about....
>
> I wish I could say more that was definite, and that I could be any help; but my name is not much of a recommendation in Nonconformity. How that article is going to live through

the next 25 years I cannot imagine. As it is, one does not want it to; but something will die with it that has cost infinite pains and meant something for the Church....It has been tried and it has not succeeded; that is the long and the short of it; and it is now running to seed, becoming more and more negative, and its people are the prey not only to the worldly drift, but to the cults. The Catholically-minded Churches will live, however bad they are, because of some principle of coherence that they possess; and just because they have lived so long already....

Nevertheless, although prospects for service in England continued uncertain, RR still felt that it was in England his future work lay. Then, in the spring of 1920, a fresh element entered the situation. RR went to deliver some lectures at the Pacific School of Religion in Berkeley, California. Some of those involved in the school approached him about becoming president of the institution. The possibilities of the job, the chance of having a hand in the education of a new generation of ministers, attracted him greatly. It was probably the only kind of opening which could, at that moment, have deflected him from his intention of returning to Britain. On the other hand—as is the lot of college presidents—the immediate plans for the development of the school would have involved him less in the lecture hall with the students than in stumping the country for large sums of money. There were, too, a few men connected with the school who, on account of RR's pacifism, and even more on account of his labour sympathies, wanted none of him. The negotiations went on through the summer, but in the end RR felt the wisest course was to withdraw his name.

As the months passed nothing clear-cut emerged on the English scene. The idea of the FOR weekly editor and continental missioner, together with the position at Headley's, seems to have faded from the picture, at least as far as RR was concerned. The negotiations with the Pacific School of Religion had seemed to offer an altogether new kind of opportunity. When they fell through, however, RR felt there was nothing to hold him in America. He had committed himself for the summer to a series of student conferences under the auspices of the YMCA, and he still had a few months to go at the Church of the Pilgrims. After that he was free. Mrs. Roberts and the three girls set off to Great Britain to establish a base of operations. RR joined the family for a brief holiday, and then he and his wife returned to Brooklyn to finish his work at the Church of the Pilgrims and prepare for the move "back home."

Part III

"He setteth the solitary in families"

15

Nan

On 19 November 1901, RR wrote to Miss Anne Catherine Thomas:

Dear Miss Thomas,

In spite of the fact that our acquaintance has been so short, I am presumptuous enough to ask you if you will meet me in the Hall of the British Museum on Friday afternoon at 4 o'clock. You will wonder at such an impertinent and blunt request. I want to see you—and as I can see no chance of a talk with you otherwise, I am forced to ask you thus. I mention the particular time because I have no other free for some while. Will you do me the honour of relying upon my good faith so far as to accede to my request? Please do.

I am afraid this is a very extraordinary way of doing things, but it can't be helped. I am a perfect ignoramus of all the "proprieties"—and let that be my excuse.

You need not trouble to reply to this, unless you care to do so. But I do hope you can see your way clear to give it the reply of coming on Friday. If the day and hour do not suit you, will you be kind enough to say when and where I may see you.

With kind regards
Believe me

Yours most faithfully
Richard Roberts

While at Willesden Green, under the rota preaching system, RR used to preach at Jewin Chapel in the City. This was always a pleasure as Morgan "Moc" Rees, one of his very close friends from college days, was a member there, along with his family. Even when not on church business RR was a frequent visitor in the Rees' home, where he was accepted as an extra son.

One Sunday when he was preaching at Jewin, Anne Catherine Thomas was attending the service. She was in London studying singing, although whether on this particular evening she sang is not on record. That she had been in London for some time is clear as there is extant a "Program of Welsh Folk Music at Westbourne Park Institute by Mary Owen," dated 28 February 1899. Among the performers listed was the contralto, Miss Annie Arthur, the professional name taken by Miss Thomas.

When Moc Rees learned of his friend's desire to meet Miss Thomas, he managed to contrive an occasion. This accomplished, RR, in due course, contrived to have her sing at a meeting at Willesden Green. It was natural that the minister of the church should see the young singer home. But these kinds of meetings could only be infrequent, and in their nature they were public occasions. Hence the letter of 19 November. Shortly thereafter Richard Roberts and Anne Thomas became engaged. And on 1 January 1902, they were married at the Calvinistic Methodist Chapel at Abergele, with RR's father performing the ceremony.

Anne Catherine Thomas was born in 1878, at Llanerchymedd, Anglesey, where her father was Master of the Work House. (Later, the children could always "get a rise" out of her by reminding her that she had been "born in a work house.") Her father's name was Meshach Thomas and, from all accounts, he seems to have been content with the title of "Master" and to have left the bulk of the work of administration to his wife. It seems typical of the man that on the certificate of marriage, under rank or profession, he should be described as "Gentleman."

Grace Pryse, Anne Catherine's mother, was the parent who made the deepest imprint on her children. She was the daughter of Robert John Pryse, better known in Wales by his bardic name *Gweirydd ap Rhys* and author of the first volume of a history of early and medieval Welsh literature. On one occasion when RR was working in the British Museum, he copied out a family tree which takes the line back to *Gweirydd ap Rhys Goch*, 1169. [Pryse, and also Price, are anglicized forms of *ap Rhys*, which literally means "son of Rhys"; *Goch* means "red."] RR's daughters used to refer to their maternal grandfather as a "potty little Welsh prince," but were secretly rather proud of his "royal" ancestry.

Twelve children were born to Meshach and Grace Thomas, eight of whom survived into adulthood; Anne Catherine was the fifth. The surviving children denied any claims the Welsh may have to being a "pure" race—they were swarthy, fair, tall, short, and, to cap it all, Anne Catherine was a redhead. And her red hair was accompanied by the traditional temperament. An older brother, Llewellyn Blackwell, familiarly known as "Gag," was a peaceable soul. One day as he was on his way home from school, he was set upon by two or three bigger boys. Nan, as she was called at home, promptly flew at them and put them to rout by the surprise and fury of her attack. This passion was to remain with her, and though she learned to control it, you could still sense it in the tone of her voice when she dismissed a person with the words "that man so-and-so!" The children knew when they heard those words and tone that "so-and-so" had been condemned to some outer fringe of the human race.

When Anne Catherine was growing up it was still not considered necessary, nor even particularly desirable, that a girl be educated for independence. It was over considerable parental opposition, then, that Nan won the privilege of studying singing in London. Nor would it have been possible but for the intervention of her eldest brother, Robert Arthur, known as "Bach," who paid a large portion of the cost out of his own salary as a clerk. (Nan blazed the trail, however; both younger sisters trained for professions, one as a teacher and the other as a nurse.) When she met RR, Nan was employed as understudy to one of the contralto soloists in the D'Oyly Carte Company, and sang in the chorus. On her engagement, however, she severed this connection, lest even so respectable a link with "the stage" should cast a shadow on her young ministerial fiancé. In later years she never sang in public as much as her friends and family would have wished. She was a perfectionist and feared to give less than her best, which was a considerable pity, as she was a fine singer with a beautiful voice.

Nan always remained conscious of her lack of formal education. When she sat down to write a letter, even to her own children, she invariably had her dictionary beside her. Her thoughts frequently outran her pen, and a new sentence would begin of its own volition before the previous one had come to its end. Writing on 27 October 1931, she made some reference to her incoherence and then said: "Dads is nasty. He says, 'The angels help us all to read your letters.'" Then she added herself: "Especially this one."

She sometimes impressed people as being a very grand lady in the old tradition, and certainly she could play that part as to the manner born. But it was often a mask for her shyness. The slightest hint of patronage brought on an exaggerated attack, however. And she could be formidable. Nan's youngest sister Beryl came up to London to train as a nurse, and the Roberts home became Beryl's home for a time. Years later Beryl remarked to the author: "You know, I was afraid of your mother. But Dick was wonderful to me." This remark reflects the attitude the Roberts children had to their parents in early childhood. From Nan the children expected, and often received, unpleasant retribution. If they could, they hid their peccadillos from their father, for they hated to see the disappointment in his face. This disappointment was never simulated for effect; nor was it frequent in spite of the fact that the children were often in scrapes of varying degrees of seriousness. RR viewed the normal misdeeds of childhood with equanimity and sympathy.

But in spite of all that has been said above, in spite of her quick, violent, and often unreasonable likes and dislikes, Nan was simple and warm-hearted, with a concern for people in general and persons in particular. During the Depression, while in Montreal, she went one day to assist with the packing of a "bale" for the West. This was a great occasion in those days. The idea was that people would bring good used clothing to be packed with a variety of new things produced by the hands of the women of the missionary society. As usual the theory was better than the practice. As the sorting went on throughout the morning, some of the used clothing had to be discarded as past redemption; some had to be mended and patched. Nan came home at lunchtime shaken and furious. What had particularly offended her was the action of the wife of one of the officials of the church, a woman of some means. "That woman" had brought a fur-lined coat of her husband's. Before she would part with it, however, she busily cut out half the fur lining, replacing it with some cheap material. What she salvaged she planned to make into a robe for a grandchild's baby carriage.

Now it was RR's invariable custom to give to his wife his wedding fees, to do with as she pleased. On the preceding Saturday he had handed her a ten-dollar gold piece. This she put in an envelope, taking it back with her to the church, where she insisted it be put into the bale. Her final remark on the incident was: "It could be me receiving that bale!"

She was a good listener. One evening a contemporary of her daughters dropped in and kept her, apparently, enthralled with a discourse on higher plane curves. When the guest had gone Nan was exhausted. "You shouldn't listen so hard, Mam," said one of the girls. "Just do as we do. We don't understand either, but we say yes and no periodically and that makes her happy." "But that would be rude," was the indignant reply. It was this quality of personal listening that endeared her throughout the years to the students with whom RR worked.

Once, in Toronto, she reproved her daughters: "You haven't been out all day." In other words, they were neglecting their health. "Neither has Mary," was the prompt reply. Mary, the maid, was about the same age as Nan's daughters. This opened her eyes to an injustice, and thereafter her maids had time off during the day so that, if they wished, they too could have a little fresh air. Not that she was a slave driver. The maids whom the author remembers were, for the most part, the good ones. They worked hard—as hard as Nan worked, and that was very hard—but they respected her and in many cases loved her. When they left the family's employ they often came back to visit. Several letters from both Nan and RR in 1932, deal at length with their concern for a maid who had left to be married, and whose marriage had gone awry. They could not have been more perturbed had she been one of their own daughters.

Nan was a pernickety housekeeper. Woe betide any of the children if they forgot to "plump" the cushions in the living room when they went up to bed! Dust and moths were personal enemies. Tidiness was a cardinal virtue in which, unfortunately, her daughters were a bit lacking. Nor could RR escape her wrath if he made a mess with his tobacco. The author still remembers the dismay on his face as he tried to sweep up the contents of an over-turned ashtray before his wife returned to the house. RR was most ineffectual at this sort of thing, for Nan was of the generation that believed housework was not a man's work, and she never encouraged his tentative efforts to be helpful. On this occasion, however, he was saved from her wrath by Dorothy, who tidied up the mess for him.

There were times when her children felt that their mother's life was one unreasonable and unending battle with laundries. The Roberts family changed laundries with noticeable frequency. The beginning of the relationship was one of wary suspicion. Sooner or later something would be missing. The end would come with Nan scornfully berating the latest sinner over the telephone. On the other hand, her dealings in shops were very personal. "I have a nice little girl in Simpson's shoe department," Nan would say. To this "little girl,"aged anywhere between sixteen and sixty, she would go for years and receive devoted service.

She disliked anything to do with the preparation of food, though she could, when circumstances forced her hand, prepare a good meal. Even with a cook in the house dinner guests caused a minor upheaval. The generously planned spread was finally introduced as "Just a picnic, you know." Through the years RR loyally, and at times enthusiastically, endured all sorts of faddy diets and nostrums. Daughter Peggy wrote in 1937:

> I phoned Mam the other night and she recommended a dose of Russian oil at night and Sal Hepatica in the morning as the unfailing prescription for a happy life! The doctors advised it for Dad after his "op," and Mam has taken it up with enthusiasm. The Hay diet has now gone the way of all other diets and has been replaced by R.O. and S.H. and an epidemic of Battle Creek foods.

Nan was devoted to RR and that devotion was reciprocated. In a letter written in 1908, while on his trip to Palestine, RR wrote: "I am more grateful than you can believe that you were given to me, and I to you, that I might be shaped for some good use. And your love has given me the strength and steadiness that I lacked before."

This was the keynote of their relationship. Always when there was a decision to be made Nan was consulted. It would have been easy for her to use her husband's love for her to deflect him from his purposes. Often in the smaller things she had her way. On major issues—leaving the pastorate for an uncertain future on account of his pacifist stand in 1914, going to America, going to Canada when, for a time, their hearts had turned to England where Nan so much wanted to be, and on through life—she never let her desires stand in the way of what he saw to be his duty. She gave him an uncompromising loyalty and backed him every step of the way. Twenty-six years after he wrote the letter quoted above, in his acceptance speech upon his election to the moderatorship of The United Church of Canada, he paid her public tribute. Pieced together from newspaper accounts, this is what he said:

You have before you a man who hardly knows where he is standing. If you knew me as I know myself, you would never have put me here. I'm not the man you think I am—but I'm a kept man. What I have I owe to two people. I hope my father knows about this. I think he does. I hope he does. It must be some satisfaction to him to know that his son has gained the confidence of his brethren in this way. He died 35 years ago.

The other is my wife. I wasn't much good till she took hold of me....

The day following his birthday in 1938, RR wrote to two of his daughters:

...I am not aware of feeling more aged than I was 20 years ago. In fact my prospects of life were, I think, less good than they are now. Only one thing has changed—namely that Mam has grown dearer and more precious to me...By that I do not mean that Gwen and you two have not also grown dearer and more precious...[But] Mam is all mine in a sense in which you no longer can be and in which she cannot be all yours. But it is a foolish thing to try to analyze our affections. Our business is to cherish them and thank God for them.

Towards the end of his life, when RR's health and memory were failing, Nan took over all the business details of life. This was no easy task for her. Up to that time RR had handled it all. In fact he had always hated to discuss financial matters. As long as he was in the pastorate he had received a good salary, and Nan, while never consciously extravagant, loved good quality and followed a policy of "economy in the long run," which might otherwise be described as lavish. Her husband's attitude to money did nothing to discourage her. It never seemed to occur to them that a time might come when money would no longer be coming in. Suddenly Nan had to learn the necessity of real economy.

In the last years of his life Nan watched over RR's every moment with tenderness and patience. When he died, she never doubted that he had simply gone "on ahead." She followed after him in January 1958.

16
RR and His Daughters

RR had a great fund of ministerial funny stories. One of his favourites was of a student sent by college authorities to meet a celebrated Presbyterian divine who was to preach on the coming Sunday at the college. Of the two men who got off the train, one had a very dismal look about him. The student decided this must be his man. "Excuse me, sir, but are you Dr. A., the Presbyterian minister who is coming to X College?" The man paused: "No, I don't always look like this. I have indigestion."

As a frequent traveller by sea, it fell to RR's lot to take part in those party dinners that mark the last night aboard ship. There was surely no more forlorn a sight than his face under a paper hat. Surrounded by the cacophony of the forced gaiety of those occasions, RR was even more miserable than he looked. He was, in fact, suffering from a kind of indigestion. For manufactured jollity he had a profound and abiding distaste.

But his capacity for spontaneous fun was abundant. He had a keen sense of the ridiculous and would, at the dinner table, tell hilarious tales on himself. The first yo-yo craze must have been in his early Toronto days. One day, fascinated by the prowess of a small boy on a street corner, RR stopped to watch. After a while, unable to bear it any longer, he begged the lad to let him try it for himself. "I collected quite a crowd," he mused.

Then there was the occasion in Montreal when he slipped on the ice and fell flat on his face. One hand was in his pocket. As luck would have it the other hand, holding his walking stick, went under him as he fell. In the straight jacket of his heavy, fur-lined overcoat he lay there, unable to extricate himself, until helped to his feet by a passerby. These and other tales lost nothing in the telling; RR was a marvellous raconteur.

In spite of RR's tightly packed schedule, his daughters never felt left out. For the greater part of the year their time was, of course, taken up with their school activities and friends. Even so, they looked forward eagerly to Saturday afternoons, for usually they could count on a long walk with RR. He, on his part, would occasionally make time for some other sort of outing, and he was extraordinarily faithful in attendance at school functions in which the girls were playing some part. It was in the summer months, however, that they enjoyed him to the full.

One June, in Montreal, a repertory company took up its stand at the Orpheum, an unpretentious theatre on St. Catharine Street. The bills were light and the acting competent, and the family saw quite a number of plays. Once, unable to get an aisle seat for himself (he had to have plenty of room for his long legs), RR splurged and bought a box. He was vastly disgusted with the women of his family in that, instead of enjoying the luxury, they fussed that they were not properly attired for the unanticipated eminence. Though the plays themselves were not remarkable—indeed the plots and characters are beyond recall—*Clothes and the Woman* stands out from the others. In the course of it RR was gripped by that sobbing laughter of a man past help. Alternately he leaned on the balcony rail in front of him, or back in his seat, seeking relief from the agony of his mirth.

They did not go to the movies as a family. This was not because RR would not have liked to go, but he had discovered that the jiggle of the action and the constant "snow and rain" of the early cinema bothered his eyes, and brought on the migraine which plagued him throughout his life. Even in later years when technical progress had overcome those hazards he was chary of the risk, and went to the movies only a few times. What he did see he enjoyed immensely.

The long evenings at a summer cottage were a time for cards. Whist was his game, and with RR at the table it was far from dull. Nan, who did not take part, would sit by urging the family not to get so excited. RR's voice would be high with triumph as he over-trumped, saying with mock contempt, "sending a boy to do a man's work." Even that quiet game of cribbage came alive with his zest.

But it was in the out of doors that RR came into his own. He was no athlete—no amount of practice could overcome the combination of acute myopia and generally poor coordination. He played golf with indifferent success. In any case, clubs and balls were not a motive; they were an excuse for striding across the golf course. The girls gladly went with him, but for the pleasure of his company rather than for the game. Their choice, and his, was a good long hike.

In Wales the family climbed Snowden and Cader Idris. With RR, rather than plodding up a steep incline, they had a sense of high adventure. There were less ambitious hikes also. One day they set off for Llwyngwril in glorious sunshine for some long forgotten objective. They had not, however, been long on the moors when a sudden heavy mist wiped out all landmarks. They pushed on for a while but eventually realized that they simply did not know where they were, where they had come from, or in what direction the objective lay. After a council of war in which each laid out the points of the compass in a different quarter, they moved on rather more cautiously. By chance they came upon a stone wall. Often, in Wales, stone walls meander on for great distances, marking some boundary. With RR in the van they pressed on with renewed optimism, expecting the wall to lead at least to some habitation. It was not long before RR burst into a roar of laughter. They had solemnly marched around the four sides of an abandoned sheepfold!

These were excursions in which Nan joined with almost as much gusto as RR. His passion for the water, however, she could not share. Water was not her element. Any craft short of an ocean liner was, to her, a sere leaf in a turbulent stream. As for swimming, she was certain that one or other family member would drown before her very eyes. Nevertheless, watching from the shore was less of an agony than not knowing what was going on.

RR was a strong though inelegant swimmer. He was always first in the water. He would hand his thick lensed glasses to one of the family and plunge in clumsily, looking rather like an outsized frog. As soon as he broke the surface he would return to get his glasses, for without them he had no idea in which direction he was going. If they had to wade in, there was a standing rule that they could not stay in unless they practised total immersion. This was not entirely because RR considered keeping one's face dry as being a sissy. There was also some theory about it being unhealthy to be in the water for a long period without the head also being wet. Since, apart from RR, all the family members wore bathing caps anyway, the girls used to be rather puzzled by this. And there was one other rule: no horseplay in the water. Horseplay was a form of manufactured jollity; moreover it could be dangerous.

The author suspects that on board ocean-liners, RR used to day-dream about his seafaring ancestors. As he ritually paced the deck, did he perhaps shut out from his mind the other passengers and imagine himself pacing the bridge? Certainly being out on deck in all weathers, breathing the salt air, and having tea with the captain in his cabin, did much to compensate for the stuffier aspects of the journey.

With small rowboats RR had become familiar in his days at Aberystwyth, and he considered himself something of an expert in this field. The lakes by which the family summered in North America gave him opportunity to teach his daughters what he knew. Even on such minor matters as shipping the oars with the spoons pointing to the bow, RR was very strict. Of course the girls went fishing with him. They never caught much, as the lakes they went to were pretty well fished-out, but rod and line made a wonderful excuse for a pro-longed outing on the water.

Boats involved, at times, a mechanical skill which RR was to-tally lacking. Preparing a mooring buoy might take the better part of a morning, and the finished product was very crude. Once when the girls were quite small, during some minor repairs to a oarlock, RR brought the hammer down smartly on his thumb. An anguished "damn" escaped his lips. Looking up at his daughters' gasps of hor-ror, RR grinned and said: "Never waste a good swear word. You never know when you may need it."

Nan did her best for some time to enjoy boating with the rest of the family. But her rigid presence was a dubious addition to the family's pleasure. Once, trying to be helpful, she grasped the wharf as they were about to land, by her action pushing the boat out again. Her fear of the water led her to cling more firmly to the wharf. Inexora-bly, as the boat and the wharf parted company, she slid into the wa-ter. As it was shallow and there was no danger, the situation was inexpressibly funny. But even RR dared not laugh. Nan knew it was ludicrous, and that aggravated her the more. Dripping from the waist down, and furious, she refused to get back into the boat, and walked the couple of miles home angrily berating Peggy who had been del-egated to go with her. She never again got into a small boat; the incident was not then, or ever, a subject for conversation. RR loved to tease, but he teased only when, and for as long as, the person involved could enjoy it.

It was, in part, the relationships established in fun that established RR's hold on his daughters' affections. But it did not stop there. When he was in the house, except when he was working on his sermon, RR was always accessible to the girls. They brought him knotty points in their homework in the simple faith that, if not solved, they at least would be clarified. They brought him their problems, fears, and joys, knowing they were important to him as persons. He gave to their opinions and queries the same courteous consideration and respect that he gave to all the others who sought his guidance.

In his relationships with his daughters there was never any pretence. They knew that his disappointment was real disappointment; his joy, real joy. They were both humbled and exalted by the knowledge that RR meant what he said when he stood in the pulpit and, after reading as his text: "And Zelophedad, the son of Hepher had no sons, but daughters...(Numbers 26:33)," went on to say: "I take that to mean that God never withholds from a man something good, unless he gives something better...."

Climbing Cader Idris, Merionethshire, N. Wales, 1923

*RR with his mother, Margaret, and
sister, Annie, about 1880*

*RR's father, David Roberts Rhiw, and
mother, Margaret Roberts, date unknown*

RR (standing, right) and classmates, Bala theological college, mid-1880s

Blaenau Festiniog, Merionethshire, Wales as it appeared during RR's youth, 1880s or 1890s

Anne Catherine Thomas, 1890s

RR and Nan, Atlantic City,
about 1939

RR and Nan, near Collins Bay, Ontario, mid- to late-1920s

A family gathering in the garden at Buckingham Manse, Buckingham, Quebec, 1938. From left to right Clifford Knowles, Gwen Norman, Nancy Norman (on Gwen's lap), RR, Donald MacVicar, Dorothy Knowles, Margaret Norman, Howard Norman, Nan Roberts, Ann Knowles (on her lap), David Knowles seated in front

Dorothy, Peggy, RR, Nan, and Gwen (author) (in front), on Great Diamond Island, New England, 1920

RR and Gwen Norman (back row), Margaret Norman, Nan (middle), Daniel and Nancy Norman [Whitla] (front), Vancouver, 1944

RR as Moderator of The United Church of Canada and ornithologist, Jack Miner, 1935

This sketch of RR, attributed to Arthur Lismer of the Group of Seven, was done in soft lead on the back of a menu dated February 25 and 26 (no year but probably mid-1930s) at the Toronto Arts and Letters Club.

Part IV

"I press on to the mark of the high calling of
God in Jesus Christ"

———

17

Montreal: The American Presbyterian Church

The month of January 1922, saw RR not in England, as he had hoped, but in Montreal. Once again G. A. Johnston Ross had a hand in the business. Before going to Union Seminary, Dr. Ross had spent two sessions as a professor at the Presbyterian College, Montreal. He had made many friends in Montreal and through them, in the summer of 1921, word reached him that the American Presbyterian Church was looking for a minister. He immediately wrote suggesting the name of Richard Roberts. The Pastoral Relations Committee had already done some extensive "sampling," but had reached no decision. They invited RR to preach early in September. On 30 September the committee recommended to the congregation that they call Dr. Roberts. And so it was ordered. As RR was anxious to spend a few months in England before settling in, the move was not made until the new year.

The American Presbyterian Church was situated on Dorchester Street, in the centre of downtown Montreal. There were in it a few wealthy families and some who were poor. By and large, however, the congregation was composed of comfortable middle-class families. It was a family church. It did not, in 1922, have the flavour of a downtown church, though even then the decline in the Sunday school pointed the direction in which the congregation would eventually go. The young couples who had grown up in the church, as they began to raise their families and set up homes in the suburbs, were already making connections with neighbourhood churches. But the real exodus was still in the future.

The sanctuary was a large auditorium in the nineteenth century nonconformist fashion. Its only beauty was in its stained glass windows. From where the congregation sat the pulpit, with the choir loft and organ high up behind it, was the focal point. There was nothing to suggest the crucified Christ to the mind of the worshipper. While RR believed that the essential element in worship was the mind and spirit of the worshipper, this did not mean that he had no use for order, ritual or symbols. Properly used they were legitimate means of reinforcing the quality of the worship. At a session meeting he suggested that a cross be placed on the communion table. No objections were raised and Mr. Gerald Birks, a member of the Birks jewellery and silver company, asked to be allowed to look after the matter. In due time Mr. Birks' gift, a simple, well proportioned brass cross, was placed on the communion table.

On the Sunday following the first appearance of the cross, an elder, puritanical and stubborn, hurried early to the church and hid the cross. Commenting on the incident another elder quoted, in a lighter mood, a revision of a line in the hymn "Onward Christian Soldiers": "...with the cross of Jesus behind the vestry door." But that was later. On the Sunday in question it was no laughing matter.

RR was not temperamental about his preaching, but it is no exaggeration to say that, at the end of a service, he was tired to the point of exhaustion. He had immediately noticed and been puzzled by the disappearance of the cross. Its absence had nagged at him throughout the service. When the cross-snatcher came into the vestry muttering and sputtering about "popery," RR lost his temper. Aware of the reputation of the Welsh for being an emotional race, RR had taken pains over the years to school his emotions. He rather prided himself on this. Normally when people let him down by not living up to the best that was in them, his reaction was disappointment rather than anger. On this occasion, however, he was for a few moments literally beside himself. Here was a member of the session taking individual action against the considered decision of the session itself. Before the blast the astonished defender of the faith scuttled away.

At home the Roberts family sat down to dinner in awed silence. RR ate little and retired for his afternoon rest thoroughly ashamed of his outburst. After tea he tried to gather himself for the evening service, but his mind refused to be quieted. Finally he announced: "There's nothing for it. I'll have to preach the sermon I preached this morning. There'll only be one man there who will notice and that's

John Gibb." (In fairness it should be added that the majority of the morning congregation rarely attended the evening service. John Gibb, who took his sermon-listening seriously and on whom RR depended greatly, was a "twicer.")

Much more characteristic than this outburst of anger was RR's answer to a man who had remained after service to accuse him of having contradicted St. Paul. "Well," said RR mildly, "I don't always agree with St. Paul." "But St. Paul was inspired!" the man proclaimed. "And so am I," RR responded. "That's blasphemy," the man cried. Upon which RR answered: "You, apparently, do not believe the Bible. I do. There is a distinct promise in it that God will give his Holy Spirit to them that ask Him. I have asked Him." A. E. Kerr, associate minister at the time [later principal of Pine Hill Divinity Hall and eventually president of Dalhousie University] had overheard the exchange. He commented: "The confession sounded perfectly ingenuous and I have no doubt it was entirely sincere. But it had the additional merit in the existing situation of preventing a lengthy dispute with the critic, who had come for another purpose than to know the truth."

In his book *The Spirit of God and the Faith of Today*, RR wrote:

> For many years I was tormented by an inability to get anything out of instrumental music. It seemed to have nothing to say to me, and in spite of the use I made of every opportunity to listen to instrumental music, I seemed to be held up before a permanently closed door. I was in college at the time, and one of my friends was an unusually accomplished pianist. One Sunday afternoon I was with him in his lodging and he was playing some nocturnes of Chopin....I well remember the unstopping of my inward ear. The music transported me to a woodland, and the sound of running water, and an amber light over the whole; and the moment remains vivid with me to this hour. The door was at last ajar. I don't know that I am much farther through it today than I was able to go that day. But at least music is no longer a dark continent to me.

This is, of course, a bit of false modesty. Over the years RR had learned to love the best in music, whether instrumental or vocal. He believed, moreover, that the word of God should be heard in the music of the service as well as in the prayers and preaching. He was singularly fortunate, for a short time in Montreal, in having as organist a distinguished musician. Bryceson Treharne, a Welshman, came to be organist at the American Church in 1923. In Treharne RR was delighted to find an expert in his field who yet believed that the music must be integrated into the purposes of worship. There was always close consultation between minister and organist. Once having discussed with Treharne the nature of the service, however, and the hymns which he would like, RR was content to let Treharne have his way with the choir and organ, confident in the results. Their friendship struck deep, and the sight of them sitting peaceably in RR's study—pipes puffing, no need to talk—was a familiar one.

Unfortunately, the untutored ears of the congregation preferred the traditional sweetmeats of musical religiosity. The church people, unaware that Sunday by Sunday they were getting a feast of the best, became restive. RR got wind that there was a move afoot to fire Treharne. As there was an official board meeting that night, he went into swift action. He phoned Treharne: "Look here, old man, I haven't time to go into it now but I want your resignation in my hands tonight." In complete trust Treharne complied. At the meeting, before any complaints could be uttered, RR announced the organist's resignation. Consternation prevailed. Where could they get a replacement at such short notice. RR let them stew for a bit. Then he offered the opinion that it might be possible to persuade Treharne to stay for a few months until a suitable replacement could be found. When Treharne left the American Church a short time later, he became the musical editor of Schirmers, New York.

There are a number of churches in Canada which lay claim to having been the first "on the air." Certainly American Presbyterian was the first in Montreal. George Lighthall, an elder, having heard a broadcast service while returning from a trip to Panama in 1922, was in the vanguard in urging the congregation to broadcast RR's sermons. The exact date of the first broadcast is not known. The best information seems to be that the broadcasts, twice a month, of the regular evening services, began in the fall of 1923, and that they occasioned a flurry of criticism. The American Church, it was said, being a wealthy congregation, was taking unfair advantage over other less affluent churches. To this RR quietly countered that American Presbyterian had no desire to monopolize the airwaves, but wished to ensure that some time might be reserved for religious broadcasting.

At one of the broadcast services the power failed. A.E. Kerr, plunged into darkness in the midst of reading the closing litany, turned to his senior in a moment of panic: "What shall I do?" "Pronounce the benediction" was the prompt reply. And so he did, to the acute chagrin of at least three irreverent young people who waited with baited breath for the all too appropriate continuation of the litany: "Lighten our darkness we beseech thee, O Lord."

RR's relations with his associate ministers were governed by his conviction that they were serving an apprenticeship. This meant two things. One was that an associate must be given every opportunity of taking responsibility in all aspects of the congregation's life, including preaching. The other was that no young man should remain too long in the position, for only as he shouldered the full responsibility for a congregation on his own could he mature.

A.E. Kerr was one of a succession of associates at the American Church. H.R.C. Avison, who later took a teaching post at MacDonald College, Ste. Anne's, and Robert Hall, who after several pastorates became a superintendent of home missions on the Prairies, were among others. Alec Kerr was later to write:

> It was characteristic of him [RR] that he would not allow me, novice though I was, to be known as an Assistant, but insisted that I be called an Associate, to avoid as far as possible any suggestion of a difference in status. This generosity of spirit, which I venture to call his distinctive mark, showed itself in a thousand ways. He saw to it that I was recognized, quite unnecessarily, along with himself, in everything that belonged to the life of the Church; and he went out of his way constantly to give me more than my share of credit for the success of any venture in which he had played the major part. He provided as fine and consistent an example as I have ever seen of that generosity without which there can be no greatness of soul.

RR believed that the temporal affairs of the church should be handled in a businesslike way. One of his first requests after he arrived in Montreal was for the installation of a proper filing system for the congregation. One evening, after a long and inconclusive debate on finances, he remarked: "Gentlemen, if you tried to run your businesses in the way you try to run this church, you'd be in bankruptcy tomorrow." This was neither the first nor last time that seasoned businessmen were brought up short by the man labelled, by those who did not know him, an impractical visionary.

At the time RR arrived in Montreal, the long processes which were to unite the Presbyterian, Methodist, and Congregational churches into The United Church of Canada were nearing fulfilment. RR was enthusiastically pro-union, and he was anxious that the American Presbyterian Church should join the venture. The session early endorsed his view. But those who were to vote on so important a move must know what it would involve. At RR's suggestion the session selected two of their number to explain the details of the Basis of Union at a congregational meeting.

It might be thought, as the union was to take place in June 1925, that by February 1924, most church members would have had a fair idea of the Basis of Union. The American Presbyterian Church was, however, literally American. Founded early in the nineteenth century by American businessmen and their families resident in Montreal, it was a congregation of the Presbyterian church, USA. As such its members had only a cursory knowledge of the protracted negotiations which had brought union so near.

Originally these Americans had been members of St. Andrew's Presbyterian Church. But in 1822, the Americans and Scots in the congregation had met in head-on collision over the choice of a minister. Each group wanted a man of their own breed. The Americans, in the end, had withdrawn and established their own congregation, making their connection with the New York Presbytery. That connection had lasted over one hundred years. The American founders had given place to Canadian sons and daughters who were ready to sever their US connections. On 20 March 1924, the congregation voted 105 to 28 to enter the new United Church of Canada.

As the American Presbyterian Church did not belong to any of the uniting bodies, a special act of the Quebec legislature was required to regularize its entry into the union. RR was advised to pay his respects to the Roman Catholic archbishop of Quebec, to ensure his acquiescence in the passage of the enabling bill. Waiting in the anteroom of the episcopal palace, he ran into Father McShane, priest at St. Patrick's, the home of the English-speaking Catholics of

Montreal. RR, who was on the friendliest terms with Fr. McShane, thought this was providential, and asked him to lend his influence with the archbishop. He received the wistful answer: "My friend, I am as much a stranger here as you."

In the event, there was no trouble in the Quebec legislature. The New York Presbytery released the congregation with its blessing and the American Presbyterian Church entered the United Church as the American Church. In due course the Montreal Presbytery received RR into the ministry of The United Church of Canada.

18

The Pace of Life

In January 1926, RR wrote the following letter:

> Dear Mr. Nelson...
>
> Rufus Holden showed me yesterday a letter which you had written to him—and I would like to say that I was very glad to see it, on many grounds. It is not good for a church that its affairs should be conducted by a few people; and I wish that there might be a wider diffusion of the spirit of your letter.
>
> But I want to say a few words about the sentence in the letter in which you refer to me; and I do so because I think your letter entitles you to know the facts....Your understanding is that I am responsible for the preaching and for the necessary services of baptism, marriage, and burial. This is quite accurate as far as it goes. But it would be more accurate to say that my responsibility begins with these things. Perhaps I can best show you what happens by transcribing two days' records from my private logbook:—and these are quite typical.
>
> Tuesday, Sept. 29: Throat a little better. Worked in the morning on sermon for Sunday evening—Adam's Apple. Afternoon: Went to Montreal and District Bank to confer with manager about the affairs of X. It appears that he has a balance of only $5.00. Called at church and did a little business. Then called on J. C. Simpson...: found him improving. Then to Mrs. W. R. Whyte...: found her gone away (this is the third time I have failed to find Mrs. Whyte). Then back to church. Dictated letters to Miss MacDonald; conferred with Mrs. MacKay about the Sunday School reports and Rev. Williams

about the proposed arrangement re St. Mark's, Mountain St., and Inspector St. Mission. Gathered materials for report on new members. Interviewed applicant who wanted clothes in order to take a job at a lumber camp. Then to YMCA to supper in honour of Mr. A. Kingman and Mr. Harrower. Left at 8:45 and thereafter worked on sermon until twelve midnight, almost completing the writing. During the day received George Lyman's membership certificate and had some conversation with R. Holden on music expenses.

Thursday, Oct. 22: Worked all morning on Sunday evening sermon. Lunched with Philips, David, and Ferguson re Men's Club. At 2:30 interviewed Mr. Duckworth of the Sun Life on the case of Miss Y. Then to Nobbs and Hyde to work on draft of guiding principles for the architecture of new churches of the United Church. There until six. Then to church. Short conference with Avison. Eight o'clock, Young People's Conference, constituted three study circles; meeting arranged for Sunday night. Afterwards worked on sermon until finished. Bed at 1:30.

You see there is neither a baptism nor a marriage nor a funeral on either day, but you can gather from those two entries the kind of things that fall to me:

(a) Sick visiting—including old and lonely folk. During these next two weeks I hope to see 10 of these all over the city.

(b) Special personal cases of a *confidential* nature—the cases of X and Miss Y have been very difficult and protracted—and there are some others. (The case of X was not simply a matter of financial insolvency; like that of Miss Y, there was serious mental instability.) Today I have to go and see about a man who attends the Church who is threatened with a sheriff in his home owing to non-payment of rent; and something new—and more or less serious—every day.

(c) The supervision of *all* the work of the Church—the business of the Session—new members—organizing new things, as with the Study Circles mentioned above. All this comes back to me.

(d) Then, it is my business to act for the Church in its external relations; to the United Church—attending Presbytery meetings and serving on Presbytery and other church committees. You will see above a reference to the Architectural Committee of the United Church—an effort to have more suitable and beautiful church buildings in the future. This week I am summoned to a meeting of that Committee, also to a conference on downtown work. I have also to serve on the Senate and the Council of the Theological College—and on the Joint Board of the Cooperating Theological Colleges. And one or two others besides.

(e) Further, because I am minister of the American Church, I have been appointed a Governor's Fellow and Member of the Corporation of McGill; and I am a member of the Board of the McGill School for Social Workers. For the same reason I have been made a Vice-President of the Montreal Council of Social Agencies. And I have been made a member of the General Committee of the National Education Conference that is to be held in Montreal next April, and of the Sub-committee on the Conference Programme.

And this is not all by a good deal. I have a Conference of Young People at the Church every Monday evening, a Men's Bible Class on Tuesdays at 5:15; and I am always at the mid-week service, not because my presence is needed there, but in order to back up Mr. MacDonald. [There were two associate ministers at this time, MacDonald and Avison.] Then I have regular and occasional Session meetings, Benevolent Fund Meetings, Sunday School Committee, and during one part of the year I have a weekly Communicants' Class. I meet once a month with a group of young rising businessmen who are discussing the relation of Christianity to modern business. YMCA workers, Social Service Workers, come to ask for advice about their work and about difficult cases; and our large clientele of McGill students gives us a handsome load of requests and consultations. And so it goes on. And it is all intensely interesting—but I confess, sometimes rather exhausting too. Apart from Saturdays, when I slack off in the afternoon and go to bed early, I am at work (including meal times) an average of 14 to 15 hours a day. Sometimes I get tired and then have to knock off for a time,—And I haven't mentioned the telephone. The other morning I had 15 calls; and you may imagine how much sermon was done that morning!

And about sermons, this may interest you. My finished manuscripts—I say *finished* because six finished sheets represent 12 to 20 draft sheets—for one year's preaching, represent the equivalent of two volumes of the size of (say) "If Winter Comes." [RR chose *If Winter Comes* as his example not because the book commended itself to him, but because, as the current bestseller, it would immediately be recognizable to his reader. Incidentally, the popularity of the book gave wide currency to Keats line, upon which the title of the book was based. RR used to remark that the end of the line, "can spring be far behind," showed that the poet had "obviously never lived in Montreal"!]

I hope this is not wearying to you. I have never written all this down before in my life; and now that I have written it, it seems grotesque that any man should attempt to cover so much ground. But it has to be done—and somehow it gets done. Of course, it can only be done by cutting out a good deal that one is asked to do otherwise. I do virtually no outside speaking, and I suppose that I refuse about 10 invitations here and there and everywhere per week. (I broke off here to attend to the telephone—a request to go to Sherbrooke to speak at the Presbytery meeting—declined!) And last night I had to spend a couple of hours studying the new Quebec Law on the collection of vital statistics, which will probably cost me an extra half-hour for every baptism, marriage, and funeral!...

I hope you will not think I write in any grumbling spirit— I don't. But I sometimes wish that folk would understand a little better what a city minister's job is really like. And in a case like ours, there is absolutely no limit to the work that might be done. We do not realize that the American Church is, in a curious way, a sort of parish church for the whole city—more than any other single church....You would be surprised if you saw the Enquiry Sheets we are now beginning to get from General McCuaig's Unemployment Committee, to discover how many people quite unknown to us report that *their* church is the American Church. Not long ago I was quite peremptorily ordered on the phone to conduct a funeral in the North End—on the ground, as it turned out, that a daughter of the dead woman used to attend the evening service in Dr. Johnston's time....

The letter reveals both the pace of RR's life and the place which the American Church held in the life of the city. Social services were in their infancy, and they suffered then, even more than they do now, from lack of resources. Funds were minimal and trained personnel scarce. Increasing unemployment was bringing a steady flow of men, women, and even children to the door of any institution that offered hope of assistance. Financial help and legal advice were common requests. At the American Church, transients in need of a meal as they "bummed" their way from place to place in search of work were a serious headache. A cash handout was an obviously doubtful procedure. To meet the daily stream of requests for meals, the church issued meal tickets on one or two downtown restaurants. Although the majority of those who came were genuinely in need, there were, inevitably, some frauds among them. Sometimes the tickets were found thrown down on the steps of the church.

Occasionally the stories offered in support of a request for assistance were ingenious. One young man declared that if only the church would give him his fare to South Carolina, he would go back to give himself up on a charge of manslaughter. His story was so convincing that Alec Kerr went to Windsor Station prepared to purchase his ticket for him, but the "killer" never turned up at the rendezvous. On another occasion Miss MacDonald, the church secretary, felt constrained to slip a note onto RR's desk as he was in the middle of an interview: "Be careful. I think this man is dangerous."

No mention is made in the letter to Mr. Nelson of RR's work with the Student Christian Movement. Many of the young people who attended the evening services were students from McGill University. "The healthy load of requests from McGill students" were personal requests—for spiritual guidance or for financial help. In those days the machinery now available within the universities for looking after students in spiritual, psychological, or financial difficulties was non-existent. RR was always available, whatever the need. When financial help was in question, he would turn to one or other of the wealthier men in the church. It was enough for these men that RR thought a person worth helping.

Through contacts with individual students, and even more through his preaching, RR became a friend of the SCM [or SCA— Student Christian Association, as it was then called]. He spoke at their services and local and national conferences. Occasionally he would be torn between amusement and exasperation with members of the SCM. Once a certain brilliant student of psychology announced with portentous solemnity that the group of which he was leader was "discussing God." That was almost too much for RR. But his exasperation and amusement never became condescension. In a tribute to RR at the dedication of a memorial plaque at Erskine-American Church in 1951, Dr. Gerald Cragg [1906–1976], then minister of the church, said:

> Older men, especially those who have reached a place of prominence and authority, usually ignore or patronize their juniors. Dr. Roberts did neither. He paid young men the compliment of treating them as equals; he would listen to their opinions, and he would discuss important matters with them as though they were his peers. Consequently there are literally scores of men now in the prime of life who are ready to rise up and call him blessed.

On Sunday evenings the Roberts family rarely returned from church without a handful of students, usually from the theological colleges associated with McGill. As he had had nothing to eat since noon save for a light tea, RR would be hungry. Family and guests would sit down to a period of relaxation and talk, punctuated by the crunching of cornflakes or shredded wheat. This once prompted a private query: "Does Dr. Roberts always have Monday's breakfast on Sunday night?"

Shortly after RR died, H. R. C. Avison wrote to RR's eldest daughter Peggy: "I used to wonder if the members of his family resented the extent to which they had to share him with other people—so many other people." Doubtless he was thinking partly of those Sunday evenings. Peggy's response—and it is the response of all the Roberts children—runs:

I do not remember that we ever did. We were a part of it and we felt especially privileged that he belonged to us in a special way. Sometimes we thought that our boy friends cultivated us with the (to us) ulterior motive of getting into our home and "sitting at the feet of Gamaliel." But it was a glorious time. The more we shared him with others, the greater our share in him seemed to be. We look with pride and affection to some of those in whom his influence lives today, who have been leaders in church and university in Canada.

19

RR's Preaching

All the multifarious business of the life of the church, and all the work he accomplished outside of its walls, were to RR an important part of spreading the word of God. Work for the church at large, in committees and other ways, and work in the community, was all God's work. But in spite of the load this work laid upon him, he never skimped what he considered to be his primary function—preaching. Lecturing some years later to students at Emmanuel College, Toronto, after expounding on the centrality of preaching in the Protestant tradition, RR went on to say:

> It is not enough that we should spend four days in good works, however good; and then for two days be scurrying about for something to say on Sunday. On these terms we do not preach at all. We simply gibber. And presently we shall be left asking ourselves why people don't come to church as they used to. The answer is simply that we are not delivering the goods. It should be a point of honour with every preacher that he religiously fences out a certain number of hours every day which are wholly consecrated to his work in the pulpit,— I do not mean, of course, that they should all be given to the preparation of next Sunday's sermons, but that they should be devoted to such studies as prepare the mind, and those devotions that prepare the soul, both for the making and delivery of sermons....
>
> Let us for a moment turn our minds to the setting of the sermon. First of all remember that you will, on Sunday morning, be addressing a company of people. I want you to ponder the wonder of this. It never ceases to be a mystery that numbers of people will come out on a Sunday morning

to listen to a man preaching. But there they are. And what is more, they come Sunday after Sunday and listen to the poor thing that you have to say. I say to you, gentlemen, that I am humbled anew every Sunday morning of my life to find a company of people gathered together that I might speak to them. Their confidence in me...seems to lay upon me a burden of responsibility heavier than I can bear. At least they deserve nothing short of the ultimate best I can give. It is no little honour to a man that people whom he knows to be better than himself should willingly and continually sit at his feet. And he should humble himself before God and ask for grace to sustain so desperate a trust.

So the weekday mornings, Monday through Friday, were spent in his study—reading, thinking, writing and, praying. Only something completely unavoidable would take him away. Normally Mrs. Roberts performed a very efficient blocking service against those who would interrupt. [She must have been out on the occasion referred to in the letter to Mr. Nelson]. By Saturday morning, both morning and evening sermons were on paper. Because of his phenomenally poor eyesight, RR had early learned not to rely on notes. He never took into the pulpit any written word except possibly some lengthy quotation. Saturday morning was spent in brooding over what he had to say. He never memorized the words; he absorbed the material so that his sermons never had the sense of being prepared orations.

Saturday afternoon RR "slacked off." The excursions across Brooklyn Bridge mentioned previously were a part of this relaxation. In Montreal these gave way to explorations of the Mountain. If there was a mildly derisory note in his voice when he referred to "the Mountain"—recalling the "real" mountains of his boyhood in Wales—nevertheless he loved the Mountain, especially in the fall when the maples were red. After a couple of hours tramping over old paths and discovering new ones, usually in company with one or more of his daughters, he would return home to tea—thin bread and butter and his favourite fruit cake. Then he would do no more work until after supper, when once again he would retire to his study to brood in quiet for an hour or two on his morning sermon.

To clear his mind for sleep, still sitting at his desk, he would play a hand or two of a card game called, "Demon Thirteen." He used to say that this particular form of solitaire occupied just enough of his mind for his "brain cells to have a chance to sit down." And then to bed rather earlier than on weeknights that he might be fresh for the worship of God on the morrow. And his dictum that the worship of God demanded a fresh mind and heart extended to his daughters. There was never any issue over this; he never gave orders. No matter if the party was likely to go on until 2 A.M., which in those days was a very dashing hour, and much as they might regret leaving, affection and respect brought the Roberts girls home by midnight.

In *The Contemporary Christ* RR has this to say about preaching:

> The first and last object of a sermon is to be the vehicle of the Word of God to the hearer. But the Word of God is not necessarily the word of the preacher, though the word of the preacher may and should convey it. As in poetry, so in preaching: the essential business is often accomplished by the undertones and the overtones of the spoken word. But the fundamental condition of preaching is the spiritual *rapport* between the preacher and the hearer, which should be created by the antecedent worship. Good preaching is not merely an affair of fine and convincing thought, of apt language, of competent delivery, though the thought should be fine, the word apt, and the utterance clear and persuasive. Yet all these things may be present and the sermon carry no word of God to any man. Over and above these desiderata there must be in the preacher and the hearer a posture of spirit which will enable the Spirit of God to give to the one, and pass on to the other, that transcendent illumination which, so far as it goes, is revelation.

These conditions were surely fulfilled at the American Church in the 1920s. Who were the hearers of the word at that time? The morning service was always well attended by the regular members of the congregation. They were responsive and loyal; many were discerning. But the evening services were different. From the four corners of Montreal came the Toms and Dicks, the Marys and Bettys, literally filling the church. There was a goodly percentage of McGill students, also. They sat on the gallery stairs, on the window sills, even on the steps leading up to the pulpit itself.

Among those who came was a young couple named Hutchinson. They had moved from Toronto to Montreal and had not yet found, near their home in a suburb, a church which answered their need for spiritual nurture. From friends in the SCM they heard of this man Richard Roberts, and how his preaching was drawing such a large and loyal following. They decided to check him out. Soon they were sufficiently "hooked" to begin attending not only the evening service, but to take part in other programs of the American Church as well.

One day RR asked if they could find time to come in for a chat. They were flattered [Jean Hutchinson's word as she told this story]. By this time they were known as Jean and Hutch. After talking about a number of things, RR turned to Jean and asked: "Do you believe in Jesus Christ?" "Of course I do," she replied sharply, just a little nettled. "Then do you intend to serve him?" "Yes, of course," was the reply, still a bit nettled. "Then why don't you throw in your lot with the rest of us?"

Jean Hutchinson would later recall that she and her husband had been eternally grateful to RR. Without that little push they might have gone on drifting, and maybe drifted out of the church altogether. They served their church loyally and well—Hutch with his financial expertise and many other gifts; Jean by entering Emmanuel College from which she received her diploma in theology in 1938. From 1945 to 1964, she was principal of the United Church Training School, and from 1962 to 1964, chair of the Board of Women. Undoubtedly there were others to whom RR gave that "little push."

RR's preaching was free from any trace of the dramatic. There were no sensational bids for popularity. Gerald Cragg explains why RR drew such crowds:

> [It was because he spoke] a word exactly suited to the needs of a generation groping for guidance, and willing to look to the pulpit in order to find it....At a time when the trend had already set toward chatty little discourses on practical psychology or on the best methods for soothing our disordered nerves, he worthily maintained the great tradition of biblical and evangelical preaching. What he offered was a message arresting in content and presented in a manner worthy of the subject. He never dishonoured his theme by

bringing to it a casual mode of expression. He was a lover of good books, a man whose mind was steeped in the best literature of our race, and he could neither write nor speak without giving evidence of that fact. Open any volume of his printed sermons and the printed page brings back the power of the spoken word. He was not so much a scholar who happened to preach, as a preacher who was also a scholar.

But he was never a literary dilettante. His preaching was in the great tradition because it had the authentic ring of conviction, and so of authority. What he had to say was rooted in the Gospel, centred in Christ, devoted to declaring the full mystery of the grace of God.

No one who heard him doubted that he believed implicitly in the message which he was commissioned to proclaim. What was equally apparent was the fact that he was a citizen, as well as an ambassador, of the unseen world. He not merely believed that it existed; he belonged by grace to that spiritual kingdom whose laws he proclaimed. When he spoke of the value of the devotional life, it was firsthand testimony he offered.

With this tribute of Dr. Cragg's there can be no quarrel. Yet there is something more that needs to be said. To speak of a person as being a citizen of a spiritual kingdom may suggest, to some, a person who has become divorced from the here and now. RR knew the world in which he lived. He knew his city. He knew its infant mortality rate, and it was a shameful thing. One Christmas morning he prophesied to his people: "If Christmas was not to become a meaningless fable, a pretty pagan festival, they must lay this shame to their hearts." On another occasion, as he spoke of the superficiality of some religion, he gave as an example an item he had culled from the daily paper. A bus load of "pilgrims" to Oberammergau had arrived there chanting, "We're here, because we're here, because we're here...." The only conclusion he could draw, he remarked dryly, was that they were obviously "not all there"!

Then, to speak of a person as a scholar, is always to run the risk of giving the impression that his study is his world, that his intercourse with the great minds of the ages unfits him for conversation with ordinary people. RR's sermons were never "difficult." If the person in the pew, the ordinary person, could not understand the word of the preacher, then, thought RR, the preacher had better "go home and examine himself." A. E. Kerr once asked RR if he ever, after preaching, had a depressing sense that he had failed. RR replied: "I have it so often that the only thing that keeps me going is my belief in the work of the Holy Spirit, who can take my poor words and use them to leave the kind of impression that He wishes in the minds of my hearers."

Perhaps the final word on RR's preaching should be that of Dr. S. P. Rose, professor at the United Theological College, Montreal: "He had to have an audience. He was a pulpit man. The pulpit was his throne. But the power exhibited there was that of the One whose servant he was."

20
The City

RR was happy at the American Church, as he had been happy at Westbourne Grove. He was deeply conscious of the loyalty and affection of his people, and particularly of the office-bearers. He had been warmly welcomed into the fellowship of the Presbytery of Montreal, and he thought of leaving with regret. Yet it had long been his opinion that five or six years was the optimum tenure for most ministers in any charge, and that he was no exception. It was time for the congregation to hear a new voice, with a fresh approach and a different emphasis. And he himself needed the stimulus of new problems and new faces.

The work he had been given to do in connection with the theological college, and his work on the Committee on Church Architecture, had been particularly congenial. It is worth noting, however, that the suggestions of the latter were not always entirely welcome. A member of the Montreal Presbytery levelled a sharp attack on the architectural committee in the columns of *The New Outlook*. RR and S. P. Rose, a former Methodist and a veritable saint, were singled out for special opprobrium. RR had already left for Toronto when the storm broke. Dr. Rose shared his hurt in a letter:

> So we are fully revealed in our true colours as poorly disguised Romanists seeking to lead the United Church away from Protestantism! I have been suspect for years, but your wickedness has taken a little longer for discovering....It would all be very funny, and Hughes' letter gave me several moments of merriment, IF. But there is an IF. Hughes has a following, mainly, I think, of former Methodists of an Orange complexion. It is a hopeless fellowship, impervious to reason, well-described in Dr. Ritchie's characterization of the Anglo-

Catholics at Lausanne, "It refuses to reason; it simply asserts. It is a most irritating opponent, for when it is manifestly vanquished and overwhelmed by fact...it simply stands up again and asserts." I pointed out months ago in Presbytery that we were trying to put nothing over on congregations, that we were responding, as we thought, to a demand for counsel on the part of many who desired to see church buildings erected more worthy of the ideals of our denomination. This answers his pitiful inquiry, why were "all the historic churches,...scenes of mighty spiritual effort and of Pentecostal victory," ignored. No plans of such buildings are needed; they are so common....[Does] Hughes suggest that mighty spiritual results are linked, like cause and effect, to a certain type of building? He knows further that there is no power within the United Church that can override the rights of congregations as to the form of architecture chosen. He seems to want some power exercised which would prohibit the erection of churchly churches.

The letter continues with a paragraph outlining the personal attack which was included in the diatribe, but then winds up:

I fear I am abusing the rights of friendship in thus writing without reserve to a fellow conspirator against the wellbeing of the U. C., but I shall be quite at peace with Hughes once more now that you have been made the victim of my emotions.

There was regret, also, in leaving the city itself. Toronto never managed to wean RR away from his love of Montreal. He had found a place for himself in the public life of the city, at least in its English speaking part. He attributed his inclusion on the various university boards and other offices to the position of the American Church. That by itself would not have been enough. His presence was desired because of what he had to contribute.

Through these varied contacts he had made many friends, particularly among the clergy. He had been active in two informal groups, the K. A. [very likely standing for *Kuklos Adelphon*, the circle of brethren] and the OEA, the former probably owing its inception to his initiative. Both of these were made up of clergy from all the denominations; both met for discussion and fellowship. They deliberately remained small. Perhaps RR had in mind what had happened in England to the Free Church Fellowship. All this, too, he would have to leave behind. But the fact remained that the English speaking community of Montreal was comparatively small, and he was feeling the need to stretch.

There was another factor in RR's decision to move. The residential areas were receding ever further from the centre of the city. Yet the changing needs of the area, bounded roughly by Dorchester and Sherbrooke Streets, and Guy and St. Denis, would have to be met if the United Church were not to default in its mission. RR knew that his type of ministry was not the kind that would soon be needed. He could also see the day coming when the dwindling core of substantial supporters of the four churches in the area would be unable to meet the financial burden. Nor did he feel that, constituted as they then were, the congregations were psychologically fitted to take up the challenge of the new situation. Radical change was called for, and that is what RR proposed. Late in 1927, after RR had left Montreal, Dr. Rose wrote to him:

> I reintroduced your proposal for the sale of our four downtown churches and the building and endowment of a worthy church, with the reservation of a good sum for church extension, at our last ministers' meeting. The Presbytery Executive was asked to secure a conference of members to talk over the question.

Nothing came of this, however. Old loyalties were too firmly entrenched.

The rigorous climate of Montreal was a further consideration in leaving. In the winter months RR would clamp his lips firmly together and utter no word that was not strictly necessary, even in walking the short distance between the church and his home in the Drummond Apartments, a matter of not more than four blocks. Rightly or wrongly he believed that the intense cold of the Montreal winters was the main cause of the trouble he was having with his throat. He must seek a milder climate.

England, of course, offered a milder climate, and in the summer of 1926, RR was again thinking of "going home." This time there was, in contrast to 1920, at least one very good prospect, Westminster Chapel. It was partly to investigate this possibility that RR took his summer holiday in England. Closer inspection proved the grass not as green as it had appeared from the other side of the Atlantic, however. And in the meantime a new field was opening for him in Canada.

21

Toronto: Sherbourne Street United

The overtures from Sherbourne Street came as a surprise. Although RR had had no thought of moving in that direction, Toronto had definite attractions. The climate was certainly a little milder than that of Montreal. The population, not yet as polyglot as it is today but fairly solidly Anglo-Saxon, offered a wider scope for his gifts. Moreover the central offices of the United Church made it the nerve centre of the church at large. But what of Sherbourne Street itself? Was it the right congregation for his kind of ministry?

Dr. George Pidgeon [1872–1971] of Bloor Street United [first moderator of The United Church of Canada] thought it was; so did Dr. Charles Bishop, who had just resigned from Sherbourne to become principal of Albert College in Belleville, Ontario. About the future of Sherbourne Street these two were of one mind. Eventually the churches in the area would have to unite. The city was growing and changing. In all the churches in the centre of the city, south of Bloor Street, death was gradually thinning the ranks of the old faithful supporters. The younger people were moving away to newer residential areas. But there was still "an opportunity for ten years at least of a fruitful ministry which would reach the entire city." Dr. Pidgeon was enthusiastic that RR should accept the invitation.

Opinion within the Sherbourne Church itself, however, was divided. One party felt they should be seeking a man whose primary interest would be in a community work program, though it is doubtful they had any clear idea of what that really meant. Another group had set their hopes on a strong preacher building up the congregation to its former powers. This latter group carried the day when the call was up for consideration. RR was not aware of how formidable the opposition had been until after he had accepted the call. He was concerned lest he be coming to a divided church. Mr. Hales, a member of the Official Board, reassured him: "While at our Board meeting questions such as those I referred to were mentioned during the discussion, at the end the resolution was unanimously and enthusiastically adopted, and I feel satisfied that when you come you will have the wholehearted support of the Board and the Congregation."

RR entered into his ministry at Sherbourne Street in January 1927. He had been there only a year when he began to feel that he was perhaps in the wrong place, that Dr. Pidgeon and Dr. Bishop had been too sanguine. Was not the nature of the situation very much like that which had caused him to propose that the four downtown churches in Montreal make a concerted effort to meet the changing needs of the area in which they were situated? A conversation with Mr. Fudger, an elder in the church, led to a letter to Sir Joseph Flavelle:

> The crux of the problem, as I see it, is that the kind of ministry that the supporting members of the church call for is not the kind of ministry that the neighbourhood needs.
>
> The alternatives before us would appear to be:
> (1) to continue as we are and where we are, and to decline steadily to second-rateness;
> (2) to move bodily to some other locality;
> (3) to make Sherbourne a definitely evangelistic centre, with the expectation that gradually such churches as Carlton Street, Parliament Street, etc. would be united with it;
> (4) to make Sherbourne a centre for a public ministry of preaching without much reference to the immediate community.
>
> As to these, No. 1 would be a sin and a shame. There is a life and power in Sherbourne which should not be allowed to run slowly to waste, and which somehow should be utilized for the sake of the future.
>
> No. 3 seems to me to have much in its favour; but it would hasten the scattering of our present strength.
>
> Nos. 2 and 4 would, I think, have to be considered with reference to the position of the United Church in the city and especially in the south-central region. And briefly this is how it appears to me. It is indispensable for a great national church such as we believe we are now creating that it should be prominently visible and powerfully vocal at the heart of every

great city in the Dominion. This is a circumstance of which the Roman Catholic Church is fully aware; and we might do well to study its strategy in this distribution of its churches....

The main function of this type of church is two-fold. First it should set the standards of worship and preaching for the surrounding areas—in city, town, and country; and second, if it is in the business section of the city, it should carry on a number of weekday ministries—midday services, early evening classes and clubs, etc.—seeking to serve primarily the business community. This latter is done in some places, but it is largely a field to be explored. To be sure, where the conditions are favourable it should also nourish a congregational life.

RR then raised the possibility of a merger with Metropolitan United, "which is in position, structure, and accessories admirably fitted" for the kind of ministry described in (4). Like Sherbourne, Metropolitan was "looking for their congregation to the city at large, and it is almost sure that each is weakening the position of the other."

The problem was placed before the Official Board. As a result conversations were initiated with other churches in the south-central area, Metropolitan, Westminster Central [later amalgamated with Old St. Andrew's to become St. Andrew's-Westminster], and Carlton Street. Carlton, it should be noted, had already embarked on a community work program which, over the years, justly commanded respect. [Carlton finally amalgamated with Sherbourne in 1959, to become St. Luke's United]. But though the writing was on the wall, there were few willing to spell out what it said. Old loyalties, even more than vested interests, blocked the way. There seemed to be nothing for it but for Sherbourne to go it alone.

The question of how and in what direction to go remained. The leadership of Sherbourne was made up of rugged individualists. Sir Edward Kemp, one of the stewards, put it neatly in a letter to RR: "The impression left upon my own mind of the evening I spent with the Committee in your study was that we were without the gripping force of men who were in love with their fellows...in work for and with them in the church with which we were associated." Eventually a plan emerged, however. Sherbourne was, for the immediate future, to remain chiefly a preaching centre, and to that end the sanctuary was to be transformed into a place where worship would be enhanced. In the meantime the congregation must prepare for the day when it would be called to serve the community without its current level of financial support. A substantial endowment fund was to be established to provide for the future. RR warned, however, that the fund should not be so large as to suppress any need for effort and initiative. The finances for these dual but related purposes were to be raised in one campaign.

The sanctuary of Sherbourne, when RR came to it in 1927, represented the nadir of Victorian nonconformist architecture. It even had red plush, tip-up cinema seats. The shell, quite accidentally, was roughly cruciform. RR dreamed dreams, and had already in the summer of 1927, consulted an architect as to what might be possible. When the board was ready to discuss renovations, RR was prepared with roughed-out plans and a tentative estimate. The board voted to proceed. The decision had been slow in coming but enthusiasm for the dual project—renovation and endowment—mounted rapidly. Dr. Russell Maltby, visiting Toronto during this period and a guest in the Roberts home, remarked one day to one of RR's daughters: "You know, your father is a most remarkable man. He has introduced me to a number of the leading men in the church, and each one of those men thinks that the whole scheme is *his* idea." By the end of 1929, the entire sum of $250,000 had been underwritten.

The dedication of the reconstructed sanctuary was scheduled for 24 November 1929. The service had been planned with care. The Lieutenant Governor of Ontario and his lady were to be among the invited guests. Early in the week preceding the dedication a representative of the company doing the work, doubtless thinking a minister of religion a soft mark, called on RR. He was sorry, he said, but owing to the pressure of other contracts the work had progressed more slowly than anticipated; the opening would have to be postponed. "The opening," RR responded, "will not be postponed. We shall hold it as scheduled. We shall apologize to our congregation and to our distinguished guests for the mess. And we shall tell them that things are as they are because your company has broken its contract!" The work was finished on time.

The year 1929, had proved a fruitful and eventful year at Sherbourne. But RR was aware that the enthusiasm of 1929, had overlaid, but not resolved, a fundamental dichotomy in the congregation's thinking. If a tentative and unofficial suggestion that he take a chair to be newly established in 1930, at Union College, British Columbia, had become firm, he might well have taken it. He considered it seriously enough to consult with Dr. Bowles, chancellor of Victoria College, Toronto about it. Bowles was doubtful, sensing that a good deal of the attraction of the job was due to conditions at Sherbourne. He concluded his letter: "I think you are going to enjoy next year even more than last. It takes a little while to 'Robertize' a congregation, if you will permit such a use of your name—and Sherbourne has been used to many sorts of preaching."

Then, in 1930, there were two or three deaths amongst the older members of the congregation, which brought about a serious financial crisis. A committee was set to work to review the entire financial situation. RR opened his report to the Official Board on the work of this committee by listing four suggestions:

(a) that it is the business of the Church to do more extensive and direct work in the immediate community;
(b) that the minister should live in the community and do more weekday work in it, more especially in the way of pastoral visitation;
(c) that the remuneration of the minister should henceforth be $7500.00 per annum, but with the understanding that this may only be temporary;
(d) that in the event of my not being able to accept these conditions and desire to resign with the close of the present church year, the Board of Stewards should grant me a year's salary.

Although RR continued with the words: "I wish at once to acknowledge gratefully this most generous undertaking," he felt, in fact, that these findings were a direct criticism of the nature of his ministry, almost an ultimatum. In his report he made a particular point of the fact that he had been notified of the committee's findings only verbally. He further commented that the first two recommendations "were not among the matters remitted to the committee; nor was the committee competent to recommend action concerning them...." In reference to (c), he added that it would have been elementary courtesy to acknowledge that the initiative in the matter of the reduction in salary had come from himself. He then continued:

> I should like to add that when I came here, I had stipulated for no salary. The amount, $10,000.00, was offered to me— it was the sum I was already receiving at Montreal. I have not at any time in my ministry stipulated for a particular salary. In any case the matter of stipend is irrelevant to the issue now raised. About that there is no difficulty at all.

Next he set forth his position with respect to pastoral visitation:

> (1) I stated explicitly before I came here that I could not undertake systematic pastoral visitation.
> (2) None the less, when I came here I made a serious effort to do so. But I did not get very far with it before all hope of carrying out my plan was swept away by the press of other work.
> (3) So far as I know, no single case of sickness or trouble or infirmity has been reported to me that I have not visited at the earliest possible moment.
> (4) I could not give any undertaking to pursue in the future a different policy in regard to pastoral visitation.

> I venture, relative to the subject of the minister's work, to say a little more which will enable you to see this matter in a better perspective. I do so not for my own sake; I have no apology to make. In the main the work of the city ministry is still conceived under the conditions of a country parish, where life is relatively simple: and it has never been clearly thought out in the conditions of city life. Let me enumerate my normal occupations....

Next follows an outline of his activities as minister of Sherbourne, being very similar to those found in his letter to Mr. Nelson of Montreal. But in his report to Sherbourne there is a measure of the didactic in his description of his work for the church at large. He was trying to get across the idea that the local church has no corner on its minister's time; that the local church and its minister are not self-sufficient; that they have a place in the larger purposes of God's kingdom:

> A minister of The United Church of Canada is expected to take his share of the general work of the Church. This is in connection with:
>
> (a) *The Presbytery*, which meets once a month. But one is also expected to serve on Presbytery committees; I serve on two, one of which is holding frequent meetings at the present time....
>
> (b) *The Conference*, which meets once a year, and of one of the committees of which I am convenor.
>
> (c) *The General Council,* it has been my privilege to serve for four years on the General Council's Committee on Church Worship and Ritual which, during this time, has been engaged in compiling the first Hymn Book of the United Church. For the greater part of the Church year this Committee has met for one afternoon a week; on alternate weeks the meetings lasted till 10 P.M.; and frequently there would be another evening meeting.
>
> This year Emmanuel College, being without a professor of Systematic Theology, asked me to take two hours' classes a week. As the Committee work on the Hymn Book was done and only an occasional meeting would be required, I thought that during this winter I might do my work for the Church at large in this way. It has taken rather less time than the Hymn Book committee work....
>
> I do not say these things in order to ask your approval of my industry. I am simply wanting you to realize why, under the conditions of a city ministry, systematic pastoral work is impossible. Pastoral visitation of this kind requires a vast expenditure of time: and most of it is wasted. Usually half the people are out when you call. If you announce that you will call in such and such a street on a certain day, a funeral or some other urgent call may, and often does, prevent you from carrying out your intentions: and the people who waited in for you are disgruntled. There is no minister in a large city congregation who can find time for it; and except in certain types of locality it is a hopeless and largely profitless

undertaking. I affirm this positively after 30 years' experience.

Allow me a word about the relation of this Church to community work. I have heard no mention of this matter that has not been made up of vague, ill-informed and unconsidered generalities....The truth is that it is idle to talk of community work in the region without taking the whole area between Sherbourne and the Don and treating it as a unit. The matter is already in hand. For some months a committee of Presbytery has been studying the subject....We are encouraged to believe that within a short time we shall be able to present a plan to Presbytery by which that area will be worked as a single whole, and in which Sherbourne will be asked to play an important and responsible part. More than this I cannot now say as the matter is not sufficiently advanced. I refer to it chiefly to put this matter in a right perspective; and also, if I may be permitted to add, to show that I have not been indifferent to the community, as it happens that it was on my motion that this investigation was set afoot....

I will not now take time to speak of the peculiar difficulties of the work at Sherbourne. But I wish to say that, as I look upon my part in these last four years, I have few regrets. On the whole things have gone, so far, much as I expected and wanted them to go. I can conceive of circumstances under which, if they had been present, we might have made more progress. But this is not the time to dwell on them. After more than 30 years of experience in the ministry, when I consider what I found here four years ago, and what we heard at the Annual Meeting the other night, I am free to say that the Congregation has reason to congratulate itself; and I am grateful to have had, with others to whose cooperation I owe much, a share in this promising advance.

After a good deal of thought I have been forced to the conclusion that the points laid down by the Committee do not include the real issue that is now being raised. I find in the action of the Committee an implied challenge to the nature and quality of my leadership in this congregation. Had this been no more than an individual view, I should have ignored it; but coming as it does from a committee, I am bound to take it seriously. I therefore wish to have this issue frankly faced; and in order that this may be done, I formally announce my intention, should this Board and Congregation concur in the opinion of the Committee, to ask the Presbytery of Toronto East at an early date to release me from the Pastoral Charge of this Congregation, as from June 30th next.

I would venture to ask members of the Board to treat the proceedings in this matter as private for the time being. It is well to avoid unnecessary publicity. I shall now leave the meeting that the subject may be discussed without embarrassment.

A lengthy discussion followed, concluding with a vote of confidence and appreciation, and a request that Dr. Roberts reconsider his resignation. Enough people had been "Robertized" to carry the day. The volcano subsided, but subterranean grumblings continued. RR never again felt entirely at ease at Sherbourne. Two years later, still conscious of the undercurrent of dissatisfaction, scrupulous to avoid offence and convinced, anyway, of the folly of such an arrangement even under the most auspicious circumstances, RR firmly rejected the suggestion of the Settlement Committee of presbytery to install either E. C. Knowles, his son-in-law, or W. H. H. Norman, his prospective son-in-law, as assistant at Sherbourne. "There is," he wrote, "a small (very small) but voluble element in the congregation that would take it as a text for grousing at me."

It would be interesting to know how far an element of personal pique was responsible for the sporadic recurrence of opposition. In 1928, RR's eldest daughter Peggy, who was Girls' Work Secretary at the Toronto YWCA, had felt called upon to resign, together with approximately 50 percent of the secretarial staff, because of a basic conflict over policy with the board of the "Y." The husbands of the board members were drawn into the fray. One was an office-bearer at Sherbourne. He conceived the idea that if Peggy could be detached from the main body, it would be an important breach in the united front. He came to RR to ask him to use his influence with his daughter. "I couldn't do that," said RR quietly. "In the first place, I've brought up my daughters to make their own decisions. In the second place, in this matter I entirely agree with Peggy." The gentleman concerned was one who was voluble in his "grouses," and he had some little following in the congregation.

In the years that followed it must have been difficult for grumblers to find anything to grumble about. The congregation was more than holding its own. In April 1932, RR wrote to his daughter Dorothy:

> The Board of Stewards reported on Tuesday that they expected to have $2000-$3000 to put back into the Endowment—which is pretty good in a bad year. The Sunday School is, I imagine, nearly doubled; and we have 250 boys and girls enrolled in groups and clubs on week days—and all of it, save in respect of about 30 girls, new work since last September. And still they come. It has been a fruitful year.

That kind of work cannot be done by the preacher and the professional church workers alone. It requires a band of eager and faithful volunteers. Though RR himself might discount it, what undoubtedly sustained those volunteers was the kind of preaching they were listening to Sunday by Sunday. Had he been inclined to apportion credit, he would have given a major part of it to Mrs. Mina McMaster, the deaconess. When, in 1942, long after he had left Sherbourne, Mrs. McMaster retired, he wrote in utter sincerity:

> Through the years I was in Toronto, Mrs. McMaster, deaconess of Sherbourne Church, was my faithful friend and fellow-worker, and I have said in another connection, it was she who, by her competency and wisdom, converted me from a prejudice against deaconesses. We had not been long in Toronto before she had become the valued and dear friend of every member of the family, and so she remains to this day. Her ready helpfulness to me in church matters relieved me of many anxieties. Her unfailing patience in difficult situations, her faithfulness to her normal duties, and her readiness to meet any call at any time—upon this I look back with deep thankfulness....No record of her work can be compiled because she is one of those rare people whose left hands do not know what their right hands are doing, and who act their religion rather than talk about it. Yet it was a deep religious life that was there to sustain her in her unwearying service.

In 1932, the five years which RR considered normal for his type of ministry were up. Some of those years had been stormy, but Sherbourne was in good shape and he could have left with a clear conscience. So it was not surprising that when the King's Weigh House in London approached him, he was attracted by the idea of a change. He was always afraid of "settling on his lees." When matters of principle were involved, RR would burn his bridges without caring for singed eyebrows. Here, however, the only question which must be canvassed was whether or not a change in pastorate would give him better opportunities for service in the kingdom of God.

W. E. Orchard, who had just resigned as minister of the King's Weigh House, was one of RR's oldest and closest friends. Orchard had not yet himself gone over to Rome, but he knew that he had gone too far along that road to retreat. As he saw it, when he did go over, some of the congregation would follow. Others who had been attracted only by his preaching, and not by his sacramental understandings and liturgical experiments, would drift back to their original nonconformist folds. Whoever followed him at the King's Weigh House would go to a broken church. All this Orchard confided to RR in various letters.

And RR had other doubts. He summed up the "cons" in a letter to daughter Gwen in the fall of 1932:

> I've had a letter from the King's Weigh House again in answer to the one you typed out. It is a series of comments on passages in that letter. The upshot of it was that they stuck to their guns on the question of a *change* in the sacramental elements, though they deprecated the word *trans*ubstantiation. But a doctrine that requires so much finessing with words seems to be a very unstable and precious affair. In any case, it all comes to the same thing: they want to believe that their Lord is *somehow* present in the elements after they have been consecrated, so that the sacrament can be "reserved" "for the sick and for the adoration." It requires a "will to believe" stronger than mine. I haven't written to them yet as a rather enigmatic cable came last week which might mean that there is another letter in the mail. I shall wait until the end of the week before I reply. Mam's opinion after reading the letter was more decisive than mine that it put an end to all possibility

of agreement. So there you are. Probably it is best so—though the prospect of a return to London was very attractive to us....

Once the uncertainties raised by this "curious episode in Congregational and Protestant history," as RR called it, were past, he returned thankfully to the task at hand. Indeed, in spite of "one or two people who would like a chance to bark," RR had much to be thankful for at Sherbourne. The bulk of the congregation loved him and supported him. When he received any honour they believed they also were honoured. The majority were glad to share him with the church at large, and, as we shall see in a later section of this book, they were generous in making provision for this sharing.

Within the activities of the church itself, the response of the congregation to his leadership made possible some momentous happenings. In October 1932, RR addressed a course of sermons to young people. He wrote to one of his daughters:

I think Mam enclosed a card of the course of sermons I am preaching—they are appearing in *The New Outlook*. They are making something of a stir—we had the largest night congregation for an ordinary Sunday that I have seen at Sherbourne. The congregation last night was 90% young men and women.

This series was followed through November and December by a forum. RR comments:

Last Sunday night was the first. It came off very well. When we came to the conference (which is held immediately after the sermon), John Line [1885–1970, professor of Systematic Theology at Emmanuel College] took it in hand: and he was superb. We were afraid that there might be demoralizing pauses and we had suborned three students to ask questions ...we had even supplied the answers. But they never got a chance. And when John Line saw the time was up there were still four people on their feet. It looks as though it is going to be a very successful experiment.

As the new year came in, further plans were afoot, this time in response to a visit to Toronto of the Oxford Group. RR wrote:

> There is no doubt that the whole episode has left us all challenged, and I think good may come of that. I wrote a letter to 150 men of the church, calling them to a meeting at the church last night, and about 75 came.

[When RR says "I wrote," he meant that literally: 90 of the letters were written with his own hand, and the rest he signed personally.]

> I put the matter up to them—Whatever we may think one way or another about the Oxford Group, it has put us in a position that we have to do something about it....We had a very good discussion; and four things emerged. First, they wanted an opportunity of fellowship in the spiritual life and asked for something like the renewal of the Class Meetings. That was agreed to; and yesterday morning they had their first meeting at 10 o'clock; over 40 men being present, led (by their own request) by Sir Joseph Flavelle, who had spoken rather impressively at the Wednesday meeting. Then a considerable number bound themselves to observe a daily period of prayer and meditation. There was a good deal of talk about our duty to go after other men to bring them into relation to God: and some of them felt a constraint to do that. And finally it was agreed to have a kind of evangelistic concentration through Lent—with a view to bringing men in. How much real drive there is in it remains to be seen; but it was quite heartening as far as it went.

Even at the start of the class meetings RR feared for their future, as "the old men are too garrulous." Sir Joseph Flavelle [1858–1939] later concurred. The group dwindled to a "dozen or 15 members, nearly all men well advanced in years, and with quite decided opinions, and religious experiences which...would not interest young folk if they were to attend." By then eighteen young men had left, asking for their own group. At the first Lenten meeting, 150 people gathered. The next week 250 came and stayed. RR wrote: "The spirit is fine on the whole—there are one or two flies in the ointment. But I think it will lead to a considerable deepening of the spiritual life of the Church."

22

Theologs, and "That Difficult Person, the Undergraduate"

The work at Sherbourne was exacting, and RR never skimped on his responsibilities to the local church. But the local church was for him no end in itself. It existed as part of, and to work for, the kingdom of God in the world. RR maintained that, as the representative of the local church, he had work to do outside its walls.

RR was always greatly attracted by the idea of academic work, of close association with theological students as their teacher. He had been disappointed when the way to the Pacific School of Religion had been barred in 1920, by the narrow views of some of its board members. The British Columbia proposal had hinged on the unlikely hope that the Board of Colleges of the United Church would, in those lean years, be able to find funds for a grant to establish a chair of systematics at Union College. The whole thing had been nebulous. Yet RR entertained these tentative and unofficial feelers seriously. That he was, at the time, feeling uneasy under the tensions at Sherbourne is without question. But it was the positive appeal of teaching theology that was the more potent influence. He had already had a taste of it in his first year in Toronto.

RR's correspondence with Dr. Pidgeon concerning Sherbourne had been quite frank. He was interested in Sherbourne, but he also mentioned that he would welcome an opportunity to teach were such an opening available. At that juncture the legal battle between the United and Presbyterian Churches over possession of the former Presbyterian colleges was unresolved. With future developments uncertain, neither of the United Church colleges in Toronto was in a position to offer a full-time appointment to an outside person. In the meantime, however, Knox College needed some temporary help. As soon as the call to Sherbourne was certain, Dr. Alfred Gandier [1861–1932], principal of Knox and already alerted by Dr. Pidgeon, invited RR to lecture in the department of systematic theology, beginning in January 1927. The subject matter, as Gandier wrote, was to be "Something along the line of the implication of the Christian Gospel in personal, social, and national life. . . ."

This appointment ran only through that winter and spring. With the cession of Knox College to the Presbyterians and the establishment of United [later Emmanuel] College as the sole United Church college in Toronto, RR's services were no longer needed. But in 1930, the chair of systematics at Emmanuel fell vacant. The first hope of the college of securing the services of Donald Baillie [1887–1954], a Scottish Presbyterian theologian who was prominent in the SCM and the Faith and Order Conferences, withered too late for an alternative full-time appointment to be made. Once again RR was called on to "pinch hit" with a course of lectures.

These were the lectures referred to in the report to the Sherbourne Official Board in 1931. In the meantime, the search for a full-time person was proceeding. Halfway through the year Dr. Bowles suggested to Dr. Gandier, now principal of Emmanuel, that there was a strong likelihood RR would be willing to resign from Sherbourne to take up the chair of systematics at Emmanuel. Possibly Bowles made this suggestion on his own initiative, because of his earlier conversations about the British Columbia possibility. It seems more likely, from the tone of Dr. Gandier's letter, that RR had made his position clear. But it was too late. In February 1931, Gandier wrote to RR:

> ...at once there came to me the vision of certain things you could do for our college and our men which few others could do.
>
> But ever since last spring when we were thinking of John Baillie's brother, a number of our men have had their minds set on securing the Rev. John MacLeod, M. A. of Kilcugan...and the chancellor and I both felt that under these circumstances you would not wish your name put up in competition with another upon whose appointment a number had already set their hearts. When, therefore, we conferred with the Council of Emmanuel College...your name was not mentioned....

I appreciate more than I can say what you are doing for our men, and wish we could have you devote all your great powers to help make [them] more effective preachers of the Evangel; but the way did not seem to open without a context which we felt was not in the interests of the college or anyone concerned.

In 1933, however, RR was again lecturing at Emmanuel. These lectures were on preaching, about which much of what RR had to say is still pertinent. The lectures begin with the nature of the preacher's overall task, and go on to expound upon the varying emphases a preacher should make:

Evangelism: You succeed in your preaching not when you win golden opinions about your preaching, but when it makes a difference in your people's lives.

Edification: We are destined for likeness to, and everlasting kinship with, the living Christ. That is what we ministers are called to promote through our ministry of edification; and after 45 years' experience with myself, and some 35 with congregations, I warn you that it is a slow and discouraging job.

Interpretation: But much that seems to be fog in St. Paul's mind is, at bottom, fog in our own minds....It is idle to expect that a Gospel expounded in the somewhat frayed ideology and imagery of the first century can come convincingly to 20th century man; and the task of the preacher is that of translating the life and experience of the primitive Christian into a familiar idiom of thought and speech.

Teaching: William James has a passage in a lecture to teachers warning against what he calls old-fogeyism. Unless a man guards himself against it, there comes over him, with the years, a certain increasing sluggishness of mental processes, a kind of hardening of the arteries of the mind which, besides making him inhospitable to novelty, indisposes him to mental activity: and he hints that the process may begin when a man is about 25. Take warning yourselves, gentlemen: and remember that most of your adult congregation have reached that unhappy condition. They will be unwilling to make any effort to follow an argument; and they demand to be spoon-fed, since they have become unable to swallow anything that they have to use their teeth upon. But that there are persons of this kind in your congregation does not absolve you from the duty of providing for those...whose minds have not gone out of business; and especially for the youth....

Prophecy: A Christian society is that which provides the conditions under which the individual is able to rise to the full human person it is in him to be. Consequently, a society which permits overcrowding, sweating, unsanitary industrial or domestic conditions, the exploitation of the public by private corporations in the matter of the necessities of life, which consents to a greatly inequitable distribution of wealth, in which the balance of justice is loaded on the side of the privileged classes—that society is in no sense a Christian society, and should not be allowed to suppose it is. And it should be brought home to individuals that they share the guilt of complicity in unjust and oppressive conditions of life if they do nothing to amend or change them....

The lectures conclude, characteristically, with a codicil on the preacher's instruments, the voice and the word. For the use of simple and apt words, and to enrich their own vocabulary, RR urged his students to use *Roget's Thesaurus*: "If you do not now own and use the book, but at my word go out and get it, you will remember me gratefully to the day of your death."

Lectures to the theological students were not RR's only contact with the university. Sherbourne was near enough to the campus that students naturally found their way there on a Sunday. And, as in Montreal, RR touched their lives not only in his preaching but in more intimate ways: counselling them in times of perplexity, and often providing financial aid through the generosity of individual members of Sherbourne Church.

From the time that RR reached Toronto the SCM laid their claim upon him, and he gladly responded to their requests for leadership of various kinds. The high point of this relationship was reached in the SCM Lenten Mission of 1933. This was the same year as the Lenten campaign at Sherbourne, the year in which RR in his letters repeatedly remarked upon the spiritual awareness and sensitiveness in the atmosphere.

The planning for the SCM mission impressed RR. There was a purposefulness about the students on the committee which was new in his experience. He wrote:

> By the way, the SCM committee was the most impressive SCM affair I've seen here at all. There were, I should say, 25–30 present; and they looked to me to be very fine persons and all of them very keen....The mission is mainly their own idea. It was time for something to happen. I'm getting rather full up for Lent; I have to preach for a week at midday services at Metropolitan; and Holy Week at Ottawa.
>
> It [the mission] begins on Monday; and things look pretty promising. There is a regular "heave" among the students just now. At Vic there has been a daily service this week—International Student Week—and the chapel has been packed yesterday and today....It looks as though we are nearing some kind of spiritual renewal. It is the same in the churches. On all hands one hears of movements of various kinds.

Dr. George Wrong [1860–1948], professor of history at the University of Toronto, wrote to thank RR for his part in the mission: "It is not easy to estimate results, but the crowd at your meetings and the interest shown did, I think, make it clear that you were reaching that very difficult person, the undergraduate. Few can do it, but you have the gift and the effect will be far-reaching."

23
To Serve His Church

The presbytery committee which studied the needs of downtown Toronto in 1931, was, through no fault of its members, a waste of time. Its plans did not come to fruition. Each of the local churches was too set on the preservation of its own entity. Each pursued its own path, to extinction in some cases, to belated amalgamation in others. This was a great disappointment to RR, for he felt that the time for piecemeal measures was already past; that concerted action and a radically new approach were called for.

There were other committees on which he served, however, which brought their work to a good conclusion. The *Hymnary* and the *Book of Common Order* of The United Church of Canada are the fruit of the work of the General Council's Committee on Church Worship and Ritual. The detailed work on these two books was in the hands of subcommittees. It was with the *Hymnary* that RR was chiefly concerned.

The *Hymnary* subcommittee met once every fortnight for four years, except in the summer months. The meetings, which began in the afternoon, often ran well into the evening. Moreover, the members had homework to do, including, in the later stages, proofreading. This rather mechanical task had compensations. RR took much delight in such memorable lines as, "I ask no dreams, no *profit* extasies."

RR never felt this task to be onerous. The preparation of a book of song for use in the worship of God was a work of joy. Moreover it was a notable body of men that sat together. It included in its number Alexander Macmillan, dean of Canadian hymnodists. RR counted friendship with Dr. Macmillan the crown of his fellowship with the group as a whole.

The subcommittee was composed of experts: experts in music,

experts in theology, experts in literature. Sometimes in the discussions the interests of fine music and good poetry threatened to override the tastes and needs of the person in the pew. Here, from his position as a pastor, RR could speak with authority. Many of the subcommittee looked askance at the old rouser, "Will your anchor hold in the storms of life...." RR defended it: "What are you going to say to the sailors and fishermen of our coasts if you throw it out?" A few weeks later he was vindicated by the roar from the throats of a congregation of landlubbers in central Ontario!

All of the traditional hymn books had made special provision for sailors and travellers by sea. Air travel had not yet become commonplace. But the new hymn book must move with the times and recognize the airman. RR was delegated to find out what was available. The hymn exchange in New York sent up half a dozen. He looked them over and found most of them disappointing. In fact, he decided he could do better himself: "I had the first two verses like that (snapping his fingers), but I had more trouble with the third. You see, I wanted it to be for more than military airmen." Finally the third verse came:

> By them bid fellowship increase,—
> O God in heaven, hear!—
> And speed the hour when wars shall cease
> And love shall cast out fear;
> Anoint them heralds of Thy peace
> To all men far and near!

The three verses completed, RR had a typed copy made which he slipped, unsigned, amongst the hymns he had received from New York. When the time came to consider the hymns, his must be considered with the others on its merits alone. The committee must not be embarrassed by its authorship. In the event RR's hymn was one of those chosen, and it was later included in an Australian hymnal.

While not so closely concerned with the preparation of the *Book of Common Order*, RR took a keen interest in it and was enthusiastic in his support. In his lectures on preaching he gave some advice on the ordering of public worship:

My own conviction is that the future lies with a form of service which is made up of both liturgical and non-liturgical elements. Its liturgical elements should not vary too much. Much of their power lies in the fact of their familiarity. I would especially plead that you procure and study the new Book of Order of the United Church, and indeed steep yourselves in it. The orders of service in that book give you the best possible guidance regarding the structure of the act of worship: and its wealth of devotional and liturgical content will make you rich in the best materials of public prayer.

A few years later he was writing to his son-in-law, the Rev. E. C. Knowles, who had recently been inducted into a new charge and was seeking to bring order to the worship services:

You are very wise in not making innovations too hurriedly: but you must not, on the other hand, be over deliberate. I would like to suggest...that one way of approach, especially with the communion services, is to get first your office-bearers, and then your people, to realize that the United Church has a liturgy of its own, which all congregations should use. It is one of my real disappointments that our congregations have been on the whole content to go on in the old slip-shod ways and have ignored the Book of Order so generally. I think that the communion service is too long—and in our use of it at Sherbourne we curtailed it. But it would be worth your while to study it and get your folk to study it too. After all it [the new charge] is a former Methodist church, and they have a tradition of liturgy; and since the UC has its own liturgy, it would at least be worth while considering its use.

"Should use" might be construed as meaning that the orders of worship in the *Book of Common Order* were obligatory. Had this been other than a private letter RR would have chosen his words more carefully. It is clear from what follows, especially the reference to the communion service at Sherbourne, that RR by no means intended that the orders should be followed slavishly and verbatim. They provided guidelines and patterns. The session might need a little education, but the final responsibility for the worship and its order in any

United Church congregation lay with that body.

RR was also a member of the Commission on Evangelism, which had been set up by the 1930 General Council. He was frequently out on its errands in neighbouring presbyteries, speaking at rallies and other meetings. In 1932, Dr. Pidgeon presented a request from the commission that Sherbourne should loan their minister to the Prairie Conferences. He wrote to the Sherbourne Official Board:

> It is impossible to tell you the strength that Dr. Roberts has been to us in the Commission and out among the Presbyteries. His counsel in the Commission has been instructive and inspiring. Then, wherever he has gone among the Presbyteries, he has lifted the whole level of the church's thought and brought new strength and inspiration. . . .

RR's reactions were mixed. He commented in a letter:

> The Commission on Evangelism and on the Social Order, which have been doing great work this year, want me to go out to speak and to lead discussions at two sessions in each Conference. It is not yet quite settled but it is likely. I don't want to go, as I hate railway travelling. But if people like Dr. Pidgeon, Mr. Rowell [Newton Wesley Rowell, 1867–1941, Chief Justice of Ontario], Sir Joseph, who are involved in the proposal—the latter is going to pay the piper—think I can render some service to the church and to the Kingdom of God, I suppose I will have to go. If I do I shall leave on Sunday night, May 22, and be away until June 5 or 6. I go first to Edmonton, then to Winnipeg, and then back to Saskatoon, and then home. British Columbia was originally included, but it holds its Conference far too early to be conveniently taken in.

When RR set off for the West in the spring of 1932, his name was already well known there. For two or three years his column "The Quiet Hour" had been appearing regularly in *The New Outlook*. These short pieces consisted of the sermons, in abbreviated form, he was preaching week by week in Sherbourne. There are still men and women, both lay and ministerial, who recall this column with gratitude. At the time he received a variety of communications thanking him, including a resolution of appreciation from the Presbytery of Dauphin, Manitoba. A typical individual reaction was this note from the Rev. A. Hinton of Montreal:

> Lest a good resolution should die at the hour of its birth, I am sitting down at an unearthly hour—considerably after midnight—to write a word of appreciation. I had just finished looking at *The New Outlook* preparatory to getting off to bed, and my last bit of reading in it had been the "Quiet Hour," when suddenly I realized that your particular column had done me good not once, nor twice. "Why not thank the Doctor!" said something within me. Hence this immediate carrying out of my resolution, lest the forgetfulness that might come with the awaking to tomorrow's cares rob you of knowing that your words have been medicine to the soul of a humble brother—sometimes tonic, not seldom purgative, always doing good.

It is not an exaggeration to say that "The Quiet Hour" had made the name of Richard Roberts a household word in the homes of United Church folk across Canada.

24
Further Afield: Psychiatric Clinic and Later Japan

Always eager to equip himself more adequately for his work RR was, in the fall of 1932, "going to school." He wrote:

> I began yesterday to attend the clinic at the Psychiatric hospital. It was very interesting and illuminating. I hope to attend every week this winter. The Psychiatry and Mental Hygiene people are very anxious for me to do so, as they say (rather flatteringly) that in the end they expect to learn more from me than I can learn from them. They are very nice modest people—no scientific swank or anything like that.

And again:

> It meets on Fridays, 3-5. It is very interesting but rather depressing in some ways. We have the patients in: and Dr. Farrar questions them. There has not been a case up so far— about 10 have been up, up to now—which I have not encountered in the course of my ministerial life—with some modifications as it were.

And several weeks later:

> My experience at the Psychiatric clinic and the reading of Lawrence have been a revelation of the harm a bad religion (I mean bad in the sense of conventionalized and secularized) will do—for it cramps where it should emancipate, and disintegrates where it should unify....

[The reference is to the *Letters of D. H. Lawrence* on which, on another occasion, RR made the following comment: "...in reacting against the religion of his boyhood (Lawrence) thought he was reacting against Christianity and Jesus Christ, but actually he was finding much of the real thing which conventional evangelicism overlaid."]

> This makes me still more certain that there should be courses in elementary psychiatry in theological colleges, not that ministers should practise psychiatry—but they should know when to send people, who come to them for help, to the psychiatrist.

Almost every summer, prior to World War II, the Fellowship of Christian Missionaries and Karuizawa Union Church would invite a preacher of repute to come to Japan for the month of August. He would preach at the regular services of the church, which was made up of missionaries of all kinds and varieties who took their summer holidays in Karuizawa. He would also be the keynote speaker at the meetings of the annual conference of the fellowship, which included missionaries from other summer resorts, for three days in August.

Neither of these groups had extensive funds, however. Persons accepting the invitation must find their own travel expenses. In RR's case it would also necessitate an extension of his regular summer holidays as, at a very minimum, travel to and from Japan in those days consumed a month. Nor was RR content with simply fulfilling his speaking engagements. He wanted, in the brief time available, to see as much as he could of the work of the church in Japan and specifically the work of the missionaries of The United Church of Canada. Furthermore, a visit to Japan without some direct contact with Kagawa was unthinkable. Toyohiko Kagawa [1888–1960] was a novelist, social worker, statesman, and evangelist. His reputation in North America was at its peak at that time, and RR had been in correspondence with him in connection with the Kagawa Co-operating Fellowship in Canada.

The Official Board of Sherbourne not only granted an extra fortnight of vacation, but with great generosity recommended that RR's travel expenses should be paid by the church. Sir Joseph Flavelle made it possible for Mrs. Roberts to accompany him.

The Roberts covered a great deal of territory in Japan that summer. RR had purchased a new set of glasses before leaving: "I wanted glasses that would enable me to see everything within sight...as I didn't want to miss anything that was to be seen this summer." He enjoyed every experience. The regular tourist sights which were reasonably within his path as he visited mission and church work, whether natural or man-made, excited his admiration. In Karuizawa the sight of Mt. Asama, with the smoke rising gently from the crater, offered a challenge. Soon a small party was gathered to make the night climb. RR recounts:

> Luckily it was a clear moonlit night—and we were up at the top sometime before four o'clock in the morning; and the moon was high in the heavens. The volcano was relatively quiescent so that we were able to look down into the crater. We could see the sizzling, panting, burning lava some 200 ft. below us. It was the likest thing I could think of to the hell of my childhood fears, especially as it sent up strong blasts of sulphur dioxide gas that almost took our breath away.

In fact, when the others of the party went a second time to the lip of the crater for a last look before the return trip to the foot of the mountain, RR excused himself.

On the complexity of the economic and political situation facing Japan, her limited natural resources, and the refusal of Canada, the United States, and Australia, to give her access to raw materials and markets or make room for her surplus population, RR made this comment: "...you give a much more cautious judgement on their Manchurian venture than you might at a distance....I confess I find the whole question very baffling." He continued:

> We have had a glorious time; and have seen and learned an enormous amount....We like the people and the country; and we have been much impressed on the whole with the missionary personnel here, especially our Canadian group, men and women. But there are some sad things here too in the missionary enterprise—there are 56 separate denominational groups trying to Christianize Japan! Many of them are small holiness and Pentecostal groups: but even in the Fellowship of Christian Missionaries, which consists

of recognized denominations, there are 32 separate units. If ever there was a need for Church Union, it's here.

The Japan trip did not end with his return to Toronto. Almost immediately RR began on a round of speaking engagements. By the end of November he had spoken on Japan in various places twenty-five times. And he was called in from time to time by the Mission Board for consultation. All this on top of his regular work, which included lecturing at Emmanuel. In January 1934, he went to speak at the North American Missionary Conference. In a letter RR wrote:

> The extra speaking I've had to do so far—the Japan meetings here [in Toronto and environs] and, on top of them, the American trip when I spoke about six times in three days (no one should be allowed by law to talk so much) has left me a little jaded and my vocal chords are tired.

This calls to mind an earlier occasion when, after speaking thirteen times in six days at Chatauqua he wrote: "I told them that there was not a man living either good enough or wise enough to be allowed to talk so much." But he went on doing it, especially during his years as moderator, until his physique rebelled.

25
RR, the Oxford Group, and Retreats

The Oxford Group made its first assault upon Toronto in December 1932. RR awaited its coming with guarded optimism. "I am sure the thing is only partially Christian, *i.e.* it specializes upon a small area within the evangelical tradition," he wrote. "But if it brings with it the breath of a new life, thank God." His reaction after the first meetings was favourable, though still guarded. In a letter to one of his daughters he wrote:

> Mam and I are frankly impressed but not converted. There is no doubt about the fine quality of life in the people that are here; they are singularly free from pose or swank....We do feel that there are some things about it which we ourselves must take more seriously than we have done—that is in a more practical way, even though we are not able to accept the whole corpus of their doctrine.

The letter continued with a discussion of the various aspects of the life of the Group. The emphasis on the "quiet hour" RR felt was wholly good. But "guidance" as practised by the Group, the jotting down of marching orders for the day at the end of the quiet time, he thought to be too subjective. There was a danger that an individual might mistake his or her own intentions for divine promptings. As RR explained:

> It seems to me not incredible that the subconscious may be so under the control of the Holy Spirit as to make this kind of guidance available, though I still think that one's own mental powers and moral insights, if these are dedicated to God, should have more share in the securing of Guidance.

"Sharing," as in the sharing of religious experience, RR saw as simply another name for "our old friend fellowship." This too he could accept, though he added a caveat that "it requires an almost superhuman sincerity if it is to be effectual." But for the indiscriminate confession of particular sins to the general public he had no use at all. On the contrary, he considered it dangerous. Of "life changing" he wrote:

> We all believe this in theory, but so far as practice is concerned we rarely deliberately go out to do it. We preachers are content to preach—to throw out the bait, hoping that a fish or two may bite. But these people go in for the sort of dip and fly fishing they do in the south of England: they aim the fly at a particular fish.
>
> Whatever else may be said of the movement, it must be studied with a good will and an open mind. We cannot allow ourselves to miss any breath of the Spirit that may be about in these needy days; and though we should try the spirits, it should not be in the light of our own prejudices and preconceptions.

After further experience with the Oxford Group, however, RR was forced to change his views quite radically. Two weeks later he was writing:

> There's not much besides in the way of news—except of course the great splash made by the Oxford Group.
>
> Splash it is—or was. My own feeling was, after the first contact, which was quite stimulating and impressive, one of continual disillusionment. I am not going to tell you the whole story here....But the whole business wound up in a flame of controversy. Creighton of *The New Outlook* published a startling attack....And the daily press took it up, and so the fat was in the fire. Pidgeon got a few people together to see whether we could agree upon a statement which would put the good side—and I agreed to join in, provided there was a specific statement inserted that some of the signatories had important reservations. But when the letter was produced I refused to sign it. It gave the Oxford Group too clean a bill of

health. That statement was for *The New Outlook*. Then Sclater and Trevor Davies started another statement for the daily press, and I refused to sign that on the same ground. Not that I agree with Creighton. It seems to me to be a good idea gone wrong. The theory, except at two or three points, seems to me sound; but the technique is open to a lot of criticism. [William Black Creighton, 1864–1946, was editor of *The New Outlook*, 1925–1937. John Robert Patterson Sclater, 1876–1949, was minister of St. Andrew's, Toronto, and later Moderator of the United Church, 1942–1944; Trevor Davies was minister of Timothy Eaton Memorial Church, Toronto, 1925–1934].

The atmosphere in which the group lives is too hot-housey. They seem never to get away into any healthy secularity: and so they live too much up against themselves and one another, and lose their perspective. One of their leaders seemed to me to have developed a palpable psychosis—and he was obsessed with the sex business; of which there was far too much in the ministers' meetings....There was a reception at Mrs. Dunlap's which Mam and I went to: but it was not edifying to us....It was very much a repetition of what we had heard before— jokes and all: and there was there, as elsewhere, a good deal of what I heard called "premeditated spontaneity."...[The] group had come to constitute themselves a sort of unconscious *claque*, which exploded synchronously and explosively at every joke, as though they had never heard it before. Ah well— that's that. A good many people seem to have been helped. But I fear the net result is a debit.

By January 1933, RR's disillusionment with the Group was almost complete. He wrote:

The visit of the Group gave us a jolt; and it has shown us that if we do not accept it we should find an alternative....Mam's encounters with members of the group were, I must say, rather disillusioning, and so were mine after the beginning. And we are both very disappointed as we had hoped that it might be the breath of God. But it wasn't. Or at least there was so much human breath about that the breath of God didn't get a chance.

Two of the alternatives which resulted from "the jolt" were the Lenten groups at Sherbourne and the Lenten mission at the University of Toronto. RR was always scrupulous to admit this. In an article published in *The Christian Century* he gave all due credit to the Group where he honestly could, while criticizing its excesses in more generalized and measured tones than appear in these extracts from letters to his family.

The Group continued to return to Toronto periodically, and some who had been caught in its coils continued to be its vociferous advocates. There were occasional repercussions. In June 1933, RR wrote:

> It's Conference week. I preach the conference sermon tomorrow morning...It's a snorter as Pat Sclater would say....We had "Ministerial Sharing" on Tuesday afternoon. I'd promised to speak about our Lenten groups—but some of the Oxford Group were so puffed up that I saw red—and rather than speak then, I left and declined to return. But I got it off my chest yesterday afternoon, in a very calm and impressive style, "The just word, the clean phrase, and no frills!" I finished up by bidding them, by the mercies of God, to preserve a sense of proportion. You'd suppose no one had ever been converted before last December....

The fuss eventually died down, but references to the Oxford Group still occasionally appeared in RR's correspondence. In September 1936, he wrote:

> I saw F. the other day, looking very well, and he is coming to see me. But I hope he won't talk O. G. For on that subject I am like Jeremiah, "I am full of the fury of the Lord, I am weary with holding it in." Buchman's admiration for Hitler because he has built the first line of defence against Communism, and all this blether of a "God-controlled Hitler" solving all problems over night, shows the man to be an unilluminated ass...You see, I'm gathering momentum already! The Gospel we want today is not the "Dictatorship of God"— Buchman's phrase (as though God were like Mussolini), but a synthesis of Karl Barth's emphasis on Revelation with John MacMurray's emphasis on Community. It's all in First

Corinthians really. I'm going to try to do it. I have four lectures to preachers to deliver in January—and I'm going to call them "The Christian Manifesto."

If the breath of the spirit was not to be found in the vapourings of the Oxford Group, it was moving in other places. Both the promise and failure of the Oxford Group led other organizations and individuals to take a long look at their religious life. RR's letters at this time were full of hope because of a spiritual sensitiveness that seemed to be in the atmosphere.

The Kagawa Co-operating Committee had been formed sometime in 1931 or 1932. It was an inter-denominational group initiated with a view to promoting in the life of the Canadian churches the ideals for which Kagawa stood. In the fall of 1933, this group examined its life and found it wanting. They took action. And the result was the beginning of a new type of activity for RR. In October 1933, he wrote: "On Monday some 30 of us are going up to Muskoka for a real retreat. They have asked me to direct it." A week later he reported:

This last week I joined some 30 ministers in a "retreat"—the real thing, not one of the usual talk fests. It was of course new country for me; but everything worked out all right and we had a very profitable experience...There was no speech-making or discussions on making sermons and programmes for Y. P. work or any of the dreary "shop" which ministers talk when they get together.

In another letter RR further described the event:

We were there for the best part of three days...and it was a very memorable and moving time. I put them under discipline in the matter of hours—we had times set apart for private self-examination, solitary meditation, and corporate intercession—and intervals of quiet and intimate conversation on the inner life and especially the meaning of our Lord's Temptation and the Cross to us as ministers and men. It was extraordinary how easily the men fell into the plan; and there wasn't one who didn't thank God he'd come.

This was the first of a number of inter-denominational retreats in which RR took part over the next few years. And there were similar sessions within the United Church. In January 1934, RR wrote:

This week we are holding a spiritual retreat for about 100 ministers, all day Tuesday...—and I am sorry to say I have to direct it. I'd much rather be directed than directing. One gets so concerned with the *chores* of the affair that one misses a good deal of the affair itself.

In March he joined George Pidgeon in Montreal for a mission planned and organized by the Layman's Association. Separate meetings were held for laymen and ministers, at noon and in the evening, and carried through from Monday to Thursday. On Friday there was a one-day retreat for the ministers. RR reported: "I don't think we had a single flop during the whole business: and the laymen are very pleased with their experiment."

These retreats were in no sense a withdrawal from life into the quiet paths of pietism. RR wrote:

Have you read any of her [Evelyn Underhill's] things? They are actually very good. My conviction is that the next movement in the religious life is going to be a strong return to the systematic culture of the inner life combined with an equally strong stress on social action. These retreats for ministers we have been having are having a very considerable response; but alongside and even within them, there is a very definite realization of responsibility for the creation of a Christian social order. Evelyn Underhill is quite clear in her recognition of the need of this combination; but her particular line is the inner life; and I think she is probably the best writer on this subject in English today [Evelyn Underhill, 1875–1941, religious writer and pacifist, published her best-known book, *Mysticism* in 1911].

RR himself, while deeply concerned and active in organizing and directing the retreats, was at the same time active in the social sphere. In March 1934, he wrote:

Perhaps the most interesting thing that is going on now is the General Council's Commission on a Christian Social Order. It was my idea—at the last General Council; and it looks as though it is going to bring in a grand report. Last night we had quite a thrilling meeting—we had two unemployed men—leaders in the Labour Union Movement but also members of the church—and we had Mr. Rundle there—he was very fine: and it all looks as though we might get a pretty radical report across. Sir Robert Falconer [1867–1943, president of the University of Toronto] is the chairman: and he's travelled a long way to the left since we began: and I expect that the final drafting will be left to him and me.

The commission dealt with all manner of issues: prices, labour codes, and standards in business. RR was greatly cheered that just at this time, H. H. Stevens, Minister of Commerce, was active in Parliament on these very matters, and from an apparently Christian standpoint. "What will come of this ferment, I cannot tell, " RR wrote; "but it is all very interesting and I think hopeful."

But RR was convinced that the right social action could come only if a person was in right relation to God. For this reason he saw the retreats as basic. Soon he was to become moderator of The United Church of Canada. Travelling from Halifax to Vancouver on evangelistic missions, he made a retreat for ministers an essential part of his itinerary in each place where he stopped.

Part V

"All my trust in Thee is found"

———

26
Moderator

As early as the summer of 1932, there had been a fairly strong movement within the United Church to nominate RR for the office of moderator. Coming as it did when he was in the midst of his discussions with the King's Weigh House, however, and when he was wondering about the future of his ministry at Sherbourne, RR found the suggestion disturbing. Yet he could see no way of withdrawing his name without appearing churlish to those who were pressing his nomination. He was greatly relieved when the issue was settled otherwise. On 24 October he wrote:

> ...Moore got the Moderatorship...I hadn't realized how much the affair had worried me until the result was declared. A great relaxation came over my whole body, and it looked to me just then the best of all possible worlds. Moore did well in the chair; he surprised me again and again by his aptness and by his spiritual resourcefulness. I was on my feet a good deal at the Council. I gave two devotional addresses....I spoke on the Foreign Mission report—and what I said led to the Council solemnly rededicating itself in prayer to the F. M. [Foreign Missions] enterprise. I presented the Report of the Committee on Church Worship and Ritual and the Report of the Committee on Peace and Disarmament.

Back in Toronto RR settled down gratefully to the work at Sherbourne and to his many other activities. In 1934, those who had come to look to RR for leadership began early to prepare their campaign to have him elected moderator. Throughout the spring it became obvious that there was general support throughout the Western Conferences. In June this support was echoed in Atlantic Canada as well. RR had been asked to speak at the Maritime Conference, and reported on 9 June what happened there:

> There was one amusing and embarrassing incident....I had finished the last address—and the President and another man had handed out some bouquets: and when I thought it was all over and got up to go Campbell Wadsworth mounted the rostrum and nominated me for the Moderatorship! I was staggered for a moment—but remembered that I had to catch a train—and fled. I do not know to this hour what the result was! I heard some cheers on my way out—so I gathered there was some approbation.

A week later, on 16 June, he reported further:

> The Moderatorship situation is pretty much as it was, save only that I understand that McGregor of London's name will be proposed in the Council. I am not quite happy about that as he is a man I like very much, and a very good man. But there's been such a spate of nominations of me that I don't see how I can draw out now....Meantime, I'm going to forget it for a couple of months. Sufficient for the day is the evil thereof.

On that note RR left for holidays in England. There he had a number of preaching engagements and, of course, there were old friends to visit. But he could not quite forget about the moderatorship. After enumerating a list of personal and professional engagements, his letter continued:

> But that isn't all....Before we left I had instructions to find someone whom we might invite to become my colleague in the event of my being elected to the moderatorship. On the very day I left Toronto I picked up a book in the Book Room called "The Finger of God." It is the story of a movement of Group Evangelism here in England, chiefly within the Methodist Church. Its leaders are a Methodist minister, Frank Raynor, and a layman named Peter Fletcher. I had had some fragmentary information about it. But I was very impressed

by the book....On the trip across it grew on me that it would be a fine thing to make Sherbourne the base of a strong Evangelistic movement by getting Raynor as my colleague. Well, to make a long story short—it involved a lot of interviews—the upshot is that both Raynor and Fletcher are coming to Canada. They work together as a unit and Raynor did not feel he could come without Fletcher. I had to decide very summarily as I had to get Raynor released by the Methodist Conference, and I had to get my request in by last Monday morning....

But please do not write about this yet to anyone in Canada. It must not be known there until after General Council.

In September RR was back in the pulpit at Sherbourne and engaged in getting the work of the congregation going again after the summer vacation. But on 12 September 1934, the General Council of The United Church of Canada, meeting in Kingston, Ontario, elected RR moderator. The entire pattern of his life changed. Dr. T. Albert Moore had told him he would not need to be away from Sherbourne for more than four months of the year. This was hardly borne out. Even when he was in Toronto, although he was not technically "away from Sherbourne," the chores of the central office of the church took a great deal of his time. As the chief representative of the United Church he had to attend a variety of functions: local, national, and ecclesiastical. These brought compensations, but they were time-consuming. The core of his work as moderator was, however, his missions to the church. Few moderators of The United Church of Canada have visited the church so widely and systematically as did RR. He gave himself with an unstinting recklessness that took a heavy toll of his physical strength.

For the two years of his moderatorship there is much in RR's letters about the chores of the office, which he liked but little, and the joys of his evangelistic missions. Other sources may provide a more objective record of his term. His letters to his daughters, however, provide a glimpse of his own view of the church and its response to him. It is a personal, family view. When he speaks, for instance, of moderatorial encyclicals and communiqués, he is not carried away by the sense of his own importance. Far from it; he expected his daughters to add the necessary seasoning of laughter—

the sort of laughter contained in the following story of his relationship with the Monsignor of the Diocese of St. Johns:

> He and I travelled together on one of the Furness Boats when I returned to England from Newfoundland during my moderatorship. We ate together and became good friends. He told me, "Roberts, if you were with us we should have made you a bishop." And I replied, "That wouldn't have been good enough for me. I'd want to be Pope!" He went off into hoots of laughter.

The letters begin on 15 September. RR wrote:

> It's very late on Saturday night, and I'm just dropping you this line to say that everything is going all right....The affair went off very happily. The voting was 170 for me and 80 for D. C. McGregor of London—that is in round numbers....There were no speeches, only nominations. They made the election unanimous on the motion of D. C. McGregor.

A week later, on 21 September he wrote en route from Kingston on the CPR:

> Mam, however, was the pick of the piece. Everybody fell in love with her and they would come to me and say admiring things about her. She really was a grand asset for me—and she was at her best in every way. I was awfully glad that she was with me, and in lots of ways she helped me very much.
> I got on in the chair a great deal better than I feared I would. I kept my head pretty well and only made two or three misprints. [RR confessed elsewhere that *The Manual* was not his favourite reading!] But I had T. Albert Moore at my elbow [the Secretary of the General Council] and he was a great resource. If I am to believe what the people say, I seem even to have come through with some credit.

On 29 September he wrote:

Everybody has been as kind as possible over the Moderatorship. We have had heaps of letters and telegrams from all sorts of people and places. The Sherbourne people have been fine. There was a reception on Wednesday evening—the best of its kind, apparently, within memory. Sir William Hearst [1864–1941, Premier of Ontario] was in the chair and made a first-class speech. And they have taken my Raynor and Fletcher proposals in the finest spirit possible. Mam came in for a bouquet also, a real one and some verbal ones as well. It was a double-decker affair—Lewis [then Associate Minister] and his wife—they were married in August, were also being fêted. Altogether "a good time seems to have been had by all."

During RR's Montreal days, articles in the *McGill Daily*, describing meetings and functions of all sorts, almost always ended with "A good time was had by all," and the phrase became currency in family exchanges.

From the first, the pace for the new moderator was hectic.

My moderatorial campaign begins in November, Montreal on the 4th for two days, then London, Ont., a mission of five days beginning on the 11th, the same thing in Ottawa, on the 19th and the last in Hamilton beginning on the 25th. It is probable I shall be at home all December—then with the New Year, I shall go to places like Peterborough, Cornwall, Sherbrooke, St. Catherine's [*sic*]: and then a little spell at home, and March and half April probably out West. That at any rate is how it looks at the moment. I shall be able to get a couple of days' rest between each mission. We shall try to get in the ministers and some lay folk from the surrounding countryside into all these places—and try to propagate a new vitality in that way. There is a spirit of expectancy in the air here—and we are hoping for a great quickening.

Getting into the swing of the work as moderator, and carrying on the load at Sherbourne, for Raynor and Fletcher had not yet arrived, made heavy going. RR felt the need of both physical and spiritual recreation, as he wrote on 6 October:

Vernon Hearst [an office-bearer at Sherbourne] and I skipped out on Thursday morning for a couple of days in the North. We went to Burleigh Falls and fished for muskellunge and bass, but got nothing save a few contemptible perch. I've had bad luck with fish this year. But we had a fine time otherwise. The spot is beautiful and the trees were on the turn—they are rather late this year. It was a pleasant break—as I had been very tied down since the General Council. On Monday I am going to the second Ministers' Retreat at Muskoka Beach....

There looks to be a promise of something of a revival. The expectation is in the air. But I'm confining my mission to church members. Raynor and Fletcher are sailing from Southampton on October 20, and will be here for Sunday, October 28: and they will begin their mission then. Pidgeon and I are trying our level best to get the Oxford Group business merged into a more thorough and solid Canadian Enterprise....He is getting the ministers who have been prominent in the O. G. to come into the bigger effort. The Sherbourne people have been very fine about the whole moderator business: and there seems already to be a real quickening in the congregation.

As he moved about the church throughout Canada, RR discovered the same "quickening" everywhere. On 9 December he wrote:

The three missions I have had have been quite astonishing. The expectancy and the response was quite extraordinary....The last one at Hamilton was packed full with young men and women from all over the conference. I had prepared a sort of card for the missions with a formula of decision on one side and a formula of reconsecration on the other. After the sermon I told them that, while we were singing a hymn, I would come down from the pulpit and stand in front of it: and any who desired to signalize either purpose I invited to come and take a card from me. I had done that at the other two places: and in that way I had exhausted about half of the 500 cards which I had had printed. But at Hamilton they came neither by ones nor in single file, they seemed to come in battalions. The cards were exhausted—and still they came. The Bishop of Niagara had come to the service and had said a word of greeting at the start. He was behind me on the platform while this was going on—but those who were near him told me that the tears were running down his face at the sight.

Then another great moment was at the Communion Service on the Thursday night. We had had a ministers' retreat from 9 A.M. to 5: and it was very good: no speechifying at all but only self-examination, meditation, and intercession. From 4 to 5 there was to be a sort of fellowship meeting, and from 4 to 4:30 I left them alone—I wanted a little rest. When I got back they had resolved to ask to come together to the altar rail to make a reconsecration of themselves to Jesus Christ. So we arranged it: and it was a tremendous moment—some 80 ministers on their knees repeating after me the dedicatory clauses at the end of the Eucharistic prayer in the Book of Order. There's no doubt that the Spirit of God is abroad in the land...and if we are able for it, there's a great harvest to be reaped.

On 18 December RR wrote: "So far Fletcher and Raynor have not made a very heavy dent in Sherbourne—but they seem to have made some impression in other places." The Raynor-Fletcher arrangement proved, in the end, a disappointment. They seemed to have remained "alien" in the Canadian atmosphere. Nor did they give Sherbourne the kind of leadership it required during RR's frequent absences. At the end of their covenanted year they returned to England and Sherbourne made other arrangements. When RR was in Toronto he preached at Sherbourne as a matter of course.

At the end of the year a new suffragan bishop of Toronto was appointed, and the moderator was invited to the consecration. RR recounts what transpired in a letter of 29 December:

On Thursday Mam and I went...to the consecration of the new Bishop Suffragan of Toronto. We were in a place of honour—the third seat from the front; and with us were the Moderator of the Presbyterian Church and the President of the Baptist Union of Ontario. It was all very impressive—and the Archbishop (Derwyn Owen) [1876–1947, Archbishop of Toronto and Primate of All Canada] conducted the service beautifully. His voice and intonation are very Welsh—and Mam and I chuckled a bit over it. The fly in the ointment was a monster—a long dreary stretch of commonplace called a sermon, by _____. But there was one interesting thing [that] happened. At the end of the service there was a communion, but only taken by the bishops and clergy in the chancel. I made up my mind that if anyone went up from the nave, I would go too. When the people in the chancel had all communicated, some officer approached the front pew in which the new bishop's wife and sons were sitting—and they went up to the altar. Then the official came to the end of our pew...evidently intending that the three non-Anglican representatives should go up. The Baptist and the Presbyterian were rather dithered: so I just stepped out past them and went up to the altar and took communion from two bishops! It has created quite a bit of interest—(the other men presently followed me) but chiefly what is interesting is that evidently the Archbishop had intended the officer to invite us to go up. There's no doubt that we and the Anglicans are drawing very close together....

Early in 1935, on 5 January, RR wrote:

Last week was comparatively quiet with us. I was down at the Moderator's office most days, but nothing much beside. On Thursday night we went to an entertainment at the Arts and Letters Club and saw a little Russian play "Michael," corkingly done by local talent....But apart from that we've stayed pretty much at home. This coming week is going to be fairly quiet too—but there is a Symphony Orchestra Concert on Tuesday to which we hope to go, my first this season. The week after that I take the road. First comes Ottawa—two days—the opening of Parliament and some functions at Government House....

In almost all of RR's letters there are references to such things as the Arts and Letters Club or the symphony—or, in season, fishing. When he went fishing he wore a bright red flannel shirt. This shirt was his pride and joy. He loved colour, but normally was very conservative in his dress. "When I want to stand for something," he used to say, "I don't want to be dismissed as the fellow who wears the funny ties." On one occasion as chaplain of the Arts and Letters Club he was, to his great delight, dressed up in a friar's robe to intone the blessing in Latin. He relished these moments of recreation; indeed, he believed that a little "healthy secularity" was a *sine qua non* of the sane and robust religious life.

He was concerned, too, for the impression which the United Church gave of itself, as evidenced in this letter written on 12 January 1935:

> We had [David] Croll, the new Ontario Minister of Welfare, in the other night. There was a row some little time ago in the course of which George Little called Croll a "Border City Russian Jew"...and I ticked off Little in a moderatorial communiqué to the press and sent a copy...to Croll, who took it very kindly and wrote me a very excellent letter. The final upshot was that he wanted to come in for a yarn: and he came on Wednesday and stayed for two and a half hours. He is a particularly fine sort of person, we think; with all the right sort of ideas for his job....
>
> Just now we are in the throes of getting in the last of the M and M [Missionary and Maintenance] money for the year. A week or so ago we were still 5% behind last year at the same date: but we are down only 3% today, and Peter Bryce [Treasurer of the United Church; Moderator of the United Church, 1936–1937] thinks that by next Wednesday we shall be on the level; and we are in good hope of getting the 5% more than last year which we are anxious to get....I wrote an encyclical to the Churches which was read last Sunday in many places and will be read in the rest tomorrow—and that has stirred up things very materially, so Peter Bryce tells me.

This was the first of several references to the financial situation of the church RR made in his weekly letters. As he became more familiar with the mechanics of the business, he became convinced that the economic state of the country was only partly responsible for the retrenchments which had been necessary. But the church, like everybody else, was feeling the effects of the Depression.

Of the political response to the country's problems RR also had something to say. The Conservatives were in power, and had been standing pat on the policy of leaving the economic hot potato in provincial hands. But the provinces, under the constitution, were powerless to effect anything but palliative measures. J. S. Woodsworth and the CCF that he had founded in 1932, had been pressing for national action. In the US the government had launched a wide-scale attack on several fronts. In this climate, Prime Minister, R. B. Bennett, was suddenly converted to a reform program consisting of social security legislation, labour statutes, and economic reform measures. This about face came as a surprise to friend and foe alike, but RR was always ready to give any person the benefit of the doubt. He wrote:

> Bennett is, I believe, very sincere and much in earnest about his reforms; and he has a surprise packet every few days. But I don't trust his party too much. So far they are swallowing it all without too wry faces, but how long it will be before there is a bolt I cannot tell. But I do not think that it will be all plain sailing for long. The Liberals are just footling: Woodsworth and his band have nothing to say but "how inadequate it all is!" I can't understand Woodsworth. If a man is going my way and is going even half way, I'm going along with him, especially if he is going to run the bus himself and at his own expense. Woodsworth is professedly a gradualist; and why he does not see that property is only having control of things, and that when you begin to check the control of the capitalist you are expropriating him, *i.e.* you are depriving him of a measure of the very essence of ownership which is control. I'm getting so exasperated with the whole lot that one of these days I will break out!

Later, on 26 January, RR reported on his trip to Ottawa:

> The great event "o'er-shadowing all"...was the visit to Ottawa.
> We got there on Tuesday evening and stayed at the Chateau

Laurier, where our night's rest was spoilt by noisy and probably drunken neighbours. The items on the programme were (after a ministerial association dinner at which I heard H. H. Stevens on Price Spreads, etc.—a very excellent and sincere presentation):

7:45...State Dinner at Rideau Hall (only me)

9:15...Reception at Rideau Hall.

I went to the dinner and sat next to Arthur Meighen and had a good time with him....The dinner didn't last long—there were no speeches. But what was, as P. G. Wodehouse would say "g and wormwood" to me, was the disproportionate number of military sticks in uniform. After the dinner the ladies came in, and Mam was the most stunning one of the lot....The greatest sight there, in its way, was R. B. Bennett in his Windsor uniform....You could almost see his tumtum wobble as he walked! But R. B. B. is all right all the same. I congratulated him on his fine leadership in the new social programme; and a far-away look came into his eye and he began to declaim there and then like an Old Testament prophet. We talked to a number of people but have no very vivid recollection of them. We enjoyed it—but it would be rather cloying as a steady diet.

The opening of Parliament the next day was also an interesting affair....Once more an excessive military show: all very straight and solemn and pompy. Then there was a real sight, Bessborough [the Governor General, 1931–1935] and his lady coming up the floor of the house. He is a well set up man, and she a beautiful woman, and she had a lovely dress with a long train carried by two pages. They walked hand in hand—their arms making a kind of arch: and I tell you, it was a sight for the gods. All silly, if you like; but those two people made one respect one's own physical human being. Then came equerries and aides and what-nots in uniform. The reading of the speech from the throne with its long catalogue of reforms—both in English and French, was quite impressive, though it took a long time. The Commons were there, crowded behind the bar of the Senate in imitation of the British practice. I found the Commons rather a depressing lot; there were a few distinguished faces among them, but the majority were appallingly ordinary. I wonder whether democracy is inevitably doomed to eternal mediocrity.

The procession went out as it came in....But there were two amusing touches. R. B. B. again going out with [Arthur] Meighen, who is the leader of the Senate [he had been Prime Minister, 1920–1921]—Meighen looking quite up to the knocker in his Windsor suit, a fine figure: and by his side R. B. B.'s disproportionate tummy showing out monstrously. The other was of a different kind. When all the cavalcade was passed—then the Judges of the Supreme Court came off the woolsack. The whole five were small men, especially in contrast to the military johnnies—they wore their red robes with ermine, and they looked like a set of marionettes—and they just waddled out of the house together. It was as though a bit of Gilbert and Sullivan had been introduced into the performance, a sort of comic relief at the end.

After Ottawa, RR went on to Kingston for a mission. He was home for two Sundays and then travelled around Ontario for the month of February. On 2 March he wrote:

I've not had much chance of letter-writing for the last two or three weeks. I have been very much on the move. I've been to North Bay, Sudbury, Sault Ste. Marie, Kingston, Morrisburg, and Oshawa—from where I returned home Thursday night. I was to have gone off today to Peterborough but I cancelled my mission there as they have been playing ducks and drakes with my plans. I send my plans ahead to these places; but they were shot to pieces in Peterborough in order to satisfy some local jealousies. So I'm home now for a couple of weeks. After that I still have to go to Owen Sound and Windsor. Then a week at Buffalo—midday Lenten services at the Cathedral there. And after that I'm done for the time being.

The missions have gone very well as a whole. Some have been better than others: and they have gone best where they have been best prepared for....Mam is pulling out of the weakness which followed the influenza. But I think that she has still to go slow for a bit. I'm all right. I was a little tired yesterday but I'm all right today. Tomorrow morning I preach at Sherbourne. On Tuesday evening there is to be a big meeting, a "Service of Witness" at the Maple Leaf Gardens, where we expect to have some 16,000 people present. All the churches are represented: and I am the sole speaker. I'm rather appalled at the idea—and haven't yet got any sort of address ready. There is no doubt that there is a spiritual movement going on here...but whether this sort of big meeting is the way to foster it, I am not sure.

Two weeks later, on 15 March, he wrote:

Mam wrote to you earlier in the week giving you the story of the big meeting. There are still some reverberations of it— and I think the total effect has been good. You will find the text of my piece in *The New Outlook*....It was a curious experience to speak in that place. The sound amplifiers were very good: but they give the voice a hollow metallic sound. And it took me some time to get accustomed to the echo of my own voice repeating my words a fraction of a second after I had spoken them. It was as though some funny man in the rafters was mimicking me! I shall have to go through it all again on June 10th. But I haven't a ghost of an idea what I am going to say then.

In the spring RR went, as moderator, to Great Britain, to attend various church assemblies. RR counted it an honour that he was invited to preach in Alexander Whyte's old pulpit while the Assembly of the Church of Scotland was in session. Whyte had been minister of St. George's Free Church, 1870–1916, and principal of New College, Edinburgh, 1909–1918. He planned to go early in August to attend the continuation committee of the Lausanne Conference which was meeting in Denmark, and thence to Switzerland to the Council of International Friendship of the World Council of Churches. En route from Denmark to Switzerland he hoped to meet with Adolf Deissman and Karl Barth and some other Christian leaders in Germany. Diessmann (1866–1937) was professor of New Testament at Berlin and a prominent ecumenist, having collaborated with G. K. A. Bell in a collection of papers by British and German scholars on Christology, *Mysterium Christi*. Barth (1886–1968) was professor of theology at Basle in Switzerland and with Paul Tillich was the greatest influence on the development of Protestant theology in the twentieth century. But before RR could leave Canada there was a great deal to be done. On 30 March he wrote:

> There have not been many happenings out of the common that I can now think of. We have had a lot of business at the office of one sort and another. The King Gordon business still smoulders, and I think that there may be a show-down at the Executive which meets on the 23rd.

The King Gordon affair was a curious mixture of principles, purses, and personalities. Gordon was a very vocal radical, one of the founders of the Fellowship for a Christian Social Order, and heartily disliked by a group of Montreal businessmen with an "armchair habit of body and a banknote habit of mind." On the grounds of economy, and under cover of a General Council order to reduce the staff of the United Theological College staff by one, the board of governors summarily dismissed King Gordon in 1933. Many of the ministers of the presbytery, particularly the younger ones, rushed to his defence on the grounds of academic freedom. A committee was formed and twelve hundred dollars raised, in small sums from all over the province, to pay his salary for one year. It is interesting to note that several members of the board of governors dissented from its action to the extent of contributing to the fund.

From the beginning RR had defended Gordon. In fact, he played some little part in persuading the executive of General Council to refuse to confirm the dismissal. When the General Council of 1934, requested that Gordon be re-established as a lecturer for two years, the board of governors refused. So the trouble lingered on. The matter was only settled when Gordon took up work elsewhere.

The letter continues:

> We have been appointing commissions for this, that and the other—Secondary Schools, Theological Colleges, the General Secretaryship, the Settlement of Ministers—and starting some of them going. It is all very interesting and I think things are hopeful. There's the usual number just now of calls and exchanges and so forth. But there is also, alas, a lot of wire-

pulling and playing politics. At the first meeting of the Committee on the Settlement of Ministers the lay members, with one consent, proposed that the question of setting up ethical codes respecting the conduct of ministers and congregations in the matter of calls, etc. be seriously discussed. That is obviously all to the good. The kind of thing that is going on in some quarters just now is thoroughly de-spiritualizing.

There was no let up of committee meetings and other obligations. RR opened a letter written in April with a long list of meetings at the head office and activities at Sherbourne at which he would have to be present. He then continued:

> I hope that there will be no unexpected additions to the list already on hand. But I can never tell. When I came in from the Retreat this afternoon [a retreat for young people held at Bloor Street Church] there were three men from Peterborough waiting to see me—there's a mess about a settlement there. Mam had been entertaining them for an hour before I came in. Incidentally, the settlement of ministers business is really an unholy mess this year. It gets worse all the time. We have, however, a very good committee, or rather a commission, which is already working on it—and I am hopeful about that. And there are other hopeful developments too. The other night I orated to the Board of Christian Education about their lack of a philosophy of Education and urged them to set about it with enough effect to move them to request the appointment of a commission to draw out a statement on Education, of the same calibre as that on the Social Order—which, by the way, has been a great success from an educational point of view in the church.

At last, due to sail from Montreal on 27 April, RR completed some unfinished business, reporting in a letter written the day before:

> Mam left last night and I go tonight. I've had a whole day on "Transfers"—shifting men from one Conference to another—

a tedious and sometimes difficult and unpleasant job. It comes on top of the Judicial Committee all day Tuesday, the Executive all day Wednesday and Thursday—and I am a bit "caved in" tonight. I am looking forward to Sunday morning, when I shall wake up with the grand and glorious feeling of having not one darned thing to do all day.

In the middle of his European trip RR had to leave his wife in England and return to Canada to be present at the Tenth Anniversary Celebration of the Consummation of Church Union at the Maple Leaf Gardens on 10 June. He wrote a long letter from the *S.S. Duchess of Richmond*, which he boarded just after attending the Assembly of the Church of Scotland in Edinburgh. He first described the King's Jubilee service which he and Mrs. Roberts attended, commenting that: "My only criticism of the service is that Cosmo Lang [1864–1945, Archbishop of Canterbury, 1928–1942] should have preached a sermon such as John Donne would have done, instead of saying harmless and hardly edifying platitudes about the King and Empire in a very impressive voice." RR had been busy otherwise with addresses to the General Assembly of the Presbyterian Church of England and the Congregational Union meetings. Of the Church of Scotland Assembly, RR wrote:

> At sea, June 4, 1935
>
> The next morning Mam and I went to Edinburgh and arrived there at 7 o'clock. We stayed at the Caledonian Hotel. The Assembly began at 1 o'clock the next day. It was an imposing affair. The Duke of Kent was there as High Commissioner to the Assembly: and Marina was with him of course. [The Duke of Kent, 1902–1942, was the fourth son of George V and Queen Mary; he served in the navy and the air force and was killed in an air crash.] A bit too much pomp and circumstance to be sure; but it gave the affair some welcome colour. The real mischief of the thing was that the entourage was so beastly military—the thing has no place in the church of God. Why in heaven can't we invent some decent democratic pageantry? I enjoyed the Assembly very much; and so did Mam. It was on the whole a very dignified and orderly business—but they had one or two royal rows, which I greatly enjoyed. But there

were some noble passages—notably the presentation of the Foreign Mission Report, three of the finest speeches I have ever heard on the subject; and the best of them by a woman representing the Women's Society. I was told, by the way, that I didn't do so badly either...They flattered my vanity exceedingly by counting me one of themselves—it was a very warm and heartening experience...

I've worked pretty steadily since I came on board. I've written out an address for the big Tenth Anniversary meeting..., a sermon for next Sunday morning: and the Hodgkin memoranda [notes on Henry Hodgkin and the early days of the Fellowship of Reconciliation for Hodgkin's biographer]. And today I shall finish off arrears of correspondence. If we get to Quebec early enough on Friday, I mean to leave the ship and take the train up to Montreal that I might be there bright and early Saturday morning. Then I am going to the "continuing" General Assembly and crave admission and the privilege of the platform for five minutes. Whether they will give it to me I haven't the faintest idea; but my conscience drives me to try.

The "continuing" assembly was, of course, the General Assembly of The Presbyterian Church in Canada—that portion of the Presbyterian Church which had not entered into Union. In Montreal RR gathered reinforcements; Dr. James Faulds, president of the Montreal and Ottawa Conference, Dr. William Munro, secretary, and William Birks. It was made very clear that this was not an official visit of the United Church moderator, but a personal one. It had been made known to RR beforehand that "telegrams protesting his appearance" had been received, though this announcement was deplored by a number of the Presbyterian brethren. Nevertheless RR was able to issue a call for the healing of the estrangement between the two churches, and for the cultivation of a spirit that would bring this reproach to the "common Master's name" to a close. He ended with good wishes for the prosperity of the Presbyterian Church. Dr. McKerroll, the Presbyterian moderator, replied "unofficially," thanking RR for his good wishes and expressing the feeling that the two churches could go forward with good will in the task to which the country called them. R. E. Knowles, in his column in the *Toronto*

Daily Star, while noting "some eddies in the stream," commented that the prevailing sentiment was one of "gratitude and joy that this initial tug at the long-closed door had come."

After preaching at Sherbourne on the 9th, and the anniversary meeting on 10 June, RR headed for Newfoundland where he visited the churches there. On 2 July he sailed for Liverpool. In Great Britain a fresh round of meetings and visiting awaited him. In early August he and Mrs. Roberts went to visit W. E. Orchard at Seaford, and from there he wrote a letter home:

> I think Mam must have told you that Eirene, Tom Jones' wife, had a stroke on June 19th. Mam brought me the news to Liverpool. It was rather a blow because they are about the oldest friends I have. Well, things went from bad to worse, and she died on the morning of July 18....The funeral was fixed for Saturday the 20th. But on the 19th Mam and I had lunch with the Archbishop of Canterbury at Lambeth. From there I went to Paddington to go to Bristol to address the Methodist Conference. The pesky train was late and the meeting was just over when I got there. I had to be up at 6 the next morning to catch a train for London—then called for Mam at the hotel and went up to the Golders Green for the funeral...: and that was a very heavy drain on me. Then later we went out to the Bristols [old friends of Crouch Hill days]—and stayed late there. So that on Sunday morning I caved in—even had breakfast in bed. Later Mam and I made a "sentimental journey" around the Serpentine; and for the rest of the day we just loafed. But on Monday I had to go back to Bristol to deliver that address: and returned that night. And by then it was pretty clear that I had come to a standstill and must rest if I was to go through the next twelvemonth without a collapse. And so here we are having a gorgeous time and I think Mam and I are both putting on strength. Mam walked today on the Downs as she hasn't walked for a considerable time.

This, of course, meant the cancellation of his commitments on the continent. But he still had a few duties to perform in Great Britain. From Southampton on 19 August he wrote:

Mam and I were twice at Llangeitho. There was a meeting of the South Wales Synod of the Welsh Calvinistic Methodists there at which they were celebrating the 200th Anniversary of the church. (Incidentally, it is now legally "The Presbyterian Church of Wales.") Llangeitho is one of the holy places, the parish of Daniel Rowlands [1713–1790, one of the founders of Methodism in Wales] who, with Howel Harris [1714–1773, another pioneer of Welsh Methodism], set the whole business going. It was rather interesting, though there was too much of the historical business and adulation of the "fathers," and too little of attention to the tasks of the present and future. I delivered a little address in Welsh (and not badly, either!) in which I told them that their next business was Reunion.

Back in Canada, RR was immediately immersed in the business of the church. In September he wrote:

There's not very good news about the M and M Fund yet. We had very much hoped that the business improvement would reflect itself in the contributions of the churches. But outside of Ontario and the Maritimes the prospects are not hopeful. Manitoba, within a month of a fine harvest, had a plague of wheat rust which reduced the crop by two-thirds, and the other provinces are also hit. Alberta is evidently sitting tight on its cash until it is sure it won't be ruined by the Social Credit government it has put into power. We shall need about 150,000 dollars more than we had last year to break even: and we are not likely to get it; and it is not likely that the banks will let us add to our indebtedness much longer. In the tenth anniversary offering we got only about $75,000 of the quarter million dollars we hoped for. The situation is pretty grave. And the policy committee of the F. M. Board is calling the Board together to consider a general retrenchment, involving about 16 percent of the whole work. I don't think myself it will go as far as that, but some retrenchment I fear there will have to be. But it depends chiefly upon how our people come up in the next four months.

Then RR headed west, continuing his program of missions to the church, but within the framework of the Tenth Anniversary Campaign. On 18 October he wrote from Calgary:

I reached here this afternoon—after a week spent in Edmonton, Lacombe, and Red Deer....I have had a reasonably good time. Evidently they were counting a lot on my visit—and I have some hope that they were not disappointed. They have been having a very difficult time in this province. Aberhart, the Social Credit apostle, has an extraordinary influence—and is dead against all organized religion (except his own!) and his hand is very heavy against the United Church. In the country a lot of people have gone quite dotty on him. Whether the man is a charlatan or a paranoiac I find it hard to tell. I had hoped to meet him at Edmonton but the opportunity never materialized. He comes here for the weekend and blazes over the air every Sunday afternoon; and his interpretation of Scripture is the most fantastic I have ever heard. My own judgement, on the evidence I have had, is that he will lead the province into a great deal of trouble before he is done. Meantime, the country churches feel the effect of him quite seriously.

From Victoria, British Columbia he wrote on 1 November:

My Vancouver Mission went very well. In spite of rain all Sunday I had two congregations of 1500 each. There were well over that at the young people's meeting on Monday: and when I challenged them to come up to the chancel steps...at least 250 responded....I must say it had been well prepared for. I begin my three days here tomorrow; and we should have a good time as the preparations here are also very good. There seem to be real signs of a renewal of life and devotion in the church....

I haven't had recent news [about the Missionary and Maintenance Fund], but the last I had was that we shall probably be able to break even this year—and I hope that we shall be able to avoid recalling any missionaries. Anyway, I'm going to have a hard shot at it. I am leaving here on Tuesday night, the midnight boat—on the homeward trail. I spend a day at Vancouver, then to Vernon and the Okanagan Valley— Nelson, Lethbridge, Medicine Hat and Moose Jaw, Regina, and Brandon—then straight home, arriving three weeks today.

Today I am a Trappist. The Vancouver mission was very exacting, and I had three (no four) meetings at Nanaimo on top of it. So I came in here yesterday rather tired....and asked to be left alone. On the job I'm talking either to congregations or to individuals or to small groups all the time: and one grows stale on it.

Back in Toronto, on 24 November RR reported:

My Western trip was very good...I had a magnificent reception everywhere...and I'm very impressed with the United Church. I have developed the conviction that our present troubles are due to poor staff work. Don't say that I say so yet—but I mean to a little later myself. The spirit of the Church is fine— I did not meet a single bad patch: and there's far less grousing in the West than there is in Ontario. But I think G. H. Q. needs some bucking up; they've fallen into routine.

For the moment I wish all railway trains and all hotels in the bottom of the sea—I'm sick of them.

Next week we are having the big "at home" at Emmanuel College; we expect some 500 guests—an entirely democratic affair ranging down or up (as you like) the whole social scale: and including Presbyterians, the Roman Catholic Archbishop (the new man, McGuigan) [1894–1974, Archbishop of Toronto, 1935 and cardinal, 1945], the Anglican Archbishop and other heretics.

Over the year-end 1935–1936, the Student Volunteer Movement held its Twelfth Quadrennial Convention at Indianapolis. Students from all parts of North America gathered, and with them representatives of the churches. On 4 January 1936, RR reported:

The Indianapolis Convention was very interesting, but whether it was a success I am not sure. There were about 3,000 students there—a rather amorphous mass of humanity;

and their appetite for meetings was insatiable. The highlight of the whole affair was the Archbishop of York [William Temple]. I heard four addresses from him, and he struck twelve every time. Whether the crowd understood what he was at is, I fear, only doubtful. But both in form and substance his stuff was magnificent....The Archbishop of Toronto [Derwyn Owen] came down too, I travelled with him both going and coming. I like him very much and got to know him better on this trip. I saw, of course, a good many people I knew—John R. Mott, Clayton Morrison, etc. [Clayton Morrison, b. 1874, was an American clergyman and pacifist.]

Back in Toronto he reflected further on 11 January:

The Indianapolis Convention appears to have had favourable repercussions all round. I have a stubborn scepticism about the ultimate value of these monster gatherings; but I seem to be quite alone in that. There is no doubt they have value: but I am quite sure that there would be more value in six regional conferences of 500 each than in one of 3000. There were some great things done there....It may interest you to know that, of the Canadian delegation of 289, 201 were from the United Church.

Then it was on the road again. From New Glasgow, Nova Scotia, RR wrote on 13 March 1936:

I'm on the tramp again, as you may see. I got to Sydney a week ago, and am going to be in the Maritimes until Wednesday of Holy Week....

When I got to Sydney it was midwinter. The harbour, which my hotel window overlooked, was frozen over. It seemed to be nearly a mile across. There were hundreds of people skating on it; ice-sailing boats, automobiles, and trotting ponies. It was a great sight. But on Monday the weather broke and became mild. I had a good time in Sydney—good congregations and very responsive....I went to Port Hawkesbury to meet the ministers of the surrounding Presbytery. But the mild weather had made the roads impassable and only a handful succeeded in getting there.

Then I went to Antigonish—a Gaelic town and countryside, most interesting; and I had a good meeting there. But the best part of the Antigonish visit was that I spent this morning at the St. Francis Xavier University—a small place, but doing wonders for the northern part of Nova Scotia. They have an extension department to promote adult education, cooperatives and credit unions among the farmers, the miners and the fisherfolk....It was to get some first hand information on that point that I went there, and I spent the whole morning....I'm going to try to use Kagawa's visit to get something of that kind going in Ontario. It looks as though these people here will work the economic redemption of the rural and littoral parts of this province. I had a letter of introduction to the Rector of the University from the Catholic Archbishop of Toronto—and I had a royal welcome. They were as cordial and friendly as they could be; and they insisted on my staying to lunch with the faculty—and the Rector even asked me to say Grace!

Here I stay until Tuesday—then Charlottetown, P. E. I. Then Sackville, Moncton, Fredericton, St. John, N. B., and then back to N. S., Yarmouth, Lunenburg, Halifax—and HOME!...And that will be the end of my travelling, save only for a brief visit to Quebec and Sherbrooke—and a few hectic days visiting the central conferences—five of them.

From New Brunswick on 21 March RR reported:

I find things down here very much what I have found them elsewhere. The present time rather difficult but the future full of promise. One thing impresses me very much. All over the country there are an extraordinary number of ministers in their thirties who are intensely spiritual in their outlook, and full of eagerness for the Kingdom of God. They are able and studious and intelligent; and I foresee a great leadership springing up from them in the next decade. Then, the young people in the church have impressed me very much. They are very keen and loyal. My own misgiving about them is that they are suffering from their education—both secular and religious—and are only moderately literate. But I hope the new Young People's Union will do something to educate them. At Sackville we had a trainload of young men and women from the country between Sackville and Cape Tormentine (where one embarks for Prince Edward Island)— they came for my Y. P. meeting there—and the CNR ran a special train for them: and they filled it up.

Back in Toronto, on the eve of Easter 1936, RR wrote:

I've finished my long travels now—mercifully. I wouldn't want to do it again. And I am grateful to have emerged from it without any material hurt. I am, however, very glad to have done it: and if people's opinions are to be trusted, it has been worth while. But the moderatorship is too heavy a job as it is now conceived: for, as the Moderator is the chief executive officer of the church, there's a lot of office work which should be loaded on someone else. Who my successor is to be God only knows. Three men have been nominated: Clarence MacKinnon, D. C. McGregor, and Peter Bryce. MacKinnon told me he couldn't take it on grounds of health; D. C. McGregor is probably going to a new pastorate; and Peter Bryce has publicly announced that he isn't standing. And at the moment I confess I see no one in sight.

And again, on 26 April:

This week has been a sort of blizzard of events....Tuesday I had to go with a mixed deputation (R. C., Pres., C. of E., and U. C.) to the Department of Indian Affairs to argue against a government cut of 15% in the grant to Indian Schools. Crerar [Thomas Crerar, 1876–1975, a Progressivist, served in the government of Mackenzie King from 1935 to 1945], the Minister of the Interior, received us—I liked him very much, especially as he agreed that we had made our case....

On Friday I attended and addressed a meeting of unemployed men—they meet every Friday afternoon at the Church of All Nations. There's a good deal of Communist propaganda among them in a quiet indirect way: and Mackay wanted me to go down to speak to them. I just talked on what was in my mind without much premeditation, and lo and behold! I sent you the *Mail and Empire* report [an article written by RR]. I hear it has given pleasure to the radicals, but I don't know yet what the conservatives think of it. I expect sheaves of letters next week.

In his speech RR made no bones about the facts of the case. The organization of society which denied people work, freedom (both industrial and political), economic security, and economic sufficiency must come under the judgment of the church. To declare the ends society is to achieve, though not the means by which they shall be achieved, is the business and the right of the church. Democracy has failed to live up to the slogan of "Liberty, Equality, and Fraternity" for lack of intelligent criticism. RR's hopes that the Antigonish co-op movement might gather momentum and replace the old "monarchic and oligarchic processes" dominating industry were not realistic. Not that even he saw the old system giving over without mounting an opposition. However, his judgement of society retains its validity:

Today we have a little liberty, but nothing like we think we have. As for equality we have a little equality before the law. And fraternity—we have mighty little of that....

It seems to me that you cannot establish liberty unless you accept a common obedience. You cannot have equality except on a basis of a common humility. Nor can you have fraternity except on a basis of mutual respect and a basis of bearing each others' burdens, call it what you will. These are the cardinal virtues necessary to any good society.

Although he made no further comment on public reactions to his speech, RR was a few weeks later writing of "stirring things up" on the problem of housing the unemployed and also of slum clearance. He had hopes of getting going "a definite church movement" "to beard the Board of Control...and try to put the fear of God in them."

On 9 May RR wrote:

Last week we finished with the Church Committees. The last

two, Executive and Transfers—and I was in the chair for three consecutive days—in all some 23 hours—and I was pretty well washed out when we finished. And now we set about preparing for the General Council. I am not too happy as I think of it....Then there is the filling up of staff vacancies—General Secretary—and the places presumably to be vacated by Endicott, Thomas, Stephenson, and Creighton. There's quite a bit of wire-pulling going on, I hear: and I fear there may be some Presbyterian-Methodist animus over the distribution of these jobs—as all who are going out are former Methodists. I fear I don't see much hope at present that we shall recover the lost ground in the M and M Fund. But there is some improvement in other ways. This time last year the statistics showed only an increase in communicant membership of 1900—this year the figure is over 6000: but that is not up to the average of the previous years....

And again, on 16 May:

I have had an interesting week. A busy Monday. You read the report of my address to the unemployed, and I got interested in the problem of housing the unemployed—which is scandalous here. So I have been stirring up things and have now a definite church movement going for not only housing the unemployed but for an immediate scheme of slum clearance and housing. We had a meeting on Monday afternoon—two hours of it, and we are going to beard the Board of Control this or next week, and try to put the fear of God in them.

Anticipating RR's frequent absences from home, in the fall of 1934, the Roberts had moved into an apartment hotel. By May 1936, they were fretting to get back into a home of their own and were beginning to look for a suitable house. RR commented, "I am longing to get back to sustained work at my desk." From time to time he had confessed to a great weariness due to the strain of so much travelling and the pressure of the executive work of his office. At no time did he refer to the prostate condition which bedeviled him throughout these two years, and which was of longer standing than that. His chief concern was not for the health of his body, but for the elasticity of his mind and the receptivity of his spirit. On 30 May 1936, he wrote:

> I shall be 62 years of age tomorrow. It happens that tomorrow is also Whitsunday. I am going to pray tonight that God will give me a little Pentecost for a birthday present. I don't see anything but some re-enacting of Pentecost is going to help this wretched world very much. We have everything—the desire, the knowledge, the technique, to make it blossom as a rose—everything but the power. As for my "advancing years," they don't bother me very much. I think that if a man can get over the 45th bunker he needn't worry very much about old age. If his mind is supple when the 45th year is past, it will be supple to the end—and in that measure a man may preserve his youth into old age. And I think that there is in me a streak of unredeemed wildness—an inheritance from my "moors and fens and crags and torrents" of long ago—that helps me along.

On 19 June he reported:

> I looked over the list of delegates to the General Council today...and by and large it doesn't look very exciting. I am afraid that once more the Council won't find itself until it is too late to be any good. Even yet it does not seem clear who the Moderator is going to be: nor the General Secretary or the *Outlook* editor. I am rather apprehensive about the whole business. We've plenty of men coming up—these "rising" 40 year-olds are everywhere magnificent. But their turn hasn't come yet. Meantime I am in odds and ends of time trying to put together, roughly, my *pronunciamento* on demitting the moderatorship.

And a few days later, on 23 June:

> We are, as it happens, in the throes of moving—and a right ghastly affair it is. We've had two days of it already—one day for the stuff from storage and today for the stuff from here. The one piece of real wisdom that emerges out of it all is:

Beware of acquiring and accumulating anything you cannot any time throw out the window and not know the difference. Mam is groaning about the amount of sheer junk there is among our...possessions—and she is resolved upon a Pride's Purge of all non-essentials!

On 4 July he wrote:

We're still alive—but it has been a pretty awful scuffle. The dining room, our bedroom and the study are habitable and comfortable. It is the best study I've had since we left England. I had a great rummage with the books. For penal servitude sentence me to stacking books...but I have done it—though I can't get all of them into one room. There's a couple of hundred in another room upstairs. And I sold another couple of hundred, some respectable fiction and some disreputable religion—Oxford Group and such like....

    We're on half-time at the Church tomorrow—no evening service. It is a great and notable mercy—and it is [to remain so] for July and August....

Toward the end of July RR's physique finally rebelled, and he was forced to enter the Toronto General Hospital for a prostate operation. Apart from the prostate condition, which proved more serious on investigation than the original diagnosis, the doctors found him in very good shape. He came through the operation very well and was "making a beeline to recovery—to the astonishment of the surgeons with respect to rapidity." He wrote from the hospital on 8 August:

I'm glad things happened as they did. The trouble was becoming more than a nuisance...And now, thank God, all that is past; and I shall be having a new beginning in a remarkably sound body. I take it as a sign that God has yet a job for me to do: and it grows more clear what it is. But about that I'll write you another time.

    Mam has been an angel and a tower of strength to me through the whole business...We were still in the midst of making the house habitable when the trouble became so acute that it had to be dealt with. How Mam has stood it all is simply only to be explained by very gracious replenishments of strength. People have been most extraordinarily kind—in spite of the fact that most of our friends have been out of town, this room has been a continuous bower of flowers. From this room I look out upon the hospital garden; and it has been a great comfort. I have not merely much, but infinite reason to give thanks; and do you give thanks with us for these great mercies....

Luckily I had pretty well finished my Nunc Dimittis address before I came to hospital....

A day or so after this letter was written, however, RR had a serious relapse. Amongst his personal memoranda were a few scraps of paper written in Welsh. One, dated Sunday, 16 August, reads:

The Great God—
Thanks: thanks: thanks: thanks: and thanks again;
praise, praise a hundred praises—to be spared thus far...
"Should I come through the wilderness"...!

Well, the end of the journey is in sight...the rest of the journey is in thy hands, and [I am] passive therein.

Thanks—simply and lowly for some peaceful visitations this last week. The week was a disappointment—pain, confusion, and bitterness. But through grace I was given the ability to see that pain and suffering was my lot just now, in the providence of my Father...and the pain became a kind of sacrament and the suffering a revelation. I now know, as I did not know before, the true meaning of the mysterious words, "that he learned obedience through that which he suffered." I, too, learned the same lesson in my own little way, and I see the world in a new light. Thanks, Thanks, Thanks.

A letter of 22 August runs:

...and tomorrow, Sunday, I'm going home. LAUS DEO! Last week was what Pat Sclater would have described as a snorter.

I had spells of delirium in the early part of it—from the fragments Mam has reported to me I gather that my conversation was "frequent and painful and free." It would really have made a famous gramophone record. But...in spite of the set-back, I am still within the average for such cures. And I shall begin life again sound in wind and limb. It looks like a new miraculous gift of life [though] I'll have to go canny for a time.

RR would have been more than content to have stayed at home until it was time to go to Ottawa for the General Council. It seemed the part of wisdom, however, to get away from Toronto. Barrie was far enough away that people would not be tempted to run to him for advice. He and Mrs. Roberts spent a quiet fortnight there. From Barrie, on 12 September, RR wrote:

We leave here for home on Monday. I want a week at home before the General Council—which begins on the 23rd. We shall go to Ottawa on the 22nd so that I may have some peace and rest before Council begins. I have a sermon and communion in the afternoon; and the constituting of the General Council in the evening, followed by my "valedictory" address and the election of my successor, whom I expect to be Peter Bryce. Then I shall be a free man—I shan't attend all the sessions of the Council—only when some things I am particularly interested in come on.

And then, from Ottawa on 24 September:

Yesterday was my big day—and I am thankful to say that I'm none the worse for it. And they say that I "retired" without manifest slump. I'm a bit flattened out today—but I'm taking nourishment in good style. And now we're going to bed.

27
Back to Normal Life

The Moderator of The United Church of Canada concludes his term at the first session of the ensuing General Council. RR realized that, after his recent experience in the hospital, he must not proceed full speed ahead. He had every intention of making himself scarce at the meetings of the council. Others, however, unaware that he was not yet back to par, pressed him into service. Reporting on the council, he wrote on 3 October 1936:

> I didn't have much of the Council itself. They put me on the committee to nominate people for the vacancies at the head office—some eight in all: and our committee sat three times a day until last Thursday morning....One interesting thing is that we elected to most of these appointments much younger men than usual.

Once the council was over, RR looked thankfully to release from the many pressures he had been under for the past two years. Having returned to Toronto, he wrote on 16 October:

> Being done with the moderatorship is a great relief...if only that I have now time to spend at my desk. My new study is fine and I am enjoying it very much. To feel when I get up that I haven't got to go down to the church offices to transact ecclesiastical business or attend committees, but can stay all morning in my study, gives me extraordinary pleasure. And to think that I haven't got to go for long journeys and sleep in pullmans and all that kind of thing is another happiness. The irony of the business of travelling for me is that, just as I was giving up, the CPR and CNR started air-conditioning their

pullmans and parlour cars, and you can't conceive what a difference it makes. There's an even temperature, continual fresh air, and no dust. If they had started two years ago, it would have added a good deal to my well-being.

But the shackles of office could not yet be shed completely. Later, on 24 October he wrote:

I am glad to be out of church politics—though I have to be on the Executive and Sub-executive. But I hope things will improve when we get our new men on the job. I am particularly hopeful of Sisco and Gerald Cragg. Sisco is a strong man and will not, I think, be a wire-puller. I was at first doubtful about the appointment of Gerald Cragg for the N. O. [*The New Outlook*] on the ground that it was bad economy to turn a scholar into a weekly journalist. But when I knew that Gerry was willing to take the job, I had no more to say but supported him vigorously.

The church continued to be plagued by financial problems. On 17 January 1937, RR reported:

It looks as though the M and M is going to be down again this year. I am convinced that the trouble lies in the whole system, which is inherently wrong psychologically and is *worked* wrong psychologically, even at that. Blanket appeals for funds may be good business on the surface. But when the *whole* appeal is sustained by the missionary interest, we are expecting too much when we expect enough to maintain four or five other enterprises—Pensions, etc. Moreover the cry of "Wolf" has been overdone. We have been crying "wolf" for the last seven years running; and either people cease to believe it, or they get too depressed to be interested in the job. The high-pressure finance idea emphasizes the wrong thing too. It emphasizes the objective (in terms of money) and not the case and the need and the work. I see no remedy except that of a thorough re-examination of the whole business. Meantime I don't see how we are going to maintain our present work...And we are behind last year already—when there is

[now] more money in the country. It is estimated that [the city of] Toronto spent two million dollars in New Year festivities.

But by March the financial situation, at least, had improved. RR wrote on 20 March:

You will be glad to know that the M and M balanced its budget for 1936—the first time in several years....

But I am pretty anxious about some other things—the lack of coordination and good feeling between the church Departments; and the very questionable condition of some of them....I have come to the conclusion, among others, that the next Moderator should be appointed for eight or ten years, armed with a good deal of authority, especially to work out and establish an organic policy for the whole church. I think Sisco is doing very well, and Gerald Cragg is doing as well as can be expected, considering his inheritance in *The New Outlook*. He was here the other day. I am a sort of "consultant" for him and Sisco.

And again, on 3 April, he reported:

Things at 299 [299 Queen Street West, the United Church offices] are not happy just now, in spite of their having balanced their budget. Owing to McLachlan's protracted and incurable illness the Board of Evangelism and Social Service is in a pretty bad mess. I think the Book Room will come in for some criticism...A biography of [Egerton] Ryerson [1803–1882, Methodist clergyman and educator, first President of Victoria College, Toronto] has been published by the Oxford Press—having been turned away from the house that bears his name! It is pretty scandalous. I imagine that there is something in the view that the best proof of the doctrine of original sin is to be found in Ecclesiastical Offices.

By the end of the year, in December, he was writing:

We were at Davidson's this afternoon to say goodbye to John

MacLeod who is going to succeed Cairns [David Cairns, 1862–1946, professor of Dogmatic Theology and principal of Christ's College] in Aberdeen...It will be a great loss to have MacLeod go—he was, I think, easily the best man at Emmanuel. I have been working with him in the committee on the statement of the Church's faith—he drew out the first draft—and it is a very good statement—the nearest to anything I have ever found to express my own faith. John Line is about the only man left in Emmanuel who has a prophetic note about him—though of course John Dow is very good within his own field. The new man, Orton, who does homiletics as well as assist Davidson in Hebrew, we met today...I am silently wild with them about this appointment. They ought to have a chair of Practical Theology, doing not merely homiletics, which is a bum subject anyway—but the whole field of the cure of souls (both traditional and modern), the pastoral task and so forth. To treat the practical end of the minister's task as a footnote to two courses in the Hebrew Bible (which is the actual arrangement in this case) is simply playing with theological education.

In the spring of 1936, an interdenominational campaign for the Evangelization of Canadian Life had been inaugurated. The United Church, of course, was to play its part. From the beginning, however, RR took a dim view of the campaign. On 7 November 1936, he wrote:

All the Protestant Churches are lined up in it—though each church does the job among its own people...But I fear it is going to be a flop. I've seen these big campaigns before—my first was in Great Britain at the end of 1900; and that was a flop: and the rest I've known were flops. Somehow these highly organized things seem to estrange the Holy Spirit—though this one is not (I think) organized as well as it should be. For *some* organization there must be. But my own deepest misgiving is that they are going out without a real "Commission" and without *the* "Word." Most revivals in Christian history that have left a permanent mark share one thing in common. "The Word" has come to some individual and he shares it with his contemporaries, as Moody [Dwight Moody, 1837–1899, American revivalist], Wesley, and Luther did. But the Word for this moment, badly needed as it is, has not yet been given. The Oxford Group hasn't got it. It seems to me to be the last kick of a decayed Moodyism. However, we shall see. Meantime I am obsessed by the fear that Pidgeon's campaign may lead us more deeply into the doldrums than we are—as a kind of reaction. I very earnestly hope for the best. But I'm scared.

Two weeks later, on 22 November, he wrote:

On Wednesday night there was a big jamboree at the Maple Leaf Gardens, a Service of Witness it was called, in connection with the Campaign for the Evangelization of Canadian Life. It was interdenominational—the crowd was not as large as at a similar meeting two years ago, nor as at the United Church's tenth anniversary. The speaker was Hugh Redwood—the journalist-Salvationist. He gave a good address, but it was hardly the address for the occasion. I had to be on the platform—*vice* Peter Bryce: otherwise I wouldn't have gone—because of the embargo I am under in the attendance of meetings. There was one rather grimly funny touch in the meeting. The Salvation Army Band played during the collection, a sort of medley affair—and the most important part of it was the Baal Chorus from "Elijah"!—that in a meeting of Christian witness!

I grow more and more suspicious of these monster gatherings. There is a sort of anonymity about them which distresses me; but my chief objection is that I am almost sure the "big" thing is alien and *au fond* inimical to Christianity. And I fear that it may be a fizzle....In some localities, I think it may have good results...But as a national movement, I cannot see much sign of it coming to anything. And we can't afford a "flop" just now.

Part of the reason seems to me to lie in the fact that it has too much of an Oxford Group tinge, and that has alienated many ministers. There's been a group of O. G. ministers, chiefly Anglican and U. C., meeting for some time; but there is very little warmth for the Oxford Group outside of these small coteries. And it belongs to the same thing, that while the campaign pays its formal respects to the social implications of the Gospel, it gives them no particular place in its pronouncements; and that has made our young lions very restive and clamorous. There is a real danger of a split in the ministry over the matter.

On 5 December, RR reported:

The campaign for the Evangelization of Canadian Life seems not to be making much headway. Here it has so far hardly made any real dent...It becomes clearer to me that the whole thing is premature and ill-organized to boot....

Meantime, one good thing may come of it. A group—interdenominational and carefully picked—is going to try to state the Christian message for the times. We had our first meeting last night—I started off by stating my own conviction that the two ideas of Revelation and Community must be regulative of our emphasis in our statement of the Gospel...and that we need to re-study the whole question of sin and forgiveness in order to find the true starting point for the social doctrine of the church. We had a good evening—but we went not very far, yet far enough to know that we are on the trail of something. Included in the group are Walter Brown, John Line, Raymond Booth (Quaker), Isherwood (Wycliffe College), Bryden (Knox College), Silcox (Social Service Council), some Anglican, Presbyterian, and U. C. parsons.

In theory RR was still taking it easy after his operation. But while he was participating in the life of the United Church as past moderator, and in the current religious life of the city, he was also engaged in the preparation of a course of lectures to be delivered in January 1937, at Bangor, Maine. Of these he wrote:

I am to give a course on preaching. But they have asked me to speak on the content of preaching rather than on the technicalities. So I'm going to lecture on "The Gospel of Today and Tomorrow," and the underlying thesis in my mind is that what we need just now, as the background of our teaching, is a synthesis of Karl Barth and John Macmurray, the linking up of the two concepts of Revelation and Community. You may have seen that I said at Ottawa [in his "valedictory" address at the General Council] that the only conclusion I can draw from the facts of the contemporary situation is that the rest of this century—and beyond—is going to be spent in universal social experimentation. It has begun—Communism, Fascism, Nazism, and the "New Deal"—and amid these confusing voices the church must have and proclaim its own doctrine of "community"—for there *is* such a doctrine. The N. T. is full of it, from our Lord's conception of the Kingdom to the apocalyptic New Jerusalem. But it is a community which must find its pattern and its creative energy in the Revelation of God in Jesus Christ Crucified: and so forth. There must be no antithesis between personal and social salvation. The one implies the other inevitably, by reason of the individual-social being of man.

But I mean by Revelation something beyond recorded revelation—I mean a new receiving and a new apprehension of the commanding, irresistible, and convicting "Word of God"—and that in terms of our contemporary confusions and needs. And if we will only get ourselves into a condition of mental and spiritual preparedness to receive that Word, the Word will be given to us.

And the groundwork of the whole four lectures—or rather, of the last three—the first is introductory, an analysis of current need—is going to be I Cor. i-ii. Before I went into hospital I made up my mind to read I Cor. through very carefully again—and as soon as I was able to I started doing so. But I didn't get beyond the second chapter. The first two chapters I read again and again and again—and every time with intenser interest and growing illumination. It was a grand spiritual experience—but it was also a revelation of the possibility of the materials of the synthesis I'm looking for. I think that before I'm through I will have something worth saying.

Letters throughout the winter of 1936 to 1937, describe the pace of RR's life. On 7 November he wrote:

> Mam went to the Symphony Concert this week (I didn't—
> one of my debilities at the moment is a persistent noise in the
> ear which loud sounds aggravate)...On Thursday there was
> the first annual dinner of the Association of Canadian
> Bookmen....Pelham Edgar [1871–1948, professor of English,
> Victoria College]...roped me in to propose the toast to
> Literature. I did so—somehow: I thought it was a pretty
> complete flop. But apparently the rest didn't...Last night was
> the anticlimax—we went to Sir Joseph Flavelle's, to a W. M.
> S. concert (to boost funds), and we had a thoroughly bourgeois
> evening...the performers were the Sherbourne choir soloists.
> But there was one outsider, a girl with a violin, and she was
> superb...a real oasis in a desert.

On 5 December:

> I've been reading this week a French novel—"Le Journal d'un
> Curé de Campagne" [Georges Bernanos]—the story of a young
> priest and his trials....I've got a row of books waiting to be
> read—Josiah Stamp's "Motive and Method of a Christian
> Order"; Micklem's "What is the Faith?"; Maxwell's "History
> of Christian Worship"; Paul Tillich's "The Interpretation of
> History."

On 17 January:

> This is Sunday night—and Mam and I are at home. I don't
> even yet go to church on Sunday nights, but I shall be
> beginning again quite soon. I'd rather like it, though, as a
> permanent institution. It gives a little elbow room to get done
> things that otherwise I cannot. I am glad to say that Mam and
> I are in pretty good form—I get now and again a day of slump,
> the hangover of the shock of the operation; and this has been
> one such day. But otherwise I'm pretty fit.
>   My chief preoccupation has been getting ready some
> lectures—I have finished the text: but I am not at all satisfied
> with them. But I fear I can't go on with them for some time—

that is, to prepare them for the press. For I must settle down to write the book on Prayer for Rufus Jones' Series: and that will want a good deal of preliminary work in the way of reading [eventually *The Contemporary Christ*; Rufus Jones, 1863–1948, was a Quaker historian and social reformer].

In February and March RR's letters refer to various engagements: a luncheon in connection with the Life and Work Conference, a week of Lenten noonday preaching at Holy Trinity in downtown Toronto, and new work on the radio:

Incidentally—we are at last likely to get the United Church on the air as a regular Sunday afternoon fixture—the Canadian National B. C. We had our first rehearsal last night—and I think it will go pretty well. When we start in I am to give the "word" for it for the first set of broadcasts....

We are sailing for England on July 2nd: We have to be at Oxford for the Life and Work Conference on Monday the 13th. We go to Cardiff for the University of Wales' "Congregation" and my DD on the 16th, and then back to Oxford for the rest of the Conference. After that we are not sure. I am supposed to go to Edinburgh for the "Faith and Order" Conference. But that would mean we should get no holiday at all. So we are wavering about going to Edinburgh.... I got an article finished for the *Expository Times* this week—it had been on the stocks for some time but I had no chance to get down to it. And I settled down to the book on prayer and worship for Rufus Jones' series. I have to provide 50,000 words by the end of June. A good deal of the stuff is really ready. But the worship part will have all to be written *de novo*— and the general introductory part. I'm on that now.

On 3 April RR reported on the pace of his life:

We have had a pretty tough week. On Wed. and Thurs. we kept open house for the members of Sherbourne—and they came! All sorts—rich and poor—young and old. It was something of a jam as you may imagine. And the business of talking to them was pretty exacting. Yesterday Mam and I felt like squeezed lemons. Besides this there were a number of other things, committees, interviews, and what not. So that we are not as fresh as we would desire to be. But no doubt we shall blossom as the rose.

I had rather a nice experience this week. We've had a problem vexing us for some time at the Church offices. One of our men had a serious operation for an abscess on his pituitary body (in the brain) a year or so ago. His sight had been going for some time and the operation was undertaken to try to save it. But he has to have it repeated next week—and he is not likely, even if he lives, to be able to work again. We can only afford him a small pension. So his wife has to look for a job. She thought that she could do some work under the Ministry of Welfare in Queen's Park: she saw two necessary people, and then reported from them that the thing to do was for me to see [David] Croll, the Minister of Welfare. When I told him the story he said, "If you have thought it worth your while to come here to ask me to appoint Mrs. X, it is certainly worth my while to appoint her!" And he thanked me for coming! Anyway, it made X and his wife and a number of other people happy. Croll is a good man at this job...but I wish he were in his job without being in the political game.

With the exception of a tonsillectomy in 1928, RR had, throughout his life, enjoyed what he called "rude" health. He had no conception of the toll a major operation takes of a person's physical resources, and he was anxious to get back into his stride. Neither experience nor temperament allowed him to take kindly to a restricted program, though he did his best to go "in low gear" and to recognize the limits of his strength with patience.

Part VI

"Be Thou still my strength and shield"

———

28
Sherbourne and the Future

Interesting and important as all these details and responsibilities were, RR's main and immediate problem in the fall of 1936, was to pick up the threads of his life at Sherbourne Street United Church. During those months he was slowly getting the feel of the place again, and it was borne in upon him that his time there was nearly completed. His long absences during his two years as moderator undoubtedly had something to do with this decision. Returning to the situation he could view it with detachment. The issues of 1929 were still present in 1937.

RR had just received news that his daughter Gwen and her husband, missionaries in Japan, might return to Canada on furlough in 1938. On 20 March 1937, he wrote to them:

> We were very much rejoiced to hear of the prospect of seeing you next year. But—*this is very private*—whether we shall be here when you come back is beginning to look rather doubtful. I am almost immediately going to propose to the Sherbourne people that they should forthwith trim their sails to the wind they shall have to sail by in the near future—that they evolve a definite policy of approach to the immediate community and reorganize themselves accordingly. And I am going to tell them frankly, that for that purpose, they will need a ministry different from my own. And I am so clear in my own mind that this is right that I shall go, in any case, when a convenient opportunity presents itself. We are not yet making plans: and we are not canvassing the future for the moment. But *some* change is inevitable.

Shortly thereafter RR urged the Official Board to set up a small commission "to survey the situation at Sherbourne and determine on a policy for its future." He did not wish to complicate things at this juncture by announcing his decision that he would be resigning. That could come later, when the commission had begun to get the feel of its work.

In mid-April, however, the situation changed significantly. Faced by the fact that any extra pressure brought on a slump of extraordinary fatigue, RR was persuaded by Mrs. Roberts to see a doctor. The doctor could find no specific trouble, but advised RR to go away immediately for a rest. This, RR declared, he could not do. However, both RR and the doctor contacted the chair of the Pastoral Relations Committee of Sherbourne to see what could be arranged. It was only natural that, when RR and the chair of the committee were discussing RR's need for a rest as soon as possible, the more general situation should come under review. Both agreed that the time had come to tell the committee, which was meeting the following Friday, 16 April, of RR's determination to resign at a fairly early date.

On that same Friday RR, returning from a quiet dinner engagement, found a phone message from the Canadian press awaiting him. As it was still early in the evening he returned the call, and was immediately asked if it were true that he had sent in his resignation to Sherbourne. Two days later RR reported:

> How it leaked out I don't know. But it put me in an awkward position. I rang up Paul Mills [chair of the Pastoral Relations Committee] and he agreed with me that I would have to make a statement this [Sunday] morning. Meantime, the Canadian Press held the matter up, very decently. I made my statement this morning—and tomorrow the world will know that I want a job after June 1938.
>
> Both Mam and I have a sense of relief that this has come about as it has. It gives Sherbourne time: and it gives us time to breathe and look around. Whatever the issue of it all may be, I am quite clear that we have done the right thing. And we have no sense of anxiety.

A week later, on Sunday, 25 April he wrote:

The fat's in the fire as Mam told you. I told the congregation this week and there's been a good deal of hubbub....

We are, of course, facing the open world: but we've done it before—and we were cared for....Of course I am communicating with my friends here and there—in Great Britain and the USA. Nothing likely seems at the moment to be in sight in Canada—and of course certain areas in Canada are impossible for me. Neither Mam nor I could acclimatize ourselves in them; and I feel no vocation either for the far East of the Dominion or the far West. But we have a year to go—and anything may happen in that time.

The hubbub died down and RR went on with his work. In June, a month earlier than originally planned, he and Mrs. Roberts sailed for England to take a three-week holiday with Orchard at Seaford, before going to the Oxford Life and Work Conference and thence to Cardiff. From Oxford he wrote on 22 July:

We have been here some 10 days now...and it has been all very interesting and in spots exciting. This is Thursday and the whole affair finishes on Sunday—but we shall go back to London on Saturday evening. We are now on the final reports—utterances to all mankind, so to speak. And there are some hefty ones. My own concern has been in the Group on International Order and War. There's a very good and forthright document to be presented to the whole conference tomorrow. It isn't a pacifist document—we could hardly expect that much, as our continental friends are not ready for it. But some of us were afraid that the official document would be so tame that we would have to issue a minority statement. Happily that will not be necessary...It is the strongest thing that has yet come from a church body on war. One of the happy circumstances for me in the matter is that I was all through working in close association with Raven whom I had not met before. I like him very much. Another was that the Archbishop of York went with us much farther than we had expected. [Charles Raven, 1865–1964, a socialist and pacifist, was professor of Theology at Emmanuel College, Cambridge; William Temple was then the Archbishop of York before moving to Canterbury in 1942.]

The University of Wales affair came off last Friday and Saturday. In the preceding November RR had written the following:

> I had the news this morning privately that the University of Wales is offering me an honourary D. D. I'm very bucked. It is now about the best Hon. D. D. there is—I don't think there have been more than half a dozen given in 20 years.

Perhaps the thought that he would be receiving a degree from the very place where he had failed to earn one as a youth gave an added savour to the occasion. RR also received other honorary degrees, the D. D. From Victoria College in the University of Toronto and another from the University of Vermont, and the D. Litt. from the University of Syracuse.

> My first job there was to address the Annual Meeting of "Coleg Harlech," where I rather flopped. But I went from that to a complimentary dinner given by the Vice-chancellor to the honourary graduands: and there I think I pulled it off. It was all very jolly. The ceremony next day was very interesting...My robes are a great sight—red gown with blue-shot-with-red facings. Solomon has nothing on me any more....
>
> There are a lot of interesting people here in Oxford in connection with the Conference. Brunner [Emil Brunner, 1889–1966, Swiss Reformed theologian from Zurich] conducted the devotions at St. Mary's Church this morning: (I have to conduct them tomorrow). It would be no use to mention all the celebrities. Best of all has been meeting old friends—I was saying this morning that I think I know more of the people at this conference than any other person! There are the British, the American and the Canadian delegations to begin with—and I find that I know more of the continentals and the Far East than I expected.

After attending the Edinburgh Conference on the Church and the Word of God, RR returned to Toronto. He was hardly back when he became the centre of a controversy which was a by-product of the Oxford pronouncement on war. On 24 September he wrote:

I've had a pretty busy time since our return. Last week I was at Hartford Seminary giving a course of lectures; and this week I gave two of the same lectures at Trinity College—where they went over with some effect, i.e. in both places. They were really rough drafts of what I hope will be a book to be entitled *The Gospel Today and Tomorrow*, or something of the sort. And it will be my sideline for this winter....

Perhaps you will see some echoes of the disrepute I have fallen into. When I was at Hartford I said, impromptu in a discussion, that if the Report of the Oxford Conference on the Church and War were to sink into the mind of the Church, there would be no more recruiting and drumbeating in the pulpits and no more prayers for victory. And the United Press broadcast them—they appeared in the Toronto papers—and there are still letters more or less cursing me by book, bell, and candle. And some of it from people who ought to know better. I don't take any notice of it—in fact I only hear of it as I don't read it even. The one thing I have long vowed I would never do is enter into public controversy with any man. But I've been getting a lot of support.

Indeed, all sorts of people rushed into print in the correspondence columns of the papers over the issue. It was several months before the furore died down. Many joined Dr. Kent of Queen's Theological College, and Dr. T. T. Shields, Toronto's maverick Baptist pastor of Jarvis Street Church, in vilifying RR's "foolish utterance." Shields had been championing Baptist Christianity and British Imperialism against liberal Protestantism and Roman Catholicism, getting him expelled from the Baptist Convention. Others spoke out in wholehearted defence of RR's position. In a personal note to RR, Gordon Sisco, secretary of the General Council, wrote:

I have no doubt you have read the very interesting letter written by Principal Kent which appears in yesterday's edition of the *Globe and Mail*. It is evident that he has missed the point, but even college professors sometimes miss a point. What I do want to say is that in this difficult time, when many of us are trying to think our way through to a Christian conclusion [concerning] the relation of Church to state, especially in times of war, we are heartened by what you said at Hartford....There are many of us who know exactly what you mean when you speak of the Church as a body of believers who must be true to the Christian ethic, as far as possible, in time of international strife. I do hope you will be encouraged to feel that many are with you. Don't budge a damn bit!

RR replied:

Many thanks for your kind letter. I had seen Kent's letter and my remark to my wife was, "Well, if Kent wants to be in the same boat as Shields, it is his funeral, not mine." But it does puzzle me, not so much that college professors sometimes miss a point, but that the Head of a Christian College so little understands the Christianity he is supposed to teach....Anyway, that kind of thing doesn't worry me personally. I've got used to it by this time.

It is doubtful that this tempest in a teapot had anything to do with the fact that, although RR was known to be available after June 1938, nothing opened up for him in Canada. Alec Kerr's opinion, as he communicated it to RR, was that it "never occurred to any Canadian church that you would be interested in anything they had to offer—after Sherbourne, whose name you have done so much to make imposing." A more serious handicap was a rumour that he had resigned on grounds of ill health.

Although RR had said that he felt that his resignation was all for the best, both for Sherbourne and for himself, he had been hurt by the breach of faith that had forced his premature announcement. He rather suspected that the rumours about the grounds of his resignation being ill health found their origin in the same source as the leak to the press. However, while he was aware that there were a few who were in a hurry to see the last of him at Sherbourne, he knew that he still had the confidence of the majority. For them, in his last months at Sherbourne, he proposed to give unstintingly of his best. And he remained unperturbed about his own future. He had accepted the fact that there was nothing for him in Canada; he remained hopeful of the USA, however, where he was booked for several lecture series here and there in the period from September 1938 to May 1939. He was confident that "the proper job will turn up in good time." On 19 March 1938, he wrote:

Our future is still enigmatic—so much so that we are unable
to make any plans—save the vague one that at some point I
shall take a fairly long rest...The place I should like to go to is
Tynllidiart [a farmhouse in the mountains of Merionethshire,
owned by Dan Thomas, his brother-in-law]! And the
possibility of going to England—for good—is not yet off the
boards. But it is all in the lap of the gods. We are sure that the
Lord has a spot for us to do a bit of work still....

But there was more trouble ahead. The "persistent buzzing" or
"a sort of letting off steam" in his ear, he passed off as a minor incon-
venience which prevented him from going to symphony concerts.
There are only hints in his letters of the physical misery he endured
in 1937. He was suffering from the vertigo and nausea characteristic
of Menière's syndrome. There was never any clear advance warning
of these attacks. Fortunately he was never stricken in public, for he
was completely helpless when the attacks hit him. Every time he
went into the pulpit both he and Nan were conscious of the fact that
he might suddenly and humiliatingly collapse in front of the congregation. Nan was haunted by the thought that he might fall down in
the street—vomiting—and be taken for a drunk. Nevertheless he
carried on with a number of outside commitments, as well as with
his work at Sherbourne. He felt not only honour-bound to do so, but
also, if he was to have any future at all, that he must.

In addition he was engaged in writing *The Contemporary Christ*.
This was one in a series being published by Macmillan's under the
editorship of Rufus Jones. He had, in the fall of 1937, promised the
manuscript by February 1938, and was making good progress until,
in December, the doctor warned him that he must ease up. Since the
work at Sherbourne must take precedence, he had reluctantly informed Macmillan's that he would be unable to complete the book
for spring publication. He added that he hoped to finish the writing
early in April. It was not until May or early June, however, that the
final chapters were sent off.

In the meantime his physical condition had deteriorated further and his doctor, once again, stepped in. On 30 April 1938, RR
wrote:

The main matter here…is that Detweiler [the doctor] has come to the conclusion that I have reached a point of fatigue at which it is imperative that I should be released from preaching and other responsibilities for some months, so that I am virtually freed from Sherbourne for good. I hope I may be able to preach there once before my term is up; but apart from that I am footloose. The Sherbourne people are being very decent about it all.…

You are not to feel anxious about me. Detweiler insists that I only need rest.

It feels funny having nothing to do—but I think I can settle down to it.

Mam is all right—but she has had a rather tough time of it these last weeks and is a bit tired.

But "having nothing to do" could not, by this time, solve the problem. The course of RR's condition had already gone beyond the point where rest alone would effect a cure. He spent two or three weeks in the hospital under observation in June and July, and then was released, as he seemed to be responding well to a stringent salt free diet. He spent the summer quietly. In the fall, after a conference with his doctors, he was greatly encouraged; in any case he was feeling very much better. The vertigo and nausea seemed to have disappeared almost completely and only the noise in the ear remained. And that he continued to regard as merely a nuisance. At the end of September, "Detweiler prophesied that I would be normal before very long, so long as I did not put undue pressure on myself. They say I may preach as soon as I like so long as I take it easy."

The General Council was meeting in Toronto that year and RR, with the blessing of his doctors, looked in on it. Of course, by this time, the state of his health was common knowledge. On 2 October he wrote:

The General Council finished on Friday—we were down several times; and at the invitation of the Moderator I took the devotional one evening—when the Anglicans, the Presbyterians and the Baptists brought greetings. The Presbyterians were there for the first time—and the quarrel is finally healed. We saw Alec Kerr a number of times; he came very much to the fore at the General Council and really distinguished himself. We heard him preach the Council sermon last Sunday—and it was very good indeed. At one point, at his initiation, attention was called to my presence at one of the meetings; I had to go onto the platform and had quite an ovation! It was rather nice but also rather embarrassing.

Several days later, on 6 October, he reported:

This week I have corrected the proofs of my book—or what is left of it. You knew, I think, that I had over-written it to the tune of some 20,000 words. The contract was for 50,000 and it had to be reduced to that. At the time when it had to be done I couldn't tackle it [he was in the hospital] so Rufus Jones did it, and did it as well as any man could have done. But the book is now little more than a torso; and the original balance has been quite destroyed. I am naturally rather sick about it....

Life seemed to be moving along quietly. RR had had three months without any vertigo and nausea. Then, suddenly, there were two very violent recurrences of the Menière's symptoms in quick succession. On 4 November he was back in hospital, undergoing an operation to sever the nerve connecting the offending ear to the brain. The operation, though effectively removing the syndrome, necessitated a further lengthy period of rest.

RR was now sixty-five years old, a time when most people are thinking of retirement. Two major operations in as many years had played havoc with his strength. Yet he remained confident that either in England or the USA some opportunity would present itself for useful service. The outbreak of World War II was soon to close the door on a return to England where, under normal conditions, his age might not have been so serious a handicap. And in the USA his age and health barred him from any call, whether to a church or a college, save as an occasional preacher or lecturer. This was something RR dared not recognize. When he had entered The United Church of Canada, it was not as a minister of one of the main uniting bodies but as an individual. Ten years later he was faced with the decision of whether or not to become a participant in the United

Church pension fund. But it would have meant contributing a considerable sum to cover back payments and had not, at the time, seemed a feasible plan. RR was not eligible, therefore, for a church pension. Though his salaries throughout his ministry had been high, neither he nor Mrs. Roberts were given to frugality, either towards themselves or others. He had always contributed generously to the church, to other causes, and to individuals. He had literally taken no thought for the morrow, nor had his right hand known what his left hand was doing. His savings were negligible; he could not retire.

29
Halifax

After his operation RR had, perforce, to proceed quietly. Throughout the early part of 1939, he undertook next to nothing in the way
of public engagements. Nor was he disturbed that no major opportunity for work presented itself. He was confident that when he was
ready for it, the job would be ready for him.

In the meantime A.E. Kerr had been appointed principal of Pine
Hill Divinity School, the United Church theological college in Halifax,
Nova Scotia. Dr. Kerr's plans for the college were hampered by a
very straitened budget. Nevertheless, knowing his old chief to be
"available," he coveted for his students something of what he had
experienced as RR's associate in Montreal. If the thing could not be
done within the budget, some other means must be found. Late in
the summer Dr. Kerr appealed to Mrs. D.A. Dunlap of Sherbourne
Street United Church. She forthwith offered a one year stipend of
two thousand dollars for a special lectureship, on the condition that
RR would accept the position. In a letter written from Montreal en
route to Halifax, RR described the nature of his duties:

> You may be wondering what I am going to do at Pine Hill. I
> am to take three courses.
> I.   The Testimony and Task of Christianity—which is an
>   attempt to state a positive central evangelical faith,
>   avoiding the "falsehood of extremes," yet trying to do
>   justice to Barth at one end and the Humanists on the other.
>   I had been working on this in the summer—without any
>   thought of Pine Hill.
> II. The Christian Ministry—the first term, General: second
>   term, Preaching.
> III. A seminar class on "Suffering, Human and Divine," based

on a book of that name by Wheeler Robinson of Oxford [in the same series as *The Contemporary Christ*].

Shortly after the arrangements had been made, and before the Roberts left for Halifax, World War II had broken out. The timing is irrelevant, however; RR's known pacifism would have made no difference to Alex Kerr. But it was an ironic turn of fate that placed RR in Halifax during wartime. Of all the cities in Canada, this Atlantic port was the most directly involved in the war.

Left to himself RR would not have felt called upon to make any statement relative to the war. He had made his stance abundantly clear over the years. Moreover, in the early days of the war he had been encouraged to think that the church was not going to be carried away by the beating of drums. On 5 October 1939, he wrote:

I think that you will be glad to hear that the attitude of the United Church as a whole to the war situation has belied my fears and exceeded my brightest hopes. In case you have not seen it I send a copy of the Moderator's letter to the ministers. (It wasn't his production, though. It was chiefly the work of Pat Sclater and R. B. Y. Scott [b. 1899, Old Testament scholar and hymn writer] edited by the sub-executive.) Even men like _____, who I should have expected would have been belligerent, take a fine Christian line....And it is not the ministers only, but the laity. Jack Duckworth...told us on Sunday night that he sat with a company of laymen, YMCA directors, who started discussing the matter, and they all agreed that fomenting the war spirit was not the business of the church—and the one I should have thought the toughest of the company said positively that the business of the church in wartime was to preach peace and goodwill. It is very cheering to me....I had to resign from my congregation in 1914 for saying the things that apparently all the United Church ministers are saying in these days. It is not that they have become pacifists, but that they have come to see that the Gospel and war are at extreme antipodes from one another.

Others, however, lacking RR's experience and perspective, were impatient with the moderator's letter. They recalled the following passages in the declaration upon war made by the General Council of 1938:

> One thing unites us all—our belief that our first loyalty must be to Christ and the cause of the building of His Kingdom on earth....We may differ on how that loyalty should be expressed, but we declare that under all circumstances, in time of war as in time of peace, a Christian must follow Christ....Neither the state or any other power has the right to compel a person to engage in what his conscience declares to be a sinful act....
>
> We reaffirm the stand taken by former General Councils of our Church relative to war, namely in brief: "The United Church of Canada, in General Council assembled, declares its unchanging conviction that war is contrary to the mind of Christ." (1932) "We believe armed warfare to be contrary to the spirit and teaching of Christ." (1934) "As Christians we positively reject war, because war rejects love, defies the will of Christ and denies the worth of man." (1936) We use the words of the World Conference of Christian Churches at Oxford (1937) to declare that "wars, the occasions of war, and all situations which conceal the fact of conflict under the guise of outward peace, are marks of a world to which the Church is charged to proclaim a gospel of redemption."
>
> Some may sincerely hold that obedience to that divine command leads them to abstain from participation in any war, some that it forbids them to participate in unjust wars, some that, in the present unredeemed state of the world, the state has a duty under God to use force when law and order are threatened or to vindicate an essential Christian principle, i.e. to defend victims of wanton aggression or secure freedom for the oppressed. The Church recognizes the conscientious right and action of each of these groups.

Quoting parts of this declaration, these men drew up a document which they called a "Witness Against War." They affirmed their loyalty and their willingness to serve as citizens so long as their service did not aid the war effort, but proclaimed their intention of standing by the declarations of the General Council. They recognized that they would be a minority, and also recognized the sincerity of those who felt they must choose another road. The "Witness" was published in *The United Church Observer* with seventy-five signatures, including RR's.

In the 1 November issue of the *Observer*, however, the sub-executive of the General Council published a statement repudiating the signatories and extolling the patriotic activities of the United Church as a whole. The statement concluded with these words:

> We are, therefore, confident that we but express the attitude of The United Church of Canada as a whole when we declare our regret at the action of the signatories in making their manifesto public. The Church is determined to adhere to its previous declarations that it will protect the individual conscience, but in our judgement, by acting collectively and inviting signatures "for later publication," the signatories of this manifesto, however sincere, have gone far beyond the limits of what is wise and proper in time of war. Even the appearance of organizing opinion against the tragic necessities of the community cannot but jeopardize the essential unity and fellowship both of the Church and of the nation.
>
> The Sub-Executive would take this opportunity of proclaiming afresh the entire and unfailing loyalty of The United Church of Canada to His Majesty, the King, and its steady purpose to support him in the present dire struggle in every way which is open and proper to the Church.

Through the grapevine the news leaked out that the sub-executive's statement had passed by only one vote, and that after intense debate. In this connection RR, as a past moderator, was hot news. Disturbed by the prominence given to RR's name in the news reports, the Rev. J. Lavell Smith, himself a signatory, wrote on 27 October to enquire whether, indeed, RR's name had been rightfully appended. RR replied:

> It was my own doing in letting my name go on the "testimony." If it was going to be published I felt that I could not afford to let anyone suppose that I was "ratting" from a conviction I

have held and publicly avowed for 20 years, and which I reaffirmed no later than March 29 last at [Charles] Raven's meeting in Toronto. All the same, I told Edis Fairbairn in my letter to him to ask the signatories to consider whether we ought not to hold our hands for the present, in view of the position in which the matter had been placed by the Moderator's letter, which was far in advance in its Christian temper of any comparable document in 1914. I think now that my "caveat" was sound, because the witness has had the effect of provoking the action of the Sub-executive, which virtually throws the Church on the side of the war. Of that document I cannot speak in moderate terms, so I leave it at that. But by a curious paradox, I am now satisfied that my name is on the black list.

RR later told a member of his family that the published "Witness" differed from the original draft which he had consented to sign, and that he had been committed to rather more than he had agreed to. Neither publicly nor privately, however, did he make any protest.

As it turned out the statement of the sub-executive rather backfired, for others shared RR's view of the matter. People who disagreed with the signatories of the "Witness" in their views about war, nevertheless staunchly defended their right to state their convictions publicly. A general reaction to the entire affair is reflected in a letter written by RR on 20 November from Halifax:

I have had a deluge of letters since the publication of the "Witness"—a considerable portion of it being abusive. But the rest of the letters prove to me that there is much more support in the church for the forthright Christian position on the matter than the Sub-executive and the "patriotic" suppose. I wonder how long Christian churchmen are going to allow their nationalism to prevent their churchmanship—especially when the Ecumenical Church is beginning to enter into our calculations.

The fuss over the "Witness Against the War" made some Halifax people a little standoffish. But there were others who made up with their warmth and kindness for this coldness. Even in the public realm this was true, for in November, while the papers were still making some play with the controversy, a group of YMCA secretaries called on him. They came with the request, as RR later reported:

> ...that I should outline for them a syllabus of forum meetings on Christianity today....[And] they wanted me to conduct the forum. I promised to do the [former]; but said that I could not undertake the leadership as I had still to "go canny" with my strength. But I also pointed out that I was a marked man just now—one of the heretic 75—and they would get into trouble if they put me in the limelight. The senior man answered quietly that they had considered the matter and were prepared to take the risk...that in fact, they wanted my point of view stated! It was very cheering. There are more than we think who have not bowed the knee to Baal.

Later this group again approached RR and asked him to conduct the forum. This time he consented to do so, as he was feeling a steady improvement in his strength.

In the meantime, other opportunities in the Halifax area came his way. He wrote to his daughter Dorothy on 14 January 1940:

> Of events, there have been few. I went to preach at one of the "Week of Prayer" meetings...in the north end of the city on Friday....We had only a handful of people there—though the congregation was twice as large as any of those on the other days of the week....I remember once hearing Joseph Parker [1830-1902, the famous Congregationalist preacher and minister] at the City Temple, after reading the verse "Where two or three are gathered in my name, there am I in the midst of them," adding: "Evidently the Lord anticipated small prayer-meetings." But I suspect that he *prefers* small prayer-meetings, if only the right people are there. I am quite convinced that if any sort of spiritual quickening is to come, it will be, as always it has been, through small bands of devoted people who covenant to pray, individually and sometimes together for it.

From time to time RR had to leave Pine Hill in order to fulfil commitments previously made. Most of these were in the USA and were normal preaching engagements. One, however, was different. In May 1939, Sidney Lovett, chaplain of Yale University and an old friend, had written to RR about taking part in the Yale Christian Conference. This was an affair which, after a life of many years, had been abandoned in 1926, for lack of interest. In 1939, at the request of the students, it had been revived. The letter to Dorothy continues:

> I am just now involved in preparation for the Yale affair, which is creating a great deal of interest and even excitement....A group of Catholic students started the idea of a joint Catholic-Protestant testimony on the campus: and the upshot is that Orchard and I are to be addressing four meetings together—the first time on record, so far as I know, that a Catholic priest and a Protestant minister are to appear together on the same *religious* platform. Apparently the Catholic authorities in the USA and England gave the required permissions without much difficulty...which may be the effect of the more liberal policy of the present Pope....The topics are:

> Sunday night: The Existence of God (O)
>   The Nature of God (R)
> Monday: The Incarnation (O)
> Tuesday: The Cross (R)
> Wednesday: The Holy Spirit (R)
>   The Spirit and the Body (O).

The program had been worked out by Orchard and RR in correspondence, of which only Orchard's letters survive. Neither he nor RR had any intention that the affair should develop into a polemic or debate. Orchard wrote: "I am looking forward to it with great expectation and it will, I am sure, be greatly blessed; and with the guidance of the Holy Spirit we shall make a magnificent united front." True, on the final evening Orchard got carried away, possibly by the convert's zeal, and spoke of reunion in such a way that, after it was all over, Father Riggs of Yale felt constrained to apologize for what he felt had been a violation of the terms of the meeting. But Father Riggs need not have worried. RR had known Orchard and the exuberance of his spirit for a very long time. Not then, nor ever, was there a breach in their friendship.

At this point the US had not yet entered the war. Opinion there was sharply divided. Some pacifist groups were very vocal against American entry into the hostilities. An article by Reinhold Niebuhr in the winter issue of *Radical Religion* castigated the pacifist position as self-righteous. Niebuhr [1892–1971], an American theologian, political philosopher, and professor at Union Theological Seminary in New York, was an influential thinker and writer on ethical issues. RR felt constrained to reply. The "open correspondence" was printed in *Christianity and Society*, a magazine of which Niebuhr was an editor. It pointed up sharply the dilemma in which Christians find themselves in time of war.

In his reply to Niebuhr RR had made reference to the "sense of alienation from my people, the coolness of friends, the suspicion of disloyalty" which the pacifist must undergo. He would have been less than human had this not hurt. But he had been through it all before and was prepared for it. Infinitely harder to bear was the inner "lacerating conflict of loyalties." The grimness of the times haunted him, as a letter written on 30 March from Halifax attests:

> There's not much news. We are both in reasonable physical condition…Our chief trouble is the spectre of the near future in Europe and the repercussions it may have on this side of the Atlantic. Whether this war is only another stage or the last stage in the collapse of the world we have known— Western civilization and all that—is ambiguous. And heaven knows what the issue may be, whichever side wins. One's only refuge is "God is in his Heaven and His purposes are sure." I find myself more and more convinced that the only thing that matters is the Gospel. If only we could get it stated in terms that fit the tragedy and uncertainty of our time. Which in my small way I am trying to do in that book. [He was working on a book on the Gospel of John which was never completed.]….What I am fearing is that there may be an outburst of apocalypticism—which is, of course, mere defeatism. I am at the moment preparing two addresses for the annual meeting of the Massachusetts Federation of Churches…in which, in a modest way, I shall try to anticipate apocalypticism and the like.

On 1 June he wrote to one of his daughters:

As to the war business as a whole—I am pretty much where I was—but with difficulty. Both sentiment and judgement make me very partisan—as between the combatants—the ethical disparity of the two sides is hardly measurable. But I am sure the church should stick to its own job—if everything is not to go with the flood. There is a hoity-toity pacifism which nauseates me—and I take it that it is something of the kind that you have in mind when you say that pacifists and Christian Scientists have a certain kinship. In this world as it is, anything that seems easy should be suspect.

We are very interested in your reaction to _____ [a leading pacifist]. Perhaps Mam and I are too hard in our judgement. But what I miss is any realization of the actual and tragic failure of pacifism which the war indicates; and that the proper [apparel] of pacifists at this time is sackcloth and ashes. Personally, I feel under conviction in the matter very keenly— and my only real comfort just now is in one verse of Emily Dickinson:

It was too late for man
But early yet for God...
Creation impotent to save -
But prayer remains our side.

Again, on 23 July he wrote:

We were glad of your letter—and hoping you are having as happy a time as these grim days allow. It is desperately hard to maintain anything like a fairly decent pacifist front at this time: and I am afraid that I don't! I think I could do it better in Great Britain than I can in this comparative peace. [RR was writing during a two-month stay in Yorktown Heights, New York.] Both Mam and I have had the feeling that we would like to be over there to share in "the fellowship of suffering." I have no hope that war can lead to anything good, *per se*. But the suffering. God only knows what grace may come out of that.

I am of the conviction, and it's not altogether wishful thinking, that the Old Country will pull through: but with a narrow margin. And that would be more hopeful than any other issue. The temper over there seems pretty good, in spite of the impending terror. And however one may criticize the politicians and all that, the folk there are the nearest thing to Christianity left in Europe now. We are praying for *them*, however the event may go.

In the meantime, the academic year at Pine Hill had run its course. RR had addressed the graduates at convocation and then had several engagements lined up for the summer.

30
The Last Years

Throughout the summer of 1940, RR was busy with student conferences, preaching engagements, and retreats with ministers. He travelled from Maine to Virginia, returning occasionally for a breather to
Yorktown Heights. There he and Mrs. Roberts had set up temporary
headquarters in the home of Gilbert and Jean Beaver. Thither, for
the next few years, they returned again and again. The house was a
gracious old structure set in a quiet countryside. There was always
room for Richard, as Gilbert Beaver always called him, and Nan. Not
least of the blessings of this haven were the persons of the hosts.

RR had not lost his touch with students. There was a vitality in
their response to him, a seriousness in their search for the things of
the spirit, that thrilled him. It was this vitality that he missed in his
meetings with middle-aged adults, even with middle-aged ministers! "Perhaps it is ever so," he commented sadly. Nevertheless he
could not confine himself to student work, and his program for the
next few months included more conventional preaching engagements. From Yorktown Heights on 14 August 1940, he wrote:

> The Northfield [Student Conference] experience was a taxing
> but happy one. Between Sunday morning and the Saturday
> morning, I preached, lectured, and otherwise spoke 15
> times—and came out alive but rather tired. It was a good
> test for me—especially as I have three months of formal
> convalescence yet to go! We set straight off from Northfield
> to Newark and I preached there twice. So "there's life in the
> old dog" yet....The conference itself was a very wholesome
> affair—though there was the usual fringe of pious
> sentimentalists.
>
> Next week we shall be in Virginia where there's another

conference. I haven't so heavy a speaking program there....Then we shall go up to Boston. I have to conduct a retreat of ministers at Cohasset—and then we go for a week to Heath where Ethel Moors has a cottage. And we shall take a month's rest somewhere before we start on the National Preaching Mission.

The month's rest proved illusory, however, for on 27 October he was heading for another student retreat to be held in Connecticut. He wrote: "There's something of a revival kindling in the New England Student Christian Movement, and it seems that I am their prophet! There won't be a very large number at the retreat; but those who will be there are hand-picked."

It had long been RR's conviction that any renewal of the church must come, as it always had, from small groups praying earnestly together. These thoughts he had summed up in an article published earlier in the year in *The Christian Century*. It was called "Companies of the Upper Room," and RR had been greatly heartened by the response to it, as he wrote on 12 June:

> The article brought me a load of correspondence. The subject of it was the conditions of a spiritual awakening. What has transpired is that
> (1) there is a group of men in Montreal (in one of the suburbs—50 or so of them) who are groping for the very thing I had written about—and they have multigraphed the article for distribution.
> (2) a lady in Virginia asked permission to have it printed in the county paper; and she is writing to all the Women's Auxiliaries in the county to have them study the article.
> (3) a group of 15—ministers, laymen, and students—met last week to consider some action along the lines of the article—this was at Yale.
> (4) the minister of the Welsh Church in New York has translated the article into Welsh and has sent it to Wales for publication.
> What will come of it all one cannot tell. But it is good that there are people seriously concerned about these things.

The demand among students for retreats seemed to RR to be a part of this same hunger for a renewal of the church.

The National Preaching Mission, under the auspices of the Federal Council of Churches, began in Indianapolis on 10 November. The atmosphere was in sharp contrast with the small groups RR had been meeting with throughout the summer. His distaste for massive campaigns is obvious from these comments written from Chicago on 21 November:

> We have finished what the local papers call "the religious blitzkrieg" on Chicago: and presently we shall be leaving for Springfield, Lincoln's old home. We open fire (to continue the figure) tomorrow morning, and will be there only two days....I haven't seen enough of the business to form any judgement on it. But so far I am not impressed. There are some very fine people in the company—but so far the evangelistic note has not been very prominent. I have two engagements daily and sometimes three: one is a seminar on the Bible, the others addresses or sermons....Mam is with me, and I am very glad that she is—she takes a lot off my load....Physically I am standing up to the job very well—I was rather apprehensive before I began lest I had not sufficient capital. But I am quite reassured now.

In fact, the pace *was* too heavy for him physically, but it was only partly because of that that he withdrew from the mission after Springfield. RR's doubts about the value of big and splashy campaigns were too strong. There was far too much of the slick salesmanship approach involved.

RR's disgust for "promotional" dodges applied to the preaching of the gospel recalls his long-standing battle against the use by publishers of irrelevant details of a person's private life in the advertising of their books. He particularly detested requests from publishers or the press for his photograph. "I will not," he burst out on reading one such request, "have my ugly old *web* [Welsh for 'face'] plastered about as an advertisement for Christianity."

When he was invited to join the Newark venture, RR turned back to his students and their eagerness as to a breath of fresh air. With his inborn optimism, he thought that this was the call for which he had been waiting.

Begun in the summer of 1939, as the field work project of two Union Theological Seminary students, the Newark project had grown to include some twenty students drawn from throughout the New England area. On their own they had pooled their resources and rented a house to live in. The project had suffered many vicissitudes. Finances were shaky and some of the original leaders had been temporarily jailed for refusing to register for the draft. But somehow the project had survived. In the summer of 1941, it seemed to be headed for a new start. In a letter describing the project, RR first outlined its beginnings and then explained how he came to be involved:

> But they had the wit to realize that their experience was too limited and that they needed a senior person with them: and their choice fell on me: so Mam and I are going to spend the next two months with them—I to be leader, chaplain, spiritual adviser and tutor. They are keen upon having regular study as well as regular prayer. It will be a very interesting experience for Mam and me. And I have some inward satisfaction that they should have asked me to lead them. Unfortunately I shall not have the best men in the group during the next two months as they will not be free until the beginning of September. They share my convictions upon what is passing in the world just now.
>
> The matter doesn't end there, though. They now propose that Mam and I join them permanently. But we are not going to come to any decision upon that point just yet. Their idea is to have the whole affair linked with (possibly) Yale: and that there shall be regular study—even to the extent of the equivalent of one year at the seminary. But the element of adventure in the affair appeals to us very much.

The Roberts settled for two months into a nearby apartment which the students had secured for them. With the possibility of a permanent association in the offing, RR watched the summer proceedings carefully. The program was ambitious—too ambitious for the numbers and capacities of the students. He drew up a report on the summer's activities for the consideration of those involved:

> Clearly the conditions under which we are living and working at present are not suitable for permanent community life.

There must, for instance, be ample provision for privacy: "a room of one's own" is essential; and set periods of quietness during the day should be determined by common consent....

For the permanent colony, it is essential that it should begin and proceed cautiously, and not involve itself in undertakings beyond its strength and experience. This may be, to some extent at least, a counsel of perfection: and the colony may find itself compelled to deal with situations beyond its experience. But in the main, it should set down a definite but modest program upon which it can build up a larger work with the passing of time and with a better understanding of the needs of the community.

RR could see that the students were dissipating their energies; trying—as the young will—to create the New Jerusalem overnight. But he was anxious to see their manifest devotion channelled. He was eager, if at all possible, to be with them. In a letter to one of his daughters he wrote:

My own feeling is that the company which we have come to know in these last two months contains the possibility of a new beginning for the Christian Church; and I should not be surprised if it became the focus of a genuine spiritual awakening. They are all very eager to develop a strong personal and corporate prayer life....I rather gather that one of the chief sources of the movement were the addresses I gave at Northfield three years ago, and afterwards at two annual summer camps at O-At-Ka in Maine, so I am partly responsible for the whole movement.

In his report to the students RR had recommended that there should be some senior body of advisers, particularly in the financial sphere. To this some of the original leaders dissented strongly. They were determined to be their own bosses. Some friends, both of the students, and of RR, were perturbed. So were some of those within the group itself, and these felt constrained to withdraw. Reluctantly RR realized that, under these conditions, the venture had only a dim future.

He turned back to such occasional work as came his way. There was still a great deal of conference work with students in the New

England area, particularly in retreats. Perhaps nothing points up more vividly the difference in the atmosphere of World War I and World War II than the fact that RR was invited and allowed to hold retreats in some of the civilian camps for conscientious objectors. There was, too, still a considerable demand for his preaching in certain of the churches.

It would have been an harassing sort of life for a younger person in reasonable health. For a man on in years and in failing health, it was doubly so. Nan did her best to spare him, making all the arrangements, doing all the packing and carrying on much of the correspondence. The opportunity for a settled existence at the Friends' Centre at Pendle Hill during the winter of 1942–43, came as a relief. There RR took part in the program as requested. Sometimes it was lectures that were wanted, but chiefly he was asked to direct retreats.

Although this type of work was congenial to him, it must have been becoming apparent that he was no longer up to it. His memory was becoming more and more unreliable. In Vancouver, where he spent the summer months of 1943, with daughter Gwen and her family, RR spent a good deal of his time at his desk. Even then it was clear that the mechanical task of writing down his thoughts was getting to be a slow and laborious business. Nevertheless, the brief radio talks he gave there on the vespers program were little classics.

Before he had set off for Vancouver, RR had been informed by Gilbert Beaver, who had interested himself in the matter, that he would very probably become the recipient of a pension from a private foundation in the USA. This made it necessary for him to live there, however. So, in the fall of 1943, he returned to New York. There he remained until the fall of 1944, doing a little writing from time to time. In September he set off for Sackville, New Brunswick to deliver the Josiah Wood lectures at Mount Allison University. He planned on spending a few weeks in Montreal on the way.

When he arrived in Montreal daughter Peggy, and Dorothy who lived in nearby Beaconsfield, were shocked at how much he had failed. They were greatly perturbed. It was not only the matter of his memory which they described as "haywire," but he was having difficulty with his speech; and his hands, never dexterous, were fumbling. They wondered how he could manage to deliver the lectures even supposing he were able to make the long journey to New Brunswick. As he was complaining of his eyes and other physical discomforts, they were able to persuade him to see two doctors who were also old friends. The diagnosis was hardening of the arteries of the brain. From what they were told, the doctors also deduced that he had already suffered one or more slight strokes. They declared that the lectures must be called off. Peggy wrote to Gwen:

> I went out [to Beaconsfield, where RR and Mrs. Roberts were staying with Dorothy] to tell Dads the next day that the doctors had said he mustn't attempt the lectures, and I don't think I have ever hated doing anything so much in my life. He reared up like an old war-horse and said, "But I *have* to give them, Pegs. I'm committed to it." We did not tell him anything about his physical condition other than that the doctors said that, with his present speech difficulty, as well as his eyes, they thought he would do himself real injury, and it wasn't fair to Mount A., Mam, or the lectures themselves to go against their advice. When he had finally accepted the decision he became quite practical for a little while: decided to mail the manuscript in the hope that they might be read by someone else; asked me to get Walter [Dr. Scriver, one of the consultants] to write to Principal Truman, etc. But a few days later he had forgotten about the whole episode and was worried about the tickets, etc. to Sackville. And then a week or two later still the whole episode came up again, and it all had to be explained again. It really is very harassing for Mam.

In order to draw his pension, RR had to be resident in the US. He and Mrs. Roberts returned to New York to spend the winter. In April 1945, Peggy went to visit them. She wrote in some detail to Gwen in Vancouver:

> I had planned all along to go to New York during the Easter holidays, and two weeks before I had sensed from Mam's letter that she was very anxious for me to go, as apparently he was a bit worse. So I went as planned on April 5th. And he had a bad turn that afternoon. He was pleased to see me when I got there though, and we had several chats during the next two-three days. But he got weaker steadily, and by Friday I knew I couldn't leave them where they were as Mam really couldn't handle the situation.

Peggy arranged for RR to be moved to a nursing home in Brooklyn where Mrs. Roberts could remain with him. After the move Peggy returned to the Van Rensselaer Hotel, to the room the Roberts had been occupying. She was called back to the nursing home not long after she had reached the hotel, however:

> Soon after 2 A.M. the phone went and the nurse called…telling me she didn't think he'd last till morning.…So I went over to Brooklyn. He was a bit better when I got there, but about 5 A.M. he relapsed into a coma which he never came out of. He died at 2:20 P.M. It was rather wonderful, Gwen. Sidney Lovett was there—came from Yale because he heard Dads was ill, and Gilbert Beaver and Cynolwyn Pugh, the Welsh minister in New York. And Dads just slept peacefully away with no suffering at all.

Mam was and is wonderful. She feels, I think, that as the person closest to him it's up to her to demonstrate the Christian faith in which he lived and died. All during the last night before he went into coma, he was moving his arms around in his old pulpit gestures and murmuring…"I want to preach—I want to preach Jesus Christ," and then every now and again [in Welsh], *Jesu Grist*. It was quite amazing and very moving. I never felt as sure in my life of the immortality ofthe human spirit—especially such a spirit as Dads'.

31

L'Envoi

In 1942, RR wrote the following hymn and dedicated it to the SCM in New England:

O God, undone am I,
 My sin prevailing;
Send Thou me, or I die,
 Thy grace unfailing;
O Love untold, unbound,
 My harried soul surround
 That I betimes be found
 Thy Triumph hailing!

My faults do Thee defame,
 Thy Name dishonour;
Aye, put Thee to open shame—
 Yet send Thy succour!
And give me, lest I yield,
 Thy Spirit's sword to wield,
 And dress me for the field
 In Thy whole armour.

O Christ, on yonder hill,
 My Captain dying,
Rebuke my coward will—
 Hear Thou my crying—
O Thou whose Face is marred
 (Thy hands and feet how scarred!)
 Nerve me to keep high guard,
 Thy banner flying.
Tune: Moab.

Part VII

Contextualizing Richard Roberts' Thought: Liberal Protestantism and the Dilemmas of the Modern Age

Catherine Gidney

Richard Roberts was in the prime of his life when he was called to Canada to minister, first to the American Presbyterian Church in Montreal, and then to Sherbourne Street United Church in Toronto.[1] Most of his theological writings date from this period. Yet the issues Roberts grappled with were not particular to the interwar years or to Canada. Rather, their roots may be located in over a century of intellectual, social, and economic upheaval that had occurred throughout the western world, and which challenged the theological underpinnings of mainstream Protestantism. While historians agree that such upheaval helped transform mainstream Protestantism at the turn of the century, the nature and effects of this transformation are greatly debated. Discussion has centred on whether the adoption of a more liberal theology—with its emphasis on social action and openness to cultural change—weakened the traditional stress of Protestantism on the Bible and personal salvation, or helped maintain continuity between older beliefs and new developments in society.[2] As a product of both the nineteenth and twentieth centuries, Richard Roberts' religious thought, his ideas on social reform, and his conception of the ministry, provide a good illustration of mainstream clerical attempts to reshape faith for the modern age.

To understand Roberts' thought we need to examine, briefly, the intellectual and social changes that had taken place in western society in the century before his birth. Traditionally evangelical Protestantism—the culturally dominant religion in nineteenth-century North America—had related faith and reason through the use of Scottish Common Sense philosophy and Baconian thought. This method had encouraged scientific study within the Christian framework of belief in God's design. Using faith and experience rather than pure reason in their defence of religion, the clergy had invoked philosophy and science to support scriptural truths and prove the accuracy of biblical facts and doctrines.[3] Yet, from the early nineteenth century onwards, geologists and biologists had begun to provide increasing evidence that the world and its inhabitants had evolved over time through numerous chemical reactions. Such arguments had gained widespread credibility and support after the publication of Charles Darwin's *Origin of Species* in 1859, challenging the authority of the Bible by questioning the accuracy of the story of Genesis and God's role in the process of creation.[4]

While scientists questioned religious interpretations of history, German theologians were at the same time reinterpreting the methods with which to study the Bible. Higher critics, as these scholars came to be called, began to treat the Bible as simply an historical document, which could be more validly interpreted through reason than through faith or theology. They suggested that scripture was the product of human rather than divine agency and, while no longer accepted as an historical and scientific account, contained profound moral and religious truths. Such critics undermined the notion of the infallibility of the Bible by questioning the historical reality of the events and facts of the biblical record.[5]

At the same time as the old relationship between religion and science was becoming uncertain, other challenges to classical Protestantism developed. Changing moral and social values made ideas of predestination, original sin, and the eternal punishment of the unredeemed seem morally repugnant and outdated. These ideas came under particular scrutiny in 1860, with the publication by a number of British clergymen of *Essays and Reviews*. The huge controversy it provoked demonstrated the extent of the challenges to traditional Protestantism. By the end of the nineteenth century, in an increasingly industrial and urban society, injustices like inhuman working conditions and city slums marked by poverty and disease were also forcing the clergy to reconceptualize the relationship between Christianity and the social order.[6]

As a result of this profusion of social, economic, and intellectual change in the nineteenth and early twentieth centuries, evangelical Protestantism gradually split into three broad expressions of faith. A fundamentalist position reaffirmed the classical emphasis on God's transcendence, individual salvation through conversion, and the importance of sin, and, in reaction to the new biblical criticism, insisted on a literal interpretation of the Bible.[7] Modernists on the other hand, concerned to adapt religious ideas to modern culture, emphasized theological concepts informed by modern scientific and intellectual thought, such as the immanence of God and the centrality of Jesus Christ, and saw society progressing towards the realization of the kingdom of God.[8] Mediating these two extremes was a liberal Protestantism of which less is known. Caught between fundamentalism and modernism, liberal Protestants were concerned to maintain a continuity with traditional elements of their faith and still remain faithful to the nineteenth century position of being open to the insights of science.

Growing up in the late nineteenth century, Roberts was exposed to and influenced by the modernist ideas which, in their call to build the kingdom of God on earth, were beginning to reshape Protestantism in the first decade of the twentieth century. Only in the interwar years did he come to realize that the modernist tendencies within pre-war liberal Protestantism needed to be tempered with elements of evangelical belief. Thus, while throughout his life Roberts wrestled with the philosophical and social concerns of modern society, he continued, in the tradition of the precursors of the United Church leadership, such as the Methodist Nathanael Burwash and the Presbyterian George Munro Grant, to attempt to reconcile modern beliefs with traditional tenets of the faith.[9] In doing so he contributed significantly during the interwar years to the re-articulation of a liberal Protestantism which avoided the extremes of modernism.

Roberts' concern to provide a relevant faith led him to write a number of essays and books on theological and professional issues. He presented what he saw as the central tensions in Protestantism in such scholarly arenas as *The Hibbert Journal* and the *Canadian Journal of Religious Thought*.[10] And he provided advice on the role and duties of the preacher in monographs such as *The Preacher as a Man of Letters*. Yet Roberts was interested not only in the tasks and intellectual concerns of ministers, but was also crucially aware of the continuing need to engage ordinary thinking people in the claims of Christianity. In works such as *The Christian God* and *The Spirit of God and the Faith of Today* he elucidated for a general reading audience central theological concepts such as God and the Spirit. Between 1925 and 1937, he wrote a weekly devotional column in the United Church's official organ *The New Outlook*. And he discussed the relationship between religion and social reform through topics such as the ideal of democracy, the role of Christian individuals in their community, and the need for pacifism in such books as *The Unfinished Programme of Democracy*, *The Contemporary Christ*, and *The Christian and War*. Many of these works were popular in nature and, as they were published with such companies as J. M. Dent and Sons, Macmillan, Allen and Unwin, and Cassells, they had a wide distribution. But Roberts spread his ideas not only through the written word, but in sermons to his own congregation, at services and missions at the University of Toronto and, when travelling across the country as moderator, in lectures to local churches and branches of the Student Christian Movement. Roberts' reach, then, was a broad one, engaging church members across Canada and encouraging them to examine and reinterpret their faith for a modern age.

During the early 1920s, as Roberts was settling in to minister to the American Presbyterian Church in Montreal, he began to realize the extent to which late nineteenth century intellectual and social changes had not only called various tenents of classical Protestantism into question, but had also resulted in their alteration.[11] In Roberts' view it was especially the widespread acceptance of Darwin's theory of evolution that had fundamentally challenged nineteenth century Protestants' conception of God. Traditionally, God had been understood as the origin and sustainer of the universe, a supernatural being who transcended human history yet continued to intervene in daily life. Evolutionary theory, however, posited an entire universe in the process of development, and thus an immanent God not only present and involved in the improvement of humanity within the natural world, but as such, also limited by its processes.[12] In 1927, Roberts succinctly described the dilemma that Protestants faced:

> Creation implies a "transcendent" God; Evolution an "immanent" God. Creation requires a God standing outside the universe, having brought it into being by his own *fiat*, and operating upon it from without in perfect freedom according to his own will. It may be true that evolution does not logically imply immanence; but there is no doubt that

the two ideas make good company in the mind. And to most minds, evolution certainly does suggest a God *within* the universe, involved in and therefore limited by its processes, and somehow fulfilling Himself in its development.[13]

Roberts believed that the development and widespread acceptance of the theory of evolution had led to the dominance, among late nineteenth and early twentieth century mainstream liberal Protestants, of the modernist emphasis on God's immanence at the expense of the evangelical understanding of God's transcendence.[14]

By the late 1920s, Roberts had become increasingly critical of the modernist tendencies in this pre-war liberal theology. Though intellectually sophisticated, he considered it incongruous in its maintenance of certain elements of traditional Protestant belief and practice. For example, in embracing modernist concepts, he argued, Protestants had allowed their thought to become fundamentally inconsistent. They believed in traditional doctrines such as, the Incarnation and the Resurrection, and practiced traditional religious exercises such as prayer—all of which suggested a transcendent God—while at the same time they fundamentally changed these doctrines by interpreting God's nature as immanent. Thus the Incarnation had come to be understood as Jesus "coming up from the ranks," while God was understood to work within or through individuals and society.[15] Roberts' critique was neither a desire to return to evangelical Protestantism nor a repudiation of pre-war liberal Protestants' attempts to incorporate evolutionary theory. What was needed, he argued, was a synthesis of these two theological traditions.[16]

In his efforts to articulate such a theology, Roberts drew on a wide and often eclectic range of late nineteenth and early twentieth century sources. In his books and lectures he referred, for example, to Romantic and Victorian poets such as, Blake and Wordsworth, Browning and Tennyson, and to scientists such as Albert Einstein and A. S. Eddington. He read widely in the area of philosophy and theology and referred to Hegel, the realist philosophy of George Santayana, the idealist philosophy of Edward Caird, Josiah Royce and R. J. Campbell, the vitalism of Henri Bergson, the liberal theology of Walter Rauschenbush, the Neo-Thomist theology of Jacques Maritain, the Neo-orthodoxy of Karl Barth, and the early existentialism of John Macmurray.[17] Guided by his desire to maintain the central tenets of the Christian faith, Roberts did not follow any particular theology or philosophy. Rather he selectively retained the thought he considered important and discarded what did not suit his purpose.

In his attempt to reconcile evolution with classical Protestantism, he found the philosophy of A.N. Whitehead most useful. This eminent philosopher and mathematician perceived the natural world as constantly developing and striving towards self-fulfilment. For Whitehead, God was part of the process of becoming, the ideal to be reached, and the element which pierced down into the natural world to aid the process of realization.[18] Whitehead, then, provided Roberts with a means for understanding a God who was both supernatural and who worked within the evolutionary process. For example, Roberts believed that Jesus was "the ultra-human 'emergent' in the course of biological development,"[19] and Christians therefore ought to shape their lives by following the example of Jesus as manifested in his life and teachings.[20] But how could a perfect human appear so early in the evolutionary process? Was not Jesus a "contradiction of a theory of gradual development?"[21] As early as 1912, Roberts had been arguing that the Cross "is not to be adequately explained except as a direct intervention of God in human affairs. God departed from His ordinary method of conducting the business of the world and broke into the world directly in the person of Jesus Christ."[22] Thus, while Christ was of this world, it was as one from the other world that he was worshipped by Christians.[23]

For Roberts it was not Jesus' birth or life, but rather his crucifixion, symbolized by the cross, which was the most significant event in recorded history.[24] He argued that Christian theology had lost the elements of reproach and shame that the cross had traditionally represented, and that it was imperative these elements be restored.[25] Where early nineteenth century evangelicals had viewed individuals as inherently sinful, turn of the century liberal Protestants had stressed the inherent goodness of humans, and the need for social rather than individual salvation.[26] Consequently, the importance placed by evangelicals on the cross as a symbol of human sin and the need for repentance had become de-emphasized in the late nineteenth and early twentieth centuries, with the notion of personal salvation achieved "through losing oneself in the social task"[27] becoming dominant. Roberts decried the modernist tendency to de-emphasize the cross, but also argued for the need to re-articulate, in a new way, the evangelical doctrine of original sin. The cross, he believed, represented the constant conflict within humans of having to choose between good and evil, and as such forced a choice upon individuals as to the path they would follow.[28] But while emphasizing the notion of individual sin, Roberts interpreted this traditional concept within the framework of evolutionary theory. Repudiating the notion of inevitable progress that prevailed in the pre-war strain of liberal Protestantism, Roberts argued that evolution implied the need for continuous struggle without which degeneracy would occur.[29] For example, in a 1928 article in *The New Outlook*, Roberts wondered how long humanity could continue to fail God:

> We are not God's last resort....In the course of evolution, more than one form of life has been discarded...because it refused to fulfil its purpose; and we cannot presume on preferential treatment if we hold up the divine traffic.[30]

Consequently, he defined sin as anything that hindered individual or societal evolution, and he considered part of the nature of sin to be a relapse by individuals and society to a standard of morality inferior to that previously attained, or to any point at which humans no longer strove to achieve the highest possible moral and spiritual level.[31]

Finally, Roberts also understood God's activity and self-revelation within the world through the concept of the Holy Spirit. Using modern scientific language to explain himself, he stated that "when I was a lad at school learning chemistry, I learned, among other things, that certain elements will combine more readily with the help of a third, which is called a catalytic agent. When God and man meet, the spirit is the unseen catalytic agent which combines them."[32] Roberts believed that the Spirit manifested itself in various ways. For example, artistic work such as poetry, music, and art were all divinely inspired and revealed God's presence.[33] Thus the spirit stimulated "high ethical passion and achievement."[34] In addition, Roberts believed that prayer was a means of God's self-revelation, for prayer was both a means of seeking God and also evidence of God's activity within humans.[35] For Roberts, then, the spirit was the divine presence in the secular and religious realms of the world.

Utilizing such basic Christian concepts as Jesus, the cross, sin, and the Holy Spirit, Roberts re-articulated these as part of his effort to synthesize key elements of modernist and evangelical thought. He affirmed central concepts of evangelicalism such as, a transcendent God, the cross as a symbol of human sin and as a reminder of the need for repentance and forgiveness, and Jesus as evidence of God's intervention in earthly affairs. Yet he combined these with the more recent emphasis by pre-war liberal Protestants on an immanent God and on the idea of the indwelling Christ.

Roberts recognized the inconsistencies in his synthesis; as he stated, "logically, transcendence and immanence are irreconcilable notions."[36] Yet he argued that "the best thought of our time leads us to the idea of a transcendent immanent eternally self-perfecting Absolute."[37] Until a more comprehensive theology emerged, Roberts was willing to live with a theological system that, while paradoxical, he saw to be more complete than anything else proposed. He did not hold this position to be final. He considered the re-articulation of theology to be a constant process and stated that "we shall probably have to build and to discard many a system of theology"[38] before achieving the one which would be absolute.

Roberts was not presenting simply a personal religion, but rather a faith which emphasized the relationship between Christians and their society. Theologically trained at the height of the social gospel movement in Britain, his ideas on social reform were a conscious shift away from the early to mid-nineteenth century conviction that reform was primarily a means of removing obstacles to individual salvation. As Roberts stated:

> The regenerated individual, no doubt, does modify his social environment; but we cannot possibly achieve a transformed society without transforming the influences which produce modern social chaos....The foundations of society must be changed *pari passu* with the character of the individual.[39]

However, during the interwar years, just as Roberts had become critical of pre-war liberal Protestants' stress on God's immanence, so he decried their exclusive focus on the idea of social transformation. For Roberts, the overriding concern with the "now" rather than the afterlife had led Christianity to be "an affair of tame humanitarianism and ambiguous philanthropies."[40] Protestants needed to integrate the personal and social nature of Christianity because, he insisted, it was impossible for them to "disentangle their relation to God from their relation to society."[41] Yet, rather than repudiate the social gospel, Roberts modified it to emphasize the fulfilment of personality[42] within society. As Roberts succinctly stated the issue:

> We are overcoming that particular fallacy that we have two parts, one of the world and the other not of the world, for which we must legislate differently. We have thought that our business in the City had no great connection with our business in regard to getting to heaven; but we are discovering that the way to heaven is through the City. We are gaining a clearer sense of the true unity of life.[43]

Thus it was imperative that Christians be involved in social reform and improve temporal conditions in order to allow for the growth of the human personality. A lasting social transformation would only occur with a spiritual and moral change, as people's lives became redirected by God's principles.

Roberts' social passion, which had developed during his youth when he witnessed the hardships faced by the men and women of his Welsh quarrying community, quickly came to shape his religious leadership. For example, sympathizing with the Independent Labour Party (ILP) he was removed from his first assignment with the Calvinistic Methodist Forward Movement, an evangelizing effort in Wales, for chairing a political meeting for MP and ILP leader Keir Hardie.[44] During his ministry at several churches in London, Roberts marched with the unemployed and protested "the living conditions of shopgirls."[45] And with the beginning of the First World War, Roberts not only reaffirmed the anti-war position that he had adopted during the Boer War but developed a pacifist stance. In 1915, he became the secretary of the Fellowship of Reconciliation (FOR), a pacifist group he had helped found a year earlier and with which he remained in close contact when called to the Church of Pilgrims in New York in 1917.[46]

This early activism, along with witnessing the carnage of World War I and the misery and suffering caused by the Depression, shaped and reinforced Roberts' view of the need for fundamental changes within society. Drawing on the post-war reform program of the Labour Party in Britain, he advocated the establishment of a real living wage and unemployment insurance so that all would be provided with economic security, housing, and leisure time. Moreover, he called for the elimination of the profit motive in the economic system and its replacement by a society based on co-operation. Profits, he contended, provoked and perpetuated conflict between individuals, classes, and nations.[47] In a co-operative society, where owner and worker were reconciled through Jesus Christ, "Capital and Labour might work out something deeper than industrial peace—a living creative fellowship in the interests of the community."[48] Despite Roberts' critique of the existing social system, he never doubted that modern democracy was the only form of government consistent with Christian principles. He defined democracy as a "society which will provide for all its members those conditions of equal opportunity that are within human control. It denies all forms of special and exclusive privilege, and affirms the sovereignty of the common man."[49] However, he also argued that democracy had not yet been completed. While Britain and the United States had extended the principles of political democracy, they had allowed the development of inequality in economic life. The economy, Roberts contended, was being maintained through oligarchical methods resulting in human exploitation for individual gain. Moreover, he argued, western democracies lacked sufficient subordination of the individual to the community.[50]

Roberts, then, was advocating a more Christian society based on the principles of a yet to be created welfare state. Although this was a radical position for the time, it did not translate into unqualified support for the Christian left. Christian radicalism, which according to historian Richard Allen emerged out of the disintegrating social gospel movement, gained a stronghold within The United Church of Canada in the early 1930s.[51] Such radicalism resulted in the creation in 1934, of the Fellowship for a Christian Social Order (FCSO), an inter-denominational organization for those interested in social reconstruction and primarily led by and composed of men and women in the United Church.[52]

Roberts' thought was similar enough to that of the FCSO that, in 1936, he agreed to write the foreword to their main political tract, *Towards the Christian Revolution*. He praised the book as an "important contribution to the current discussion of the ends and values of a Christian society, and the ways and means of achieving it."[53] Yet for Roberts it was simply that—part of a discussion needed within the church. He was less willing to endorse their attempts to have their beliefs adopted as official church policy. When Christian socialists put forward a report at the 1933 Toronto Conference of the United Church aimed at transforming society, Roberts voted against it. While the reasons for his position are sketchy, he seems to have believed that Christian socialists focused on improving economic conditions at the expense of spiritual development.[54] An examination of Roberts' involvement in the Commission on Christianizing the Social Order can help clarify how his approach differed from that of Christian socialists within the United Church. Concerned about the problems caused by the Depression, Roberts called for the establishment of this Commission at the United Church's General Council of 1932. For the next two years he aided the chair, Sir Robert Falconer, in drafting the commission's report. The purpose of the commission was to articulate Christian standards and principles for the social order, to determine to what extent these principles prevailed, and to establish measures for their implementation.[55]

The commission, like the FCSO, identified the main problem in the social order to be that of economic insecurity, the result of the dominant "unsocial" spirit of acquisition. It advocated that basic material needs be met and that worker and manager work co-operatively for the general good. To this end it suggested Christians practice their faith both in their personal and public lives, that they study the existing social order in groups in order to arouse their consciences against injustices within the system, and that the church take action once a consensus had developed.[56] While the FCSO welcomed the report as a sound analysis of the injustices of capitalism, its members felt the commission had not gone far enough, and wondered whether any tangible changes were possible while the existing system survived.[57] For Roberts, however, the report was simply a beginning, intended to address Canada's economic situation. It provided a strong basis for discussions within the church out of which a consensus for action could be developed. But perhaps more importantly, the report addressed his own concerns in that it linked social reform to the need for Christians' to practice their faith in a more diligent manner.

Where Roberts did side with the more radical wing of the United Church was on the issue of pacifism. While only a small number of Canadians held pacifist sentiments during the first half of the twentieth century, a significant number of these came from within the left wing of the United Church, particularly from among the membership of the FCSO.[58] Taking a progressive stand in the mid-1930s, the United Church had declared war "contrary to the spirit and teaching of Christ."[59] Yet with the outbreak of World War II, it quickly proclaimed its support for the war effort. As a result, a month after Canadian entry into the war, Roberts, along with over sixty-eight other pacifist ministers, signed a manifesto entitled "A Witness Against War." At first Roberts had hesitated in taking this radical action. He completely repudiated the United Church's declaration of support for the war effort. Yet he felt the church's position to be somewhat redeemed when, in mid-September, he received a general letter from the moderator, John D. Woodside, to all ministers, stating that "we must affirm for ourselves and our brethren the paramount authority of conscience under the leadership of Christ."[60] Roberts had spent the years during World War I championing the rights of the conscientious objector, and consequently felt his activities and lifelong efforts had been vindicated by the moderator's letter. Writing to his daughter he stated that:

> ...the attitude of the United Church as a whole to the war situation has belied my fears and exceeded my brightest hopes....I had to resign from my congregation in 1914 for saying the things that apparently all the United Church ministers are saying in these days. It is not that they have become pacifists, but that they have come to see that the Gospel and war are at extreme antipodes from one another.[61]

Nevertheless, fearing he would be seen as compromising his pacifist position, Roberts reluctantly signed the manifesto.[62] But the manifesto created a furore within the church; and shortly after it appeared, the sub-executive of the General Council issued a statement that, while supporting the individual's right to object to war, condemned the manifesto as contrary to the interests of the community and exceeding the bounds of what was proper in wartime.[63] At the same time, the sub-executive reaffirmed the United Church's loyalty to "the King, and its steady purpose to support him in the present dire struggle in every way which is open and proper to the Church."[64] Roberts considered the sub-executive's patriotic position to be a support for nationalism rather than Christ's teachings, and its condemnation of the manifesto "rather feeble and cowardly"; he was now glad that he had put his name to the "witness."[65]

Roberts' position against war was consistent with the position he had taken on the social and economic order. War, he believed, was a direct negation of the creation of personality and the realization of the Christian aim of shaping and stimulating "fellowship in every part of life."[66] A lasting solution to war, he believed, could not be found in peace treaties. Only by accepting Jesus' ethic of right, which Roberts defined as "that which creates, deepens, expands fellowship and restores it when it is broken,"[67] could the roots of war be eliminated.

For Roberts, then, individual belief and action were intricately connected. The development of the human personality—or, in other words, the growth of the human spirit—could only be achieved in a social setting. The purpose of community was to provide the opportunity for human creativity and thus enable the elevation of humanity. When creative growth was being restricted, it was imperative that the conditions of that restriction, whether economic, political or social, be changed. Reform on a vast scale, however, could not be successfully achieved overnight, but had to occur gradually and through consensus. At the same time, Roberts emphatically insisted that in order for reform to lead to a lasting social transformation, society had to be based upon Christian principles.

Yet if reform was to create the potential for the development of human personality, how, in fact, did Roberts believe individuals would learn to accept and to become guided by Christian principles? During the nineteenth century, evangelicals believed that such a change could only be brought about through individual salvation, a process involving "repentance and conversion and the acceptance of a disciplined life that reflected a spiritual transformation."[68] Often this was achieved through the means of revivalism, a form of evangelization whereby a preacher exhorted people to repent of their sins, receive the word of God, and be converted.[69] By the early twentieth century, historians have noted, this traditional understanding of evangelization had either disappeared from most mainstream Protestants' religious beliefs, or had been replaced by a non-revivalist approach to piety.[70]

During the interwar years Roberts voiced the importance of spiritual change through evangelization. Indeed, he placed this notion at the centre of his conception of the church and of the ministry. But he also radically changed the traditional understanding of the process. His views on evangelization came out with particular clarity in his response to the Oxford Group movement, which took Canada by storm in the early 1930s. Led by Frank Buchman, an American Lutheran who had devoted his life to evangelizing efforts in the western world, the Group arrived in Canada in the fall of 1932. During the 1920s Buchman had gathered together a "team" of evangelists and traveled throughout the USA and Britain before reaching Canada. His approach was evangelistic, using the methods of confession and exhortation in order to encourage individuals to conversion and thus to effect their salvation. Upon arriving in a city, the Group would hold a large meeting to attract as many people as possible. They would then hold smaller "house parties" in private mansions or luxury hotels, such as the Château Frontenac or the Banff Springs Hotel, to which only the local elite were invited.[71]

The Oxford Group movement has generally been assessed as a conservative movement which, by stressing personal evangelization, offered a method of escape from the economic and social problems facing Canadians in the 1930s.[72] While Roberts repudiated its over-emphasis on a personal religion, he also felt it brought a needed element to the church. While on the one hand decrying, in his candid letters to members of the family, the movement's absence of social concern, and writing of the movement as "a passing phase," a "side-show," and a "good idea gone wrong," on the other hand he contended that, despite its faults, it presented a challenge both to himself personally and, he believed, to all church members.[73] While he believed some of its methods to be wrong, he considered the Group's expression of a simple evangelical faith and its revival of personal evangelization to be important. The Group's message, he claimed, had challenged people's moral self-complacency, changed many people's lives, and revived the corporate life of many congregations.[74] Indeed, for Roberts himself, that message acted as a springboard to his own attempt to re-articulate the concept of evangelization for the twentieth century.

Roberts believed the Group's emphasis on daily quiet time was important. He argued that he had, for some time before the arrival of the Group, encouraged all members of his congregation, both on their own and in small groups, to engage in this practice in the form of daily prayer. He believed that the action of prayer revealed the movement of God within the individual. On the one hand God provoked prayer, and on the other hand the act of prayer directed one's life towards God.[75] As Roberts stated: "God Transcendent and God Immanent, who are strangers in logic, meet in experience. Our prayers go up from God; the answering sign comes down from God."[76] Such fellowship with God through private and corporate prayer was, for Roberts, the first step towards transforming society.[77]

Roberts, however, found the Group's belief in the need for an immediate conversion experience more problematic. He believed that there were different ways of achieving redemption for, as he stated: "God saves us one by one, each after his own fashion."[78] Roberts' own conversion to God had occurred gradually over the course of his youth. Moreover, the process of surrendering to God was not a one time event but rather, he claimed, "something I find that I have to be going on doing again and again, in the faith and the hope that every time I do, some new area of my life is annexed to his Kingdom."[79]

For Roberts, then, revivalism was a long-term process, involving the cultivation of the movement of the spirit within the individual. Here the role of the preacher was especially important in preparing the pathway and harnessing the spirit of revivalism. To this end preaching needed, through both rational and emotional appeal, to provoke a commitment from the congregation to Jesus, to move them to lead a disciplined and devotional life, and to encourage fellowship with God and other individuals through individual and corporate prayer. Evangelistic efforts, he believed, ought to occur in small groups within individual churches, led by the preacher, emphasizing religious growth through Christian nurture rather than sudden conversion, and should appeal to both emotion and reason.[80]

Roberts' activities as moderator of the United Church provide a further illustration of his attempt to re-articulate the traditional understanding of evangelization. In 1934, Roberts was appointed moderator for two years. Within a few months of his appointment he set out in *The New Outlook* his impression of the particular direction

United Church members seemed to feel the denomination ought to take, as well as the type of leadership he would attempt to provide. Church members, Roberts believed, desired a spiritual renewal:

> There is today a rising tide of earnest and persistent desire for definite and sustained concentration upon the spiritual offices of the Church, evangelism, the culture of the inner life, the revivification of public worship, the study of the Scriptures, and the quickening of fellowship in the deep things of God. These are the things that give the Church its meaning; when these fail, or cease, then the Church's life falls into routine and dullness and its impact upon the unregenerate world is compromised and may even cease altogether.[81]

Essentially, Roberts believed his task as moderator was to provide the necessary leadership to help initiate the process of spiritual quickening within the United Church. To this end he planned to travel to strategic centres across the country. He wanted to remain in one location for five days, from Sunday to Thursday. While his agenda would be organized by local committees, he would address congregations on Sunday, Tuesday, and Wednesday evenings. As well, Thursday would be reserved as a day of spiritual retreat for ministers.[82]

Roberts did not, however, see renewal as a task for the ministry alone. Only if church members participated in the process would his mission succeed. He not only believed that the laity should be involved in church life—organizing and leading church activities, for example, but also that they had a direct role to play in the process of evangelization and spiritual renewal. Consequently, he asked every church member to undertake spiritual preparation through personal prayer in order to receive the visitation of the Spirit.[83] At the same time, the spiritual renewal which Roberts hoped his mission would accomplish was not solely for the spiritual betterment of United Church members. He believed that such renewal would lead to "a new passion for social righteousness" and to a Christianity which would "find its proper corporate expression in the creation of a Christian social and world order."[84]

Roberts took this approach to evangelization to the local level—to his own church in Toronto. When he was called to Sherbourne Street United Church in 1927, death was thinning the ranks of the older members of the congregation, younger members were moving to newer residential areas outside the vicinity of the congregation, and the incoming residents to the district could not be attracted.[85] The congregation was divided among itself as to the type of minister needed for Sherbourne, and while those who wanted a scholarly preacher won out, division remained, centred mainly on the need for greater pastoral care and for evangelization in the neighbourhood.[86] To address such criticism Roberts attempted to develop a new vision of the ministry and church appropriate for a changing urban community. In keeping with his re-articulation of evangelization and his conception of the inner life of the church, he attempted to reinvigorate the religious spirit within the church.

In 1931 the Sherbourne Street Forward Movement was begun with Roberts as originator and mainspring. In response to the congregation's poor financial position in 1930, the movement was established to increase funds, membership, and participation in church activities. Participants desired "the deepening and the devel-opment of the personal and corporate spiritual life of the present membership of Sherbourne."[87] They proposed that this be achieved primarily through "a recovery of our prayer life, both in private and in fellowship."[88] Church members were asked to pray daily for the congregation and the work of the church, and to attempt to extend opportunities for common prayer. In addition, members of the For-ward Movement stated that:

> We look to a greater loyalty and regularity of the members of the Church at the Sunday Services, to the enlistment of a larger number in the actual work on behalf of the Church....And we trust that many members of the Church will be stirred to undertake personal work looking toward the winning of others into the fellowship of Jesus Christ.[89]

At the end of 1932, the Official Board claimed that the move-ment had helped solve the financial problems of the church. In addi-tion, the board stated that it felt "that the Movement has greatly stimulated interest in the work of the church and that we are from this standpoint in a much healthier condition than we were a year ago."[90]

Roberts also encouraged members of the congregation to increase their opportunities for prayer in fellowship. After questioning male adherents of the congregation about their Christian life and their service to their church, Roberts suggested they revive the old Methodist class-meeting. This the men enthusiastically did under the leadership of Sir Joseph Flavelle. Older boys, desiring to increase their opportunities for fellowship but feeling uncomfortable among the men, set up their own prayer meetings.[91] Similarly, in 1933, sensing a widespread desire for spiritual renewal among Torontonians, Roberts launched an intensive Lenten campaign from his church. While regular church services were held, special group meetings for fellowship, prayer, and further discussion about the Christian message were also organized.[92]

While Roberts' concept of evangelization was not a return to the position held by nineteenth century evangelicals, he did maintain a continuity with the older tenets of his faith. Roberts affirmed traditional forms of piety such as daily prayer, spiritual renewal through belief in Jesus Christ, and commitment to a disciplined life. Yet, in important ways, he also sought to transform piety. For example, conversion need not be an immediate religious experience, and evangelization was to occur in individual congregations rather than large scale campaigns.

In his religious thought, in his understanding of the relationship between Christianity and society, and in his conception of evangelization, Roberts neither wholeheartedly embraced liberal theology nor compromised the supernatural elements of his faith. Rather, he sought to combine elements of the old evangelical creed with liberal thought. In his theology he emphasized central concepts of evangelicalism such as a transcendent God and the cross as a symbol of human sin and a reminder of the need for repentance.

Yet he combined these with more liberal notions such as divine immanence and Jesus as a fully human person and yet still divine. Similarly, in his religious and social thought and in his advocacy of the reform of society he blended the social gospel idea of the need for a social transformation with the traditional evangelical belief in individual spiritual growth. Neither individual nor social regeneration was sufficient in and of itself for social transformation. That goal, he argued, could only occur as individuals accepted God's word. Indeed, Roberts' stress on the importance of evangelization was primarily aimed at achieving this spiritual renewal. To this end he re-articulated a traditional evangelical practice for modern society by offering opportunities for revivals in small groups within individual churches, led by a preacher with a solid grounding in the Bible and a life of prayer who drew on both emotion and reason to aid people to accept Christian truth and commit their lives to its principles.

This attempt at a synthesis of traditional and more modern beliefs was a result partly of Roberts' awareness that the older forms of faith had to undergo some re-articulation in order to incorporate new scientific discoveries and address modern socio-economic conditions. Such a reformulation was especially necessary, he argued, because of the inability of the pre-war expression of liberal Protestantism to provide a theological base for understanding central concepts of traditional belief, or to provide the strong spiritual motive to ensure lasting social transformation. During the interwar years, Roberts was involved in a major reinterpretation of the liberal Protestantism that had arisen prior to World War I. Indeed, in his attempt to develop a synthesis of what appeared to be logically opposed theological concepts in evangelical and liberal Protestantism, Roberts sought to reconcile an abiding Christian faith and piety with the intellectual, social, and economic changes occurring within modern society.

Endnotes

1 I would like to thank M. Van Die, R. D. Gidney, W. P. J. Millar, and J. M. F. Dawson for their continued support and encouragement.

2 The literature on Canadian religious history can be roughly divided into the work of those historians who argue that the changes in mainstream Protestantism helped create a more secular society, and of those who believe that such changes were part of the ongoing process of theological reformulation. For the former position see Ramsay Cook, *The Regenerators: Social Criticism in Late Victorian English Canada* (Toronto: University of Toronto Press, 1985); David Marshall, *Secularizing the Faith: Canadian Protestant Clergy and the Crisis of Belief, 1850–1940* (Toronto: University of Toronto Press, 1992); and A. B. McKillop, *A Disciplined Intelligence: Critical Inquiry and Canadian Thought in the Victorian Era* (Montreal: McGill-Queen's University Press, 1979). For the latter position see Nancy Christie and Michael Gauvreau, *A Full-Orbed Christianity: The Protestant Churches and Social Welfare in Canada, 1900–1941* (Montreal and Kingston: McGill-Queen's University Press, 1996); Phyllis D. Airhart, *Serving the Present Age: Revivalism, Progressivism, and the Methodist Tradition in Canada* (Montreal: McGill-Queen's University Press, 1992); Marguerite Van Die, *An Evangelical Mind: Nathanael Burwash and the Methodist Tradition in Canada, 1839–1918* (Montreal: McGill-Queen's University Press, 1989); and Brian J. Fraser, *The Social Uplifters: Presbyterians, Progressives and the Social Gospel in Canada, 1875–1915* (Waterloo: Wilfrid Laurier University Press, 1988).

3 Mark Noll, *A History of Christianity in the United States and Canada* (Grand Rapids: William B. Eerdmans, 1992), 155–56; Michael Gauvreau, "Protestantism Transformed: Personal Piety and the Evangelical Social Vision" in *The Canadian Protestant Experience, 1760–1990*, ed. George A. Rawlyk (Burlington: Welch, 1990), 77–78; Van Die, 42.

4 Marshall, 45–46.

5 Gauvreau, 75, 111; Marshall, 45.

6 Marshall, 47; Richard Allen, *The Social Passion: Religion and Social Reform in Canada, 1914-28* (Toronto: University of Toronto Press, 1971), 11–13.

7 William R. Hutchison, *The Modernist Impulse in American Protestantism* (Cambridge: Harvard University Press, 1976), 2; George M. Marsden, *Fundamentalism and American Culture: The Shaping of Twentieth-Century Evangelicalism, 1870–1925* (Oxford: Oxford University Press, 1980), 117.

8 Hutchison, 2.

9 Van Die, 12; Airhart, 8, 142.

10 "The Theological Dilemma in America," 140–41; "Imago Dei," 328–36.

11 This argument was first developed in my article, "Richard Roberts: A Case Study in Liberal Protestantism in Canada During the Interwar Years," *Historical Papers 1995: Canadian Society of Church History*, 83-86.

12 "The Theological Dilemma in America," 140-41; "The Scope of Theology," unpublished lecture, 1927, 15-17 (Box 4, 112, Richard Roberts Papers [hereafter RR Papers], United Church of Canada/Victoria University Archives [hereafter UCC/VUA]).

13 "The Scope of Theology," 15.

14 "The Theological Dilemma in America," 140-41; "The Scope of Theology," 15-17.

15 "The Theological Dilemma in America," 142.

16 "The Scope of Theology," 4.

17 I derived this classification of philosophers and theologians with specific intellectual traditions from two sources: John Macquarrie, *Twentieth-Century Religious Thought* (London: SCM Press, 1963), and Randolph Carleton Chalmers, *The Happy Science: An Introduction to Schools of Contemporary Theology* (Toronto: United Church Observer, 1975).

18 Cf. Macquarrie, 264-66. For Roberts' use of Whitehead, see "The Scope of Theology," 14.

19 "The Scope of Theology," 18.

20 *The Christian God*, 69.

21 *The High Road to Christ*, 94.

22 Ibid., 96–97.

23 Ibid., 91.

24 *The Christian God*, 63–64.

25 "The Quiet Hour," *The New Outlook* [hereafter NO] 5 Dec. 1928, 7.

26 Cf. Allen, 4–7.

27 Ibid., 18.

28 *The Christian God*, 65, 67.

29 "The Scope of Theology," 49–51; "Discipline of Life," *NO* 31 July 1935, 755.

30 "The Homeless Stranger," *NO* 28 Nov. 1928, 7.

31 "The Scope of Theology," 49–51; "Discipline of Life," 755.

32 "Spirit of Adoption," *NO* 18 Jan. 1933, 55.

33 *The Spirit of God and the Faith of Today*, 47–142; *The Preacher as a Man of Letters*, 106.

34 *The Spirit of God and The Faith of Today*, 112.

35 "Discovery of God," unpublished sermon, 1932 (Box 6, 167, Unpublished Sermons, RR Papers).

36 *The New Man and the Divine Society,* 16.

37 "The Scope of Theology," 26. For an earlier reference see "Imago Dei," 328–36.

38 "Wheels and Systems, A Plea for Another Theology," unpublished lecture c. 1929, 11 (Box 3, 77, RR Papers).

39 *The Renascence of Faith*, 252–53.

40 "If Only in This Life," 419.

41 *The New Man and the Divine Society*, 181.

42 By personality Roberts did not mean individuality, but the essence within humanity that all held in common. Cf. "The Awakening of Personality," unpublished sermon, 1932 (Box 6, 169, Unpublished Sermons, RR Papers).

43 *The High Road*, 160.

44 Cf. Christopher Turner, "Conflicts of Faith? Religion and Labour in Wales, 1890–1914," in *Class, Community and the Labour Movement: Wales and Canada, 1850–1930*, ed. Deian R. Hopkins and Gregory S. Kealey, with an introduction by David Montgomery (Wales: Society for Welsh Labour History and Canadian Committee on Labour History, 1989), 68.

45 Cf. Vera Brittain, *The Rebel Passion: A Short History of Some Pioneer Peacemakers* (London: George Allen and Unwin, 1964), 79.

46 Cf. "Richard Roberts," Finding Aid 118, UCC/VUA; Thomas P. Socknat, *Witness Against War: Pacifism in Canada, 1900–1945* (Toronto: University of Toronto Press, 1987), 100-01.

47 Cf. *The Unfinished Programme of Democracy*, 88–9, 124; "The Creation of Community," unpublished lecture (in "Three Lectures c. 1934–37," Box 4, 116), 2–4; *The Contemporary Christ*, 136; "Jesus and the Unemployed," *NO* 6 May 1931, 419; *The Untried Door,* 57.

48 *The Untried Door*, 115.

49 *Unfinished Programme*, 9.

50 "Personality and Community," 4–8; "The Creation of Community," unpublished lecture (in "Three Lectures c. 1934–37," Box 4, 116, RR Papers), 5-7; *The Contemporary Christ*, 12–14.

51 Allen, 356.

52 Cf. Robert Wright, "The Canadian Protestant Tradition 1914–1945," in *The Canadian Protestant Experience, 1760–1990*, ed. George Rawlyk, 178. Many FCSO members also participated in the League for Social Reconstruction and the CCF. Cf. Michiel Horn, *The League for Social Reconstruction: Intellectual Origins of the Democratic Left in Canada, 1930–1942* (Toronto: University of Toronto Press, 1980), 3–14.

53 Foreword to *Towards the Christian Revolution.*

54 Cf. Report No. 2, Committee on Evangelism and Social Service, *Record of Proceedings*, 20, Nineth Toronto Conference, 1933, United Church of

Canada. See also my article, "Richard Roberts: A Case Study in Liberal Protestantism in Canada During the Interwar Years," 87–88.

55 Cf. Richard Roberts to Gwen, 16 March 1934 (Box 1, 13, Correspondence, RR Papers); Richard Roberts to E. Knowles, 24 March 1934 (Box 1, Correspondence, RR Papers); "Report of the Commission on Christianizing the Social Order," 235, *Record of Proceedings, Sixth General Council, 1934*, UCC.

56 "Report of the Commission on Christianizing the Social Order," 236, 241–44, 246–47, *Record of Proceedings, Sixth General Council, 1934*, UCC.

57 Cf. Roger Charles Hutchinson, "The Fellowship for a Christian Social Order: A Social Ethical Analysis of a Christian Socialist Movement" (Th. D. diss., Toronto School of Theology, 1975), 40; "Report of the Commission on Christianizing the Social Order," 248, *Record of Proceedings, Sixth General Council, 1934*, UCC.

58 Cf. Socknat, 10, 142–48.

59 Quoted in Ernest Thomas, "General Council on War and Peace," *NO* 9 Jan. 1935, 30.

60 John D. Woodside, "Dear Brother in the Ministry," 1939 (Box 3, 64, RR Papers).

61 Richard Roberts to Gwen, 5 Oct. 1939 (Box 1, 13, Correspondence, RR Papers).

62 Cf. Richard Roberts to Gwen and Howard, 20 Nov. 1939 (Box 1, 13, Correspondence, RR Papers).

63 Cf. "Sub-Exec Issues Statement," *United Church Observer*, 1 Nov. 1939, 4, and David R. Rothwell, "United Church Pacifism—October 1939," *The Bulletin* 22 (1973), 47–52.

64 "Sub-Exec Issues a Statement," 4.

65 Cf. Richard Roberts to Gwen and Howard, 20 Nov. 1939 (Box 1, 13, Correspondence, RR Papers).

66 *The Basis of the Ethics of Jesus*, 4.

67 Ibid., 3.

68 Van Die, 9.

69 Airhart, 4, 12–13.

70 For the former position see Marshall, 28, 69–70. For the latter position see Airhart, chapters 4 and 5; Gauvreau, 289; Van Die, 193.

71 Cf. Robert Wright, 174–75.

72 Cf. Robert G. Stewart, "Radiant Smiles in the Dirty Thirties: History and Ideology of the Oxford Group Movement in Canada 1932–1936" (M. Div. thesis, Vancouver School of Theology, 1975), 43, 49, 66; N. K. Clifford, "Religion in the Thirties: Some Aspects of the Canadian Experience," in *The Dirty Thirties in Prairie Canada*, ed. D. Francis and H. Ganzevoort (Vancouver: Tantalus Research Ltd., 1980), 125.

73 Cf. Richard Roberts to Dorothy, 29 Oct. 1932 (Box 1, Correspondence, RR Papers); Richard Roberts to Dorothy and Cliff, 18 Dec. 1932 (Box 1, 5, Correspondence, RR Papers); Richard Roberts to unknown, 24 Dec. 1932 (Box 1, 13, Correspondence, RR Papers); Richard Roberts to Dorothy, 6 Jan. 1933 (Box 1, 5, Correspondence, RR Papers).

74 Cf. Richard Roberts to Dorothy and Cliff, 23 Jan. 1933 (Box 1, 5, Correspondence, RR Papers); Richard Roberts, "The Oxford Group."

75 Cf. Richard Roberts to Gwen, 10 Dec. 1932 (Box 1, Correspondence, RR Papers); "Prayer, the Human Response to God," *NO* 25 Sept. 1929, 973; *What's Best Worth Saying,* 68.

76 *What's Best Worth Saying,* 68.

77 Cf. "The Spirit of Fellowship," *NO* 11 July 1934, 533; "The Quiet Hour," *NO* 29 April 1936, 400.

78 "The Oxford Group."

79 Richard Roberts to E. Knowles, 24 March 1934 (Box 1, Correspondence, RR Papers).

80 Cf. *The Preacher as a Man of Letters,* 194, 203; "Lectures on Preaching," unpublished lectures, n. d. (Box 4, 114), 6-10; "The Spirit of Fellowship," *NO* 11 July 1934, 533; *The Contemporary Christ,* 81, 102, 108; "The Quiet Hour," *NO* 4 March 1931, 203.

81 "Moderator to the Church: II. The Moderator's Mission," 954.

82 Ibid., 954.

83 "The Moderator to the Church: III. The Matter of Spiritual Preparation," 978–79.

84 "Moderator to the Church: II. The Moderator's Mission," 955.

85 This was a situation which all of the churches of the area were facing in the 1930s ("Report of the Down Town Committee," 6 May 1930, 400, Minutes 1930–1937, Toronto East Presbytery, UCC).

86 Cf. Vernon Grant to Richard Roberts, 4 March 1931 (Box 2, 46, Correspondence, RR Papers).

87 "Report of Sherbourne Forward Movement," Annual Report of Session 1932, Correspondence 1929-50, Sherbourne St. United Church Records, UCC/VUA.

88 Ibid.

89 Ibid.

90 "Report of Official Board," Annual Report of Session, 1932, Correspondence 1929–1950, Sherbourne St. United Church Records, UCC/VUA.

91 Richard Roberts to Gwen, 28 Jan. 1933 (Box 1, 8, Correspondence, RR Papers); Richard Roberts to Gwen, 24 Feb. 1933 (Box 1, 13, Correspondence, RR Papers).

92 Richard Roberts to Dorothy, 4 March 1933 (Box 1, 5, Correspondence, RR Papers); Richard Roberts to Gwen, 11 March 1933 (Box 1, 13, Correspondence, RR Papers).

A Bibliography of the Writings of Richard Roberts

compiled by William Whitla

I. Manuscript collections and archival materials

The papers of Richard Roberts, including clippings of a number of his articles, are located in the United Church of Canada/Victoria University Archives at the University of Toronto:

Box 1: Family Correspondence, Personalia, and Biography
   File 20: Autobiographical Manuscript by Richard Roberts
Box 2: Correspondence
Box 3: Official Correspondence, Newspaper Clippings, Articles, and Lectures
Box 4: Lectures and Sermons
Boxes 5 and 6: Sermons
Box 7: Miscellaneous
Proceedings of General Council, United Church of Canada. 1932-36. United Church of Canada Archives.
Proceedings of Toronto Conference, United Church of Canada. 1933. United Church of Canada Archives.

II. Books and Pamphlets

Many of the books of Richard Roberts were published in both Great Britain and the United States, often in the same year, as indicated below:

Are We Worth Fighting For? London: Humphrey Milford: Oxford University Press, 1914 [Papers for War Time, No. 2] [pamphlet].
The Ascending Life. New York: Woman's Press of the YWCA, 1924; London: Student Christian Movement, 1925.
The Basis of the Ethics of Jesus. New York: Fellowship of Reconciliation, 1921 [pamphlet].
Christ and Ourselves. London: Student Christian Movement, 1914.
Christ Crucified. London: Friends' Tract Association, 1915 [pamphlet extracted from *Christ and Ourselves*].
The Christian God. London: Hodder & Stoughton, 1929; New York: Macmillan, 1929. [The Merrick Lectures for 1928.]

The Church and the Next Generation. London: James Clarke, 1909.

The Church in the Commonwealth. London: Headley, 1917 [New Commonwealth Books No. 2]; New York: Frederick A. Stokes, 1917; repr. New York: Frederick A. Stokes, 1918.

The Church Tower. New York: Committee of Ninety-Nine, 1923.

The Contemporary Christ. Introduction by Rufus M. Jones. New York, Macmillan, 1938. [Great Issues of Life Series]

The Discipline of Interior Prayer. New York: Association Press, 1940.

The Evolution of the Soul. Michigan: William F. Ayres Foundation, 1936.

The Faith for the New Age. London [no publisher] 1925[?] [pamphlet].

Florence Simms: A Biography. New York: Woman's Press of the YWCA, 1926.

For God and Freedom. Sackville, NB: Mount Allison University, 1945. [Josiah Wood Lectures, 1944]

For the Kingdom of God. London: Student Christian Movement, 1933. [Addresses delivered in Lent to Students of the University of Toronto].

The Gospel at Corinth. New York: Macmillan, 1924.

The High Road to Christ: a Popular Essay in Re-statement. London: Cassell, 1912.

The Jesus of Poets and Prophets. London: Student Christian Movement, 1919; repr. 1920; repr. PortWashington, NY: Kennikat Press, [1971].

Jesus, Son of Man: Short Studies in the Gospel Portrait of Our Lord. London: Cassell, 1913; New York: Cassell, 1913.

The Kingdom of Heaven. London [no publisher], 1928.

The Meaning of Christ as Interpreted by Poets and Patriots. London: H. R. Allenson, 1906.

The Meaning of Christ: Studies in the Place of Jesus in Human Thought and Action. London: H. R. Allenson, 1906.

The New Man and the Divine Society: A Study in Christianity. New York: Macmillan, 1926. [Southwark Lectures delivered at the Theological School, Harvard University, 1926.]

On Digging In and Going Over the Top. Toronto: United Church Publishing House, 1927 [sermon].

"On, to the City of God." New York: Woman's Press for the YWCA, 1921.

Opening Up New Ground in Japan. London: International Review of Missions, [1934?].

The Papers of John Pererin, by A Modern Mystic. Boston: Universalist Publishing House, Murray Press, 1923.

The Pardoned Offender. London: RTS, 1934 [pamphlet].

Personality and Nationality: a Study in Recent History. London: Headley Brothers, 1914; repr. 1915.

The Preacher as a Man of Letters. New York: Abingdon, 1931; London: J. M. Dent and Sons, 1931.

The Profiteer and the Prophet. London: The Crusader, 1919 [pamphlet reprinted from *The Crusader* 5 and 12 Sept. 1919].

The Red Cap on the Cross. London: Headley, 1918.

The Renascence of Faith. Introduction by G. A. Johnston Ross. New York: Fleming H. Revell, 1912; London: Cassell, 1912.

Robert Owen. Caernarfon: Swyddfa "Cymru," 1907. 2 vols. [in Welsh].

The Spirit of God and the Faith of Today. Chicago: Willett, Clark & Colby, 1930.

Still No Room at the Inn. London: National Council of Evangelical Free Churches, 1915 [pamphlet].

That One Face: Studies of the Place of Jesus in the Minds of Poets and Prophets. New York: Association Press, 1919.

That Strange Man Upon His Cross. New York: Abingdon Press, 1934; London: Allenson, 1935. [Four lectures delivered at Yale University on the Kent Shaffer Memorial Foundation.]

The Unfinished Programme of Democracy. London: Swarthmore Press, 1919; New York: B. W. Huebsch, 1920.

The Untried Door: An Attempt to Discover the Mind of Jesus for Today. New York: Woman's Press of the YWCA, 1921; New York: George H. Doran, 1921; London: Student Christian Movement, 1921.

Two Sermons on the Bible. Toronto: United Church Publishing House, 1931. [Preached at Sherbourne United Church, Toronto, 11 and 18 January, 1931, pamphlet.]

What's Best Worth Saying: A Present Day Discussion of Christian Faith and Practice. New York: George H. Doran, 1922.

The Will to Love: An Address to Christian Parents and Sunday School Teachers. London: Fellowship of Reconciliation, 1915.

III. Chapters in Books

The Christian and War: An Appeal, by M. F. McCutcheon, Alan P. Shatford, W. A. Gifford, Richard Roberts, W. D. Reid, and T. W. Jones. Toronto: McClelland and Stewart, 1926.

The Conquest of War: Some Studies in the Search for a Christian World Order, by Norman M. Thomas, W. Fearon Halliday, F. W. Armstrong [and] Richard Roberts. New York: Fellowship Press, 1917.

"Faith in the Spirit of God." In *A Faith for Today: Sermons in the College Chapel, Victoria University, Toronto*. Ed. E. M. Wallace.

Toronto: Ryerson Press, 1932.

"Foreword." In *Towards the Christian Revolution*. Ed. R. B. Y. Scott and Gregory Vlastos. New York: Willett, Clark, 1936; London: Victor Gollancz, 1937; repr. with an Introduction by Roger Hutchinson. Kingston: Ronald P. Frye, 1989.

IV. Articles

"1517-1917: A Retrospect and an Anticipation." *The Hibbert Journal* 16 (Oct. 1917–July 1918): 319–28.

"Authority Endangers Conscience." *The Christian Pacifist* Feb. 1946, 773–76.

"Baron Friedrich von Hügel: A Personal Tribute." *Canadian Journal of Religious Thought* 4.5 (Sept.–Oct. 1927): 401–15.

"The Beatitude of Giving and Receiving." *The Expository Times* 48.10 (July 1937): 438–41.

"Beyond the Four Walls." *The World Tomorrow* 10 (Oct. 1927): 394–96.

"Christianity and Justice." *Canadian Journal of Religious Thought* 6.3 (May-June 1929): 149–55.

"Christianity at the Crossroads." *The New Outlook* 29 April 1931, 395, 411.

"A Call to Fidelity." *The New Outlook* 19 June 1935, 622–23, 641. [Address at the Tenth Anniversary of the Establishment of the United Church, Maple Leaf Gardens, Toronto].

"Companies of the Upper Room." *The Christian Century* 58 (14 May 1941): 650–51.

"Considerations Bearing Upon a Christian Doctrine of Personality." *Canadian Journal of Religious Thought* 3.2 (Nov.-Dec. 1931): 379–87.

"The Discipline of Life." *The New Outlook* 31 July 1935, 755.

"The Doctrine of God." *Hibbert Journal* 23 (Oct. 1924): 20–31.

"Elijah: Strong, and Soul-Sick." *The Sunday School Times* 28 Jan. 1911, 44–45.

"Foreword" to Vera Brittain. "Massacre by Bombing: The Facts Behind the British-American Attack on Germany." *Fellowship* [special issue of the Journal of the Fellowship of Reconciliation] 10.3 (March 1944): 49. [Foreword also signed by Harry Emerson Fosdick, E. Stanley Jones, Rufus M. Jones, Kenneth Scott Latourette, and others].

"Freedom of Speech," *The New Outlook* 27 Dec. 1933, 918–19, 924. [Sermon on Luke 11:33].

"The Golden Grove." *Canadian Journal of Religious Thought* 7.5 (Nov.–Dec. 1930): 381–83.

"How the Fellowship Began." *Fellowship* [The Journal of the Fellowship of Reconciliation] 9.1 (Jan. 1943): 3–5.

"If Only in This Life." *The New Outlook* 24 April 1935, 419.

"Imago Dei." *Canadian Journal of Religious Thought* 2.5 (Sept.-Oct. 1925): 328–36.

"In Praise of Humanism." *Canadian Journal of Religious Thought* 8.2 (March-April 1931): 119–24.

"In the Midst of the Years." *The New Outlook* 13 March 1935, 259–60, 268-69. [Address at the Service of Witness, Maple Leaf Gardens, Toronto, 5 March 1935]

"Jesus and the Unemployed." *The New Outlook* 6 March 1931, 419; repr. *Federal Council [of Churches of the USA] Bulletin* Sept. 1931, 7–8.

"Lamennais." *Canadian Journal of Religious Thought* 7.3 (May-June 1930): 189–96.

"The Lure of the Disinherited." *The World Tomorrow* (1927 [?]): 240–44.

"Makers and Destroyers." *The New Outlook* 18 May 1932, 465, 480.

"The Moderator to the Church: I. Clearing the Decks for Action." *The New Outlook* 24 Oct. 1934, 930–31.

"The Moderator to the Church: II. The Moderator's Mission." *The New Outlook* 31 Oct. 1934, 954–55, 968.

"The Moderator to the Church: III. The Matter of Spiritual Preparation." *The New Outlook* 7 Nov. 1934, 978–79.

"The Moderator to the Church: IV. The Beloved Community." *The New Outlook* 14 Nov. 1934, 1002–3.

"The Moderator to the Church: [V. Untitled]." *The New Outlook* 2 Jan. 1935, 6.

"The Moderator to General Council." *The New Outlook* 30 Sept. 1936, 906–7, 915–17.

"The Old and the New." *The Aldersgate Magazine* (1913): 78–79.

"The Old Apocalyptic and the New." *The Christian World Pulpit* 24 May 1911, 323–24.

"One Fine Hour." *The New Outlook* 14 Oct. 1931, 969. [Sermon on Hebrews 2:9].

"An Open Letter [to Reinhold Niebuhr in answer to his "Christian Moralism in America," in *Radical Religion* 5.1 (Winter 1940): 16–20]." *Christianity and Society* 5.2 (Spring 1940): 41–43. Niebuhr replied: "An Open Letter to Richard Roberts." *Christianity and Society* 5.3 (Summer 1940): 30–33.

"Opening Up New Ground in Japan." *International Review of Missions* 23 (Oct. 1934): 547–54.

"Our Eternal Contemporary." *The New Outlook* 9 Dec. 1936, 1144–45.

"Out of the Night." *Religion in Life* 11 (1942): 119–24.

"The Oxford Group." *The Christian Century* 50 (1 Feb. 1933): 147–49.

"A Pastoral Prayer." *The Christian Century Pulpit* (May 1936): 115.

"Pentecost." *The New Outlook* 28 May 1937, 491–92. [An address broadcast 16 May 1937 over CRCT on the programme presented by the Radio Committee of the United Church of Canada].

"The Preacher as Interpreter." *Canadian Journal of Religious Thought* 3.2 (March-April 1926): 101–10.

"The Problem of Conscience." *The International Journal of Ethics* 29 (April 1919): 332–38.

"Protestantism and the Altar." *The Christian Century* 43 (9 Dec. 1926): 1518–20.

"The Quiet Hour." *The New Outlook* 1928–1937, as follows: from N. S. 4.48 (28 Nov. 1928) to 5.52 (25 Dec. 1929), and from 6.43 (22 Oct. 1930) to 13.17 (30 April 1937). [A column, usually weekly, on a specific topic. Most were separate articles, though some were in a series]: "Be Renewed in the Spirit of Your Mind." *The New Outlook* 25 Dec. 1935, 1251; 1 Jan. 1936, 7 [Parts I and II]. "The Body of Christ in Canada." *The New Outlook* 23 Jan. 1935, 81–82, 101; 30 Jan. 1935, 116, 128 [Parts I and II]. "The Discipline of Life." *The New Outlook* 26 June 1935, 652–53 [I. "The Wrong Use of Salt"]; 3 July 1935, 675–76, 685 ["The Wrong Use of Salt (Concluded)"]; 10 July 1935, 695, 705 [II. "The Right Place for Candles"]; 31 July 1935, 754–55, 762 [III. "The Wrong Place for Pearls"]; 14 Aug. 1935, 795, 806 ["The Wrong Place for Pearls (Concluded)"]; 21 Aug. 1935, 816, 825 [IV. "The Right Use of Fundamentalism"]; 28 Aug. 1935, 836, 847 ["The Right Use of Fundamentalism (Concluded)"]; 4 Sept. 1935, 856 [V. "The Middle-of-the-Road Man"]; 11 Sept. 1935, 876, 885 ["The Middle-of-the-Road Man (Concluded)"]; 25 Sept. 1935, 920–21 [VI. "On Telling the News"]; 30 Oct. 1935, 1047 ["On Telling the News (Concluded)"]; 6 Nov. 1935, 1068 (VII. "Peter Filled with the Holy Ghost"]; 13 Nov. 1935, 1092 ["Peter Filled with the Holy Ghost (Concluded)"]; 20 Nov. 1935, 1116, 1125 [VIII. (wrongly numbered VII). "What God Sees in Man"]; 27 Nov. 1935, 1137, 1154 ["What God Sees in Man (Concluded)]; 4 Dec. 1935, 1164, 1177 [IX. (wrongly numbered VIII). "The Fine Art of Forgetting"]; 18 Dec. 1935, 1228 ["The Fine Art of Forgetting (Concluded)"]. "Faith and Sanity." *The New Outlook* 6 March 1935, 235–36; 20 March 1935, 287–88 [Parts I and II]. "The Guiding Hand of God." *The New Outlook* 25 Oct. 1933, 757; 1 Nov. 1933, 773 [Parts I and II]. "In a World Gone Mad What Is a Christian To Do?" *The New Outlook* 31 Jan. 1934, 69 [I. "The First Thing Is To Keep His Head"]; 7 Feb. 1934, 85, 92 [II. "The

Second Thing Is To Keep His Eyes Open"]; 14 Feb. 1934, 101, 111 [III. "The Third Thing Is To Use His Brains"]; 21 Feb. 1934, 117 [IV. "The Fourth Thing Is To Watch His Step"]. "The Inner Chamber." *The New Outlook* 22 April 1936, 376, 390; 29 April 1936, 400–1 [Parts I and II]. "The Recapture of Christian Experience." *The New Outlook* 28 March 1934, 223 [II. "Prodigals All"]; 21 March 1934, 205 [I. "The Breaking of Bonds": the publishers note that these two articles were inadvertantly numbered in the wrong order: they are correctly ordered here: that is, the first article in the series is "Prodigals All" and the second, "The Breaking of the Bonds"]; 4 April 1934, 237 [III. "The Home-Coming"]; 11 April 1934, 256 [IV. "Son Once More"]; 18 April 1934, 284 [V. "The New Mind"]. "The Salutary Doctrine of the Second Place." *The New Outlook* 25 May 1932, 491–92 [I. "More Than Conquerors"]; 1 June 1932, 515, 521 [II. "Hewing Agag in Pieces"]; 8 June 1932, 539, 552 [III. "Thou Shalt Love..."]; 15 June 1932, 563 [IV. "Fear not, little flock: for it is your Father's good pleasure to give you the kingdom"]; 22 June 1932, 587, 598 [V. "The Riches of the Second Place"]. "The Sower and the Soul." *The New Outlook* 11 March 1931, 227; 18 March 1931, 251 [Parts I and II]. "The Spiritual Foundations of the Christian World Order." *The New Outlook* 23 Nov. 1932, 1087, 1103 [I. "God and the World"]; 30 Nov. 1932, 1111, 1124 [II. "Right and Wrong"]; 7 Dec. 1932, 1133, 1148 [III. "The Chief End of Man"]; 14 Dec. 1932, 1162, 1176 [IV. "The Pattern of Human Life"]. "The Ultimate City" *The New Outlook* 6 July 1932, 635, 649 [I. "The city which hath the foundations" Heb. 11]; 13 July 1932, 659, 671 [II. "The Street of the City" - Rev. 21:21]; 20 July 1932, 683, 693 [III. "The City Without Walls" - Zech. 11:5]; 27 July 1932, 703, 712-13 [IV. "The City Without a Church: 'I saw no temple therein'" - Rev. 21:22]; 3 Aug. 1932, 721 [V. "The City Without a Police Department: 'The gates thereof shall in no wise be shut by day'" - Rev. 21:25]; 10 Aug. 1932, 743 [VI. "The Children of the City"]; 17 Aug. 1932, 763, 771 [VII. "The Life of the Citizens: 'And they shall serve Him day and night in His temple'"- Rev. 7:15]; 24 Aug. 1932, 783 [VII. "The Life of the Citizens" (Continued)]; 31 Aug. 1932, 801, 812 [VIII. "The Skirt of a Jew: 'In those days ten men...shall take hold of the skirt of him that is a Jew, saying, We will go with you, for we have heard that God is with you'" - Zech. 8:23].

"Radical Religion Forty Years Ago." *Christianity and Society* 5.4 (Fall 1940): 32–34.

"Religion in 1950." *The Aldersgate Magazine* (1913): 139–40.

"Religious Japan." *The New Outlook* 3 Jan. 1934, 5.

"Revival Without Tarrying for Any." *The New Outlook* 30 Sept. 1931, 923. [Sermon on Psalm 95:6–7].

"Solid Ground in a Shaking World." *The New Outlook* 7 Oct. 1931, 947–48. [Sermon on Hebrews 12:28].

"Spirit of Adoption." *The New Outlook* 18 Jan. 1933, 55.

"The Spirit of Fellowship." *The New Outlook* 11 July 1934, 533.

"Stored-up Sunshine." *The Aldersgate Magazine* (1913): 120.

"The Theological Dilemma in America." *Hibbert Journal* 25 (Oct. 1926-July 1927): 140–47.

"This Do." *The New Outlook* 23 Sept. 1936, 870–73. [Sermon to General Council of The United Church of Canada].

"The Threshold of the Church." *The Aldersgate Magazine* (1913), 63–64.

"Toward a National Church." *The New Outlook* 23 Oct. 1935, 1022.

"Treasure Trove." *The Christian World Pulpit*, 12 Feb. 1925, 79–81 [Sermon preached in Appleton Chapel, Harvard University].

"Two Confessions of Faith." *Canadian Journal of Religious Thought* 5.1 (Jan.–Feb. 1928): 18–22. [Review of Ronald Knox, *The Belief of Catholics*, and Julian Huxley, *Religion Without Revelation*].

"Why Freedom?" *The New Outlook* 4 Feb. 1931, 103, 114. [Sermon on 1 Peter 2:16–17].

"William Blake Comes Back." *Methodist Review* 110 (Sept. 1927): 637–84.

"With Christianity It Is Always Sunrise Somewhere in the World." *The New Outlook* 13 May 1931, 443.

About the Author

Gwen Rhianon Prys Roberts Norman was born the third child of Richard and Nan Roberts in London, England, on October 3, 1909, not long before the beginning of World War I. In 1917 she moved with her family to Brooklyn, New York, and then to Montreal, where she completed her secondary school at Trafalgar Institute. She went on to McGill University, taking a B. A. in honours German and History and her M. A. in Medieval History in 1932.

In 1932 she married Howard Norman and together they sailed to Japan to be missionaries for the Overseas Missions Board of the United Church of Canada to work under the direction of the United Church of Christ in Japan. They returned to Canada with their three children just before World War II broke out.

Following the war the family returned to Japan. For a number of years Howard and Gwen taught at Kwansei Gakuin University, Gwen teaching oral English, Latin, and History, and coaching the English Drama and Public Speaking Clubs. While at Kwansei Gakuin, Gwen and Howard were instrumental in the post-war re-establishment of the Canadian Academy, a school for missionary and other foreign children in Kobe and its environs. Gwen remained on the CA Board until her retirement, with the exception of two years when she served as Field Representative of the Japan Mission, both to the Home Board of the United Church and to the Japanese Church. Later Howard and Gwen moved to Nagano Prefecture and engaged in evangelistic work until their official retirement in 1970. It was during this last period that she found time to write the biography of her much-loved father.

Upon return to Canada, Gwen resumed her early love of history. Until her eightieth year she worked at the United Church Archives, compiling finding-aids on overseas mission papers. With Howard Norman she wrote a history of the first one hundred years of United Church missions in Japan which was published by the Division of World Outreach in 1981. Gwen is currently writing her autobiography.

Index

Abergele 116
Aberhart, William 208
Aberystwyth 24 ff.
Allen, Richard 272
Alternative Service Man 94
American Civil Liberties Union
    129
Anderson, David 82
Anglesey 44
Angus, Chris 87
Antigonish 211
Asama, Mt. 178
Asquith, Herbert 45
Avison, H. R. C. 133, 141

Baillie, Donald 167
Bala 3, 28, 29, 30, 40
Bala Theological College 3
Bangor 24
Barth, Karl 201, 218, 255, 267
Beard, Charles A. 101
Beaver, Gilbert 251, 256, 258;
    Jean 251
Bell, G. K. A. 86, 201
Bennett, R. B. 198–99
Bergson, Henri 267
Bernanos, Georges 226
Bessborough, Lord 199
Bevan, Edwyn 86
Birks, Gerald 130
Birks, William 205
Bishop, Charles 153
Blaenau Ffestiniog 3, 12, 15
Blake, William 267
Blatchford, Robert 38
Boojum 81, 85
Book, Anthony 22
Book of Common Order 171–73
Bookman, The 87
Booth, Raymond 224
Bowles, Dr. 157, 167
Bristols, the 204
British and Foreign Bible Society
    29
British and Foreign School
    Society 18
British Peace Society 92
British Weekly, The 64, 77, 87
Brockway, Fenner 93
Brown, Walter 224
Browning, Robert 267

Brunner, Emil 234
Bryce, Peter 18, 197, 212, 223
Buchman, Frank 183, 276
Burtt, Philip 107
Burwash, Nathaniel 265

Cader Idris 124
Caernarvonshire 3
Caird, Edward 267
Cairns, David 222
Calvinistic Methodist Church 3,
    14–15, 32, 43, 47, 115, 207,
    274
Campbell, R. J. 267
Campbellites 15
Canadian Journal of Religious
    Thought 265
Cardiff 35
Carlton Street United Church
    155
Carruthers, Haldam 76
Cattell, James McKeen 101
Charles, Thomas 29
Chatauqua 179
Christian Age 46
Christian Century, The 39, 183,
    252
Christianity and Society 39, 282
Church of England 14, 15
Church of Scotland 201
Clarion, The 38
Clark, Rev. L. Mason 102
Clifford, Dr. John 44, 76
Collegium 88, 89
Commission on Christianizing
    the Social Order 273
Committee on Church
    Architecture 149
Conglywal 12
Congregationalists 15
Constantinople 55
Conway 20
Cragg, Dr. Gerald 141, 146,
    220, 221
Creighton, William Black 181,
    214
Crerar, Thomas 212
Croll, David 196, 228
Cymanfu Bregethu 16
Cymanfu Ganu 16

Daily News 87
Dana, Edward Salisbury 101
Darleston 77
Darwin, Charles 26, 264
Davies, George 90, 91, 95,
Davies, John, of Bontddu 4
Davies, Trevor 182
Deissman, Adolph 201
Dell, Floyd 105
Dickinson, Emily 249
Donne, John 204
Dow, John 222
D'Oyly Carte Opera Company
    117
Duckworth, Jack 242

Eastman, Max 105
Eben Fardd 3
Eddington. A. S. 267
Edgar, Pelham 226
Education Act 44–45
Edwards, Dr. Lewis 3, 28
Edwards, Dr. Thomas Charles
    16, 28, 40
Edwards, Ellis 31
Einstein, Albert 267
Eisteddfod 17
Ellis, Thomas E. 10
Emmanuel College 143, 159,
    164, 167, 191, 209
Endicott 214
Essays and Reviews 264
Evangelical Movement 14, 29
Evangelical Revival 29
evolution 266, 268

Falconer, Sir Robert 186, 273
Faulds, Dr. James 205
Fellowship for a Christian Social
    Order (FCSO) 86, 272–73
Fellowship of Reconciliation
    (FOR) 69, 83–96, 97, 98,
    205, 271
Flavelle, Sir Joseph 154, 165,
    177, 226, 280
Fletcher and Raynor 190–91,
    193
Forsyth, P. T. 63
Forward Movement 33, 35, 271
Francis St. Xavier University
    211

Free Church Council 56
Free Church Federation 78
Free Church Fellowship 151

Gandier, Dr. Alfred 167
Gardner, Lucy 89
Garegddu 12
Gibb, John 131
Gordon, King 202
Grant, George Munroe 265
Gweirydd ap Rhys Goch 116
Gwynedd 3

Hardic, Kier 36, 271
Harris, Howell 207
Headley Brothers 107, 110
Hearst, Sir William 192
Hegel 267
Hibbert Journal, The 265
Hillis, Dwight 101
Hinton, A. 175
Hitler, Adolf 183
Hodgkin, Henry 88–93, 97,
    107–09, 127, 205
Holden, Rufus 136
Holmes, John Haynes 102
Holy Land 54
Hughes 149
Hutchinson, "Hutch" and Jean
    146
hwyl 16
Hymnary 171–72

"Ilico" see Micklem, Nathaniel
Independent Labour Party (ILP)
    36, 271
Ireland 109
Isherwood 124

Japan 177–79, 231
Jennie 22
Jerusalem 54
Jones, D. Trevor 39
Jones, E. P. 63
Jones, Eirene 44, 206
Jones, Margaret 8
Jones, Richard 8
Jones, Rufus 227, 236, 239
Jones, S. T. of Rhyl 16
Jones, Tom D. 44, 206
Joshua, Seth 35, 37

Kagawa, Toyohiko 177
Kagawa Co-operating
    Committee 184
Karuizawa Union Church 177
Kemp, Sir Edward 155
Kennedy, Dr. Stoddard 48
Kent. Dr. 235–36
Kerr, A. E. 131, 133, 140, 148,
    236, 238, 241

King's Weigh House 108, 109,
    173, 189
Knowles, Dorothy 119, 161,
    246, 257
Knowles, E. C. 161, 173
Knox College 166, 167
Kuklos Adelphon ("K.A.") 150

Labour Party 36, 106, 271, 172
Lang, Cosmo 204, 206
Lathrop, John Howland 101
Lausanne Conference 201
Lawrence, D. H. 177
Lewis 193
Lewis, Warburton 77
Lincoln College 14
Line, John 164, 222
Little, George 196
Liverpool Institute 21
Llan Ffestiniog 15
Llanberis 3, 11
Llanerchymedd, Anglesey 116
Llangeitho 207
Llanwnda 3
Llewellyn, Richard 35
Lloyd George, David 10
Lloyd George, Mrs. 91
Lloyd, Morgan 9
Lovett, Sidney 247, 258
Luther, Martin 223

MacDonald, Miss 136, 140
MacDonald, Ramsay 105
Mackay 212
MacKinnon, Clarence 212
MacLeod, John 167
Macmillan, Alexander 171
Macmurray, John 70, 183, 224,
    266
MacVicar, Peggy 120, 141, 161,
    257, 258
Maltby, Dr. Russell 77, 156
Manod 12, 13, 19
Mansfield College, Oxford 77–
    78
Maritain, Jacques 267
Marshall, Newton 77
Masses Publishing Company
    105
Maxwell, William D. 226
McGregor, D. C. 190, 192, 212
McGuigan, James, Cardinal 209
McKerroll, Dr. 205
McMaster, Mrs. Mina 162
Meighen, Arthur 200
Melish, John Howard 101
Merionethshire 3, 4
Methodism 4, 14
Micklem, Nathaniel 77, 80, 92,
    94, 226
Military Service Act 94

Moelwyn 13, 19
Moody, Dwight 223
Moore, Dr. T. Albert 189, 191–
    92
Morgan, Herbert 77
Morrison, Clayton 210
Morrison, Walter 47
Mott, John R. 26, 210
Munro, William 204
Mussey, Henry Raymond 101
Mussolini, Benito 183
Myers, F. W. H. 92

Nation, The 95, 102
National Association for the
    Advancement of Colored
    People 102
New Harmony 44
New Lanark 44
New Outlook, The 149, 164,
    174–75, 181–82, 201, 220,
    266, 269, 277
Newtown 44
Nicoll, Robertson 87
Niebuhr, Reinhold 242
No Conscription Fellowship 93,
    96
Norman, Gwen 121, 163, 231,
    254, 256
Norman, W. H. H. 161
Nyth-y-Gigran 12

Oberammergau 147
Orchard, William Edwin 85,
    108, 163, 206, 233, 247
Orton 222
Owen, Derwyn 196, 210
Owen, Robert 44
Oxford Group 165, 180–84,
    276-77

Pacific School of Religion 111,
    166
Palestine 35
Parker, Joseph 246
Parry, Dr John 3
Passive Resistance Movement
    44, 54
Paton, William 64, 87
Peace Society of London 88
Philips, Evan 16
Pidgeon, Dr. George 153, 166,
    174, 185, 223
Pine Hill Divinity School 241
Presbyterian Church in Canada
    205
Presbyterian Church of England
    46, 56 et passim
Presbyterian Church of Wales
    15, 207
Price, Dr. Hugh 78

Primitive Methodist 36, 43
Pryse, Grace 116
Pryse, Robert John 116
Pugh, Cynolwyn 258
Pugh, John 33–34
Puritan theologians 5

Ramsay, Dr. Alexander 59, 83, 105
Raven, Charles 233, 245
Raynor and Fletcher 190, 192, 194
Red Lion Square 89
Redwood, Hugh 223
Rees, Morgan "Moc" 115
Rhiw, David Roberts 3
Rhiwbryfdir 3, 4, 12
Rhys 115
Richards, Richard 86
Riggs, Father 247
Ritchie, Principal 51
Roberts, Annie 8
Roberts, David (Rhiw) 3, 14, 28
Roberts, Dorothy see Knowles, Dorothy
Roberts, Gwen see Norman, Gwen
Roberts, Margaret 8-17
Roberts, Anne Catherine ("Mam," "Nan") 44, 62, 64, 115-24, 125, 144, 177, 180, 182, 192, 195, 196, 201, 203, 204, 206, 217, 218, 249, 251, 253, 258
Roberts, Richard, publications:
Are We Worth Fighting For?
87; The Christian and War
266; The Christian God 265;
Church and the Next
Generation 51; "Companies
of the Upper Room" 39, 252;
The Contemporary Christ
145, 227, 237, 239, 242, 266;
"How the Fellowship Began"
83; The Meaning of Christ 52;
The Preacher as a Man of
Letters 265; Quiet Hour 174–
75, 180; "Radical Religion"
39, 248; The Red Cap on the
Cross 103; The Renascence of
Faith 63; Robert Owen 44;
The Spirit of God and the Faith
Today 11, 131, 265; The
Unfinished Programme of
Democracy 266
Roberts, Robert David 8
Robinson, Wheeler 242
Robson, Sir Henry 59, 60
Rose, Dr. S. P. 148, 149, 151
Ross, Dr. G. A. Johnston 97, 129
Rowell, Newton Wesley 174

Rowlands, Daniel 207
Royce, Josiah 267
Russell, Bertrand 104
Ryerson, Egerton 221

Santayana, George 267
Saunders, David 16
Sclater, Robert Patterson 182, 217
Scotch Baptists 15
Scott, R. B. Y. 242
Scriver, Dr. Walter 257
Sephton 23
Shaw, Bernard 53
Shields, Dr. T. T. 235
Silcox 224
Sisco, Gordon 220, 221, 235, 236
Skinner, Dr. 71, 87, 98
Smith, Rev. J. Lavell 244
Snowden 124
Society of Friends 93
Speer, Robert 26
Spencer, Malcolm 77
Stamp, Josiah 226
Stephenson 214
Stevens, H. H. 186, 199
Stevenson, Miss 103
Stowell, Ellery Cory 103
Student Christian Association
(SCA) 140
Student Christian Movement
(SCM) 64, 85, 140, 141, 146, 169, 258, 266
Student Volunteer Movement
209
Sunday Strand 46, 51
Swanwick 75

Tatlow, Tissington 26, 64
Taylor, Tom 36
Temple, William 86, 210, 233
Tennyson, Alfred 267
Thomas, Anne Catherine see
Roberts, Anne Catherine
Thomas, Beryl 118
Thomas, Dan 90, 214, 237
Thomas, Ebenezer 3
Thomas, Llewellyn Blackwell
("Gag") 116
Thomas, Meshach 116
Thomas, Norman Mattoon 102
Thomas, Robert Arthur ("Bach")
116
Tillich, Paul 202, 226
Treharne, Bryceson 132

Underhill, Evelyn 185
University College of Wales 234
University of Syracuse 234
University of Vermont 234

Venturer 92, 93
von Hügel, Baron Friedrich 48

Wadsworth, Campbell 190
Wesley, John and Charles 14, 29, 223
Whitefield, George 14, 33
Whitehead, Alfred North 268
Whyte, Alexander 64, 201
Williams, Griffith John 19, 20
Williams, Hughes 30
Williams, John 16
Wilson, Edmund 100
Wilson, Woodrow 101
Woodsworth, J. S. 198
Wordsworth, William 367
World Council of Churches 201
World Tomorrow, The 102
Wrong, Dr. George 170